# Seven Pillars
*of*
# SERVANT
# LEADERSHIP

# Seven Pillars

*of*

# SERVANT LEADERSHIP

### Practicing
### the Wisdom of
### Leading By Serving

*Revised & Expanded Edition*

## James W. Sipe and Don M. Frick

Paulist Press
New York / Mahwah, NJ

Cover image © by John Aikins / Corbis
Cover design by Sharyn Banks
Book design by Lynn Else
Index prepared by Eileen Quam

Library of Congress Cataloging-in-Publication Data

Sipe, James W.
    Seven pillars of servant leadership : practicing the wisdom of leading by serving / James W. Sipe and Don M. Frick. — Revised & expanded edition.
        pages cm
    Includes bibliographical references and index.
    ISBN 978-0-8091-4926-1 (pbk. : alk. paper) — ISBN 978-1-58768-490-6 (ebook)
    1. Servant leadership. I. Frick, Don M., 1946- II. Title.
    HM1261.S565 2015
    658.4´09—dc23

                                                                2014044332

ISBN 978-0-8091-4926-1 (paperback)
ISBN 978-1-58768-490-6 (e-book)

Published by Paulist Press
997 Macarthur Boulevard
Mahwah, New Jersey 07430

www.paulistpress.com

Printed and bound in the
United States of America

# Contents

To Rachel Irene and Christopher James.
It has been my greatest pleasure
to serve as your father.
J.W.S.

And to Linda Linn, the Frick family's
natural Servant-Leader
D. M. F.

# Foreword to the
# Revised & Expanded Edition

Seven years ago I was given the opportunity to serve as the CEO of Popeyes Louisiana Kitchen. I was a member of Popeyes' board of directors when the CEO unexpectedly quit. After interviewing a slate of potential candidates, the board asked me if I would consider leading the turnaround of Popeyes. In my mind, this was a once-in-a-lifetime opportunity to develop both the strategies and the organizational culture for high performance. I had some anxiety about doing this transformation under the scrutiny of public shareholders, but if we succeeded, we would be a case study.

A case study in what? A case study in leading a successful turnaround with a Servant Leadership approach.

The first step was to assemble a quality Popeyes leadership team for the journey—eight people to lead the functional disciplines. Second step was to create a turnaround plan for the company—our Roadmap to Results—with four strategies: we would rejuvenate the treasured elements of this Louisiana-inspired food brand, run better restaurants, improve speed of service for our guests, and boost restaurant operating profits for our owners. If we did these things well, we would be able to build more restaurants, the source of value creation for the shareholders.

More important was the decision of whom we would serve.

Our first conversation was the standard discussion about stakeholders. Would we serve the guests who paid us their hard-earned dollars for a good meal, the employees who dedicated their time to taking care of our food and our guests, the franchise owners who invested in our people and our assets, or the shareholders who provided the capital for growing the company?

Conventional thinking was you had to serve them all. We decided instead that we would focus on serving one group well—

our franchise owners. They had taken the most risk by signing a twenty-year agreement to represent Popeyes, and they had made substantial financial and human capital investments. Franchise owners were in it for the long haul; without them, Popeyes did not exist.

The primary metric of our success would be franchise owner satisfaction measured in both an annual survey and restaurant operating profit—the indicator of restaurant financial health.

Fast forward to today. Our franchise owner satisfaction is very high: 95 percent give positive ratings to the quality of our franchise system and 90 percent say they would recommend our brand to a new owner. The average restaurant operating profit has increased from $170K, 17 percent of topline sales, to $280K, 22 percent of topline sales—a 59 percent increase in five years. Our shareholders have also prospered as the enterprise value of the company has quadrupled.

The business plan and the success metrics were important—but how we led was more important; Popeyes' purpose and principles guided the way we served our franchisees.

When we put Popeyes' purpose and principles in writing, we went in search of advice on the traits of servant-leaders. One of the first books we read on the topic was the original edition of *Seven Pillars of Servant Leadership*. In fact, it was the only concrete "how to" book we found on implementing a culture of Servant Leadership. Many of Popeyes' principles were inspired by the thinking in this book and, as forecast by authors James Sipe and Don Frick, these principles have delivered superior performance results at Popeyes.

Our plan started with Pillar I, People of Character—the leadership team of Popeyes. Each person was selected for his or her insightful, ethical, and principle-centered mindset. They are all skilled in their disciplines and high achievers, to be sure, but their ambition is for the people of Popeyes more than for themselves. Their egos are in check. Integrity is evident in their actions.

Pillar II, Putting People First, was the principle behind our decision to serve our franchise owners well. As mentioned, we decided that our actions would demonstrate genuine care and concern for the franchise owners who were deeply invested in Popeyes. Our success would be measured by their success.

Our business model is highly dependent upon persuasive communication skills. To implement any decision, we must convince over three hundred franchise owners of its merits. Until they are convinced, our strategies sit on a piece of paper, invisible to the guest. Few leadership models contemplate the importance of being a skilled communicator, but you will find it cited in Pillar III of this book.

If we singled out one behavior that has been most central to the turnaround success of Popeyes, we would cite collaboration with the leaders of our franchise system. Each quarter, we meet with ten elected leaders of our Popeyes International Franchise Association (PIFA). The purpose of these meetings is to review upcoming plans and build alignment with our franchisees. We have used these three-day work sessions to listen carefully to the concerns of our owners, to review performance data and adjust accordingly, and to build the teamwork essential to success. Pillar IV—Compassionate Collaborator.

Too many people believe Servant Leadership is a giant group hug without a business strategy. Nothing is further from the truth. Serving people well requires a compelling business strategy. How on earth could people be well served if the business strategy flops? Sipe and Frick call this Foresight—Pillar V—and it has been the foundation of Popeyes' performance.

When we began this journey at Popeyes, we had fallen into the trap of many corporations—functional silos. People were focused only on their functional areas, with little knowledge or cross-functional connection to other departments. We only had about eighty people in the home office building, but we were sending emails to the people in the office three doors down. We broke out of this dysfunctional mindset by establishing cross-functional teams for each critical business strategy. We assembled one team to build a strong new product pipeline, one team to improve speed of service in our restaurants, and another team to save money for the restaurants. This new way of working—Systems Thinking, Pillar VI—led us to better, faster performance results.

One value that has helped us build trust with our franchise owners is personal accountability, which is a commitment to do your piece of the puzzle. At Popeyes, the franchisor is responsible for building the brand with strong marketing and new product innovation. The franchisor creates the restaurant operating system and provides low-cost, high-quality ingredients. The franchise owner is responsible for building and operating the restaurants to Popeyes' standards with high-quality people. When both the home office and the franchisor do our parts well, the business performs. If either of us falls short, the business suffers. Trust, a component of Pillar VII—Moral Authority—is built on accountability.

No discussion of Servant Leadership is complete without touching on the overarching value of humility. I prefer the definition given by C.S. Lewis: "True humility is not thinking less of yourself; it is thinking about yourself less." At Popeyes we say,

"We value humility, because as soon as you claim to be humble, you are off course."

Nothing is more difficult or aspirational than serving others over our own self-centered thinking. It is a daily struggle, and we are imperfect practitioners. But overcoming our selfish nature is the test of our commitment to Servant Leadership. The best question to ask yourself is, "How have I served others today?"

Sipe and Frick give us the handbook for practicing Servant Leadership. If you do the things they recommend, your team and your organization will be blessed with superior performance results. But don't take my word for it, give it a try.

*Cheryl A. Bachelder*
*CEO, Popeyes Louisiana Kitchen, Inc.*

# Preface

*Leaders are made, not born. Each of us contains the capacity for leadership.* —Warren Bennis

Leadership lessons can come from surprising sources. One of my (Don's) most treasured lessons came from Roger, my barber.

Roger was unfailingly polite, genuinely interested in his customers, and of course, a genius with the shears. But underneath I sensed his sadness, vulnerability, and deep, abiding wisdom. One day, as he added new details to his life story, I discovered why.

Roger, whose given name is Nao Tou Vang, is a resettled Hmong from Laos. By the age of seventeen, his mother had died and his uncle and father—both former CIA employees—plus his brother had all been killed by the communists. With his family wiped out, Roger fled across the border to a refugee camp in Cambodia.

Roger was bright but illiterate. He never had an opportunity to attend school. With the help of international agencies, a group of educated refugees in the camp set up a school and Roger eagerly enrolled. His goal was to complete what was called a "Level Three Education," and he did so within two years. I asked what subjects he mastered to accomplish this education.

"The three levels were reading and writing—in two languages—and leadership."

He noticed my look of surprise. "Leadership? What did you learn about that?"

"I was taught that a leader is responsible to seeing to the needs of the people. For example, my job as a leader was to ensure that one hundred families had enough food every day." Then he added softly, "And I did it."

Roger moved to other camps, used several dictionaries to teach himself English, and was eventually sponsored in America by a church group. Today he is a vibrant member of the La

Crosse, Wisconsin, community and continues to lead by serving the needs of his fellow Hmong. He is one of my heroes.

Roger's story goes to the heart of leadership, as Robert K. Greenleaf, in his classic text *Servant Leadership*, has helped us understand it. Reading and writing—that is, basic skills and competencies—are just the beginning. We study and learn, gain insights and get promotions, not for their own sake, but in order to earn the final honor of leadership. Our education is incomplete, however, until we learn to meet the needs of those entrusted to us—to act as a leader who serves or, to be more precise, a servant who leads.

Significantly, Roger first had to prepare and feed himself before he was ready to feed others. Then he needed to learn where to start—who needed food, where he could find it, how he could deliver it, and at the same time, create a system that could be efficiently maintained and easily replicated.

## About This Book

The goal of *Seven Pillars of Servant Leadership* is to help complete the education of Servant-Leaders because, like Roger, leadership competencies coupled with a desire to serve is not enough. We also need to learn where to start our journey of leading by serving, how to stay on the path day in and day out, and how to correct our course when we begin to stray.

This book was born of a desire to be concrete about how to implement Servant Leadership without turning Robert Greenleaf's formulation—leading by serving first—into a collection of "tips and tricks." This aspiration arose from our frustration over searching for—and never finding—help in converting the insights of Servant Leadership into sustainable, measurable competencies without neglecting matters of the heart and soul, which make leading by serving truly worthwhile. Perhaps our experience parallels your own.

Have you ever been inspired by the ideas in a leadership book or workshop but were left hanging when, on the last page of the book or during the final session of the seminar, the guru said,

"Good luck!" and ended things just when they were getting interesting? It was as if his duty was done by showing you the leadership mountaintop, providing a brochure on how to climb, and then flying away in a helicopter just when you were ready to leave base camp. Still, you were so moved by the insights that you were determined, this time, to do something about them! Within days, however, your enthusiasm waned and you found yourself back in the pattern of same-old, same-old. What happened?

Perhaps you came away with a bullet-point list of leadership "how-to's" that were not framed as actionable, measurable skills and competencies. St. Paul wrote, "I can will what is right, but I cannot do it" (Rom 7:18). Knowing the right principles of leadership does not mean that you will carry them out.

Or maybe you were not provided with clear direction on how to replace old behavior patterns with new ones or how to apply what you learned to real-world, on-the-job challenges. Perhaps the leadership expert did not mention the deep reflection and "heart-work" necessary to engage in personal transformation.

We are determined to take you beyond leadership base camp. As "scientist-practitioners," leadership consultants and coaches, we are long-time students of the principles and practices of Servant Leadership and the dynamics of adult learning and development. We therefore intend to help you take a series of concrete steps to evolve Servant-Leader behaviors in your own way, in your own time, so you can begin integrating them into the daily rhythms and routines of your life—at work, home, and in the community.

You could say that we wrote this book for you because we needed it ourselves. Because when it comes to leadership, and especially Servant Leadership, information, insight, and motivation are not enough. Only congruent, persistent, and meaningful action combined with regular practice, feedback, and accountability, completes our Level Three education.

We offer no guarantee of results, only an abiding belief that, like Roger, you too can learn to be responsible for seeing to the needs of the people—to lead by serving first.

# Our Vantage Point

*There is nothing as powerful as an idea whose time has come.*
—Victor Hugo

The authors have witnessed firsthand how Robert Greenleaf's brainchild of Servant Leadership has come of age. The notion of leading by serving has been around for several millennia in the teachings of every major religious tradition, but Greenleaf, who began to evolve the idea as an AT&T executive, coined the term in a 1970 essay entitled *The Servant as Leader*.[1] He was the first to describe it as a personal journey and a management strategy, for both the public realm and the private sector.

# Don's Story

When I first read the essay *The Servant as Leader* in 1986, Greenleaf's writings had already deeply affected a small but influential group of thought leaders like Warren Bennis, Peter Drucker, Peter Senge, Margaret Wheatley, university and seminary presidents, corporate CEOs, the Eli Lilly Endowment, sisters in Catholic orders, and several originators of the service learning movement, among others. I clearly remember my response the day I first read the essay: I was stunned. Its ideas gave a language to my personal mission and context for all the inner seeking and professional experiences that had prepared me to receive the wisdom of Bob Greenleaf's thinking. I knew the trajectory of my life had changed.

I worked at the Greenleaf Center in Indianapolis during the early 1990s when its Executive Director Larry Spears and other dedicated people began bringing Greenleaf's ideas to a wider audience through publications, conferences, and international centers. Back then, Servant Leadership seemed like a subterranean movement of hope that erupted here and there, with the potential to bubble to the surface of consciousness around the planet and change humans' understanding of leadership greatness. Those were exciting times indeed.

During the course of researching and writing Greenleaf's 2004 biography, *Robert K. Greenleaf: A Life of Servant Leadership*, I was deeply affected by my encounter with the intellect, humility, and spirit of Bob Greenleaf and decided I would dedicate the rest of my career to understanding and sharing the ideas of Servant Leadership. This book is part of that effort.

## James's Story

As a psychologist, family therapist, and corporate consultant, I was intuitively following the principles of Servant Leadership when I was introduced to Greenleaf's work in 1998, during a brief stint as the training manager of a nonprofit, youth-serving agency. I soon realized that Greenleaf's writings described who I aspired to be as a professional, what I believed about helping and developing others, and what I hoped to accomplish with my life's work. I went on to cofound Magellan Executive Resources in Minneapolis, an organizational consulting firm steeped in the principles and practices of Servant Leadership. My colleague Jeff Pauley and I followed a personal and organizational mission "to improve the quality of life on earth, by helping individuals in leadership roles practice and promote the principles of leading by serving first."

At first glance, this undertaking sounds grandiose—or blatantly unrealistic. However, as Robert Greenleaf reminds us, "Nothing much happens without a dream. And nothing great happens without a great dream….[Certainly] it takes more than a dream to bring a thing to reality. But the dream must be there first."[2]

In 2007, my mission followed me to Personnel Decisions International, a global leadership solutions company, with twenty-five offices around the world. Subsequently, in 2013, PDI was acquired by Korn Ferry International, one of the largest executive recruitment, leadership development, and talent management firms on the planet, with over eighty offices in forty countries. I now find myself in a position to serve and influence leaders on a much grander scale, bringing "this thing," my dream, another step closer to reality. I hope this book will further contribute to making that dream come true.

## A Quiet Revolution

*As many small trickles of water feed the mightiest of rivers, the growing number of individuals and organizations practicing Servant Leadership has increased into a torrent, one that carries with it a deep current of meaning and passion.*

—Larry Spears

For several decades, Robert Greenleaf's concepts have inspired a quiet revolution. It has now become noisy. A bibliography found on the Greenleaf Center's website (www.greenleaf.org) lists hundreds of articles about Servant Leadership in academic and popular journals. It has been the subject of many masters and doctoral theses. Over a quarter of a million copies of Greenleaf's original essay, *The Servant as Leader*, have been sold, in a dozen languages, and scores of book titles have sold many thousands of copies worldwide. Centers for Servant Leadership are active in ten countries. In 2004, ten million viewers saw a televised feature on Servant Leadership aired by NBC's *Dateline*.

The topic speaks to a deep longing for a way of being and acting in the world that reflects inner truths. Through the years, thousands of people whom Greenleaf referred to as "seekers" have had an "Aha!" experience when they encountered this idea— a shock of recognition, a realization that what Stephen Covey calls a natural, universal "force of nature," was hidden in plain sight all along.[3]

But what happens then? Where does one find the path to becoming a Servant-Leader and what are the steps to travel it? In the words of John Schneider, who spent years working with his team to understand and implement Servant Leadership at Indianapolis-based Schneider Engineering, "Greenleaf needs to be operationalized." He is right, and that is the way Robert Greenleaf wanted it.

Greenleaf did not provide a universal checklist or a formula for becoming a Servant-Leader. He wanted each person and organization to apply the principles and values in ways that made sense to them. Nevertheless, Greenleaf did believe that certain core skills of Servant Leadership could be taught, developed, and measured. His work was conceptual and concrete, idealistic and pragmatic.

Greenleaf's strategy fit his personality and the zeitgeist of the 1970s. Yet, while times have changed, the truths he tapped into have not. Mountains of leadership research since his death confirm his key insights, and a global Servant Leadership movement is afoot, creating a groundswell of interest in developing step-by-step, actionable and measurable competencies for becoming a Servant-Leader.

## Welcome to the Revised Edition

When we first envisioned creating a competency-based framework for Servant-Leaders, we were responding to a need expressed by our clients. They wanted a set of concrete, practical steps for applying the principles and practices of leading by serving. We were determined to accommodate them without turning Robert Greenleaf's Servant Leadership philosophy into a set of facile bullet points, "tips and tricks," or abstract, watered-down principles that avoided the tough work of learning new skills, measuring outcomes, and embarking upon a deep inner journey of honest reflection.

We had no way of knowing how extensive the need for such a book was. Now we do. Since publication of the first edition in 2009, we have been delighted and humbled to learn how it has been used to introduce and integrate Servant Leadership in a wide range of organizations: for-profit businesses, not-for-profit foundations and service organizations, religious organizations, higher education curricula, even public sector organizations. The Seven Pillars has spawned study circles, influenced strategic decisions and cultural transformations. Even more satisfying are reports of the spill-over influence of Servant Leadership behaviors into individual lives, families, and community involvements. But don't take our word for it. Read about the success of Popeyes Louisiana Kitchen in the foreword to this revised edition or the measurable results reported in the new chapter, "The Seven Pillars in Action."

This updated version includes some new research as well as additional insights gained by applying the Seven Pillars approach to our clients' challenges. A new chapter, "The Seven Pillars in Action," offers a case study that shows how one organization in the public sector has used the Seven Pillars as a key resource to introduce Servant Leadership into their operations—the Minnesota Department of Transportation (MnDOT). The larger story, however, is not about this book, because *The Seven Pillars* is only one of MnDOT's many sources they consulted to help rebuild public trust after the catastrophic 2007 bridge collapse. The story we can all benefit from describes the process of using Servant Leadership for positive transformation: where to start; how to translate abstract principles into vision, mission, strategy, and policy guidelines; ways to promote internal cultural change through research and stories; the power of champions who model congruent servant behaviors.

Even though every organization implements Servant Leadership differently, we chose a story from the public sector for two reasons: First, many people despair of public institutions undergoing any kind of transformative change. This mental model is supported by commonly held views: "Government organizations are too bureaucratic. They are bound by laws, hide-bound to traditional ways of doing things, and subject to political whims. They serve their own survival, not the public good." History offers abundant evidence for some of these views, but they are not representative of every public sector organization staffed by people who take seriously their roles as public servants. If a state cabinet-level agency like MnDOT can use Servant Leadership to help regain public trust and transform its internal culture, so can small and large organizations in the private and nonprofit sector that are more nimble by nature. Second, you will be able to immediately apply lessons learned from the experiences of the remarkable people you meet in these pages, and will be inspired by them.

This profile also illustrates the efficacy of Robert K. Greenleaf's enduring philosophy of Servant Leadership that, because it springs from the universal human impulse to serve, applies to people of all cultures, languages, religious doctrines, nationalities, and personality inventories. That is good news for you and your organization, religious and community involvements, and family.

# Acknowledgments

I (James) have learned so much from so many about leading by serving. Some of their stories grace the pages of this book. To all the others I am unable to recognize individually, I sincerely thank you.

I would also like to acknowledge Jeff Pauley for his enormous contributions to the excavation and construction of the Seven Pillars and Don Frick, my colleague and friend.

Well done, good and faithful servants!

I (Don) wish to thank the many old and new friends who have allowed us to share their Servant Leadership stories or have contributed in other ways, especially the following: Nao Tou Vang (Roger), Ann McGee-Cooper, Haley Fox, Jai Johnson, Sr. Georgia Christensen, Elizabeth Brindel, and Jeffrey Dols.

Robert Greenleaf would have loved Viterbo University in La Crosse, Wisconsin, where I worked while completing this manuscript. At Viterbo, I learned from colleagues and master teachers like Rick Kyte, Tom Thibodeau, Trevor Hall, Tom Knothe, David Banner, and Earl Madary, and from the dozens of Master of Arts in Servant Leadership (MASL) students—bright, engaged seekers whose spirits emitted sparks, every one of them. The lessons they shared have worked their way into this book.

# Introduction

*The first and most important choice a leader makes is the choice to serve, without which one's capacity to lead is severely limited.*
—Robert Greenleaf

People who are new to Servant Leadership may wonder what the fuss is all about. What distinguishes it from all other leadership philosophies? What is it about its foundational principles that has inspired so many? Why is it so often described as "transformative?"

Simply put, it is the leader's commitment to serving others that matters most of all. According to Greenleaf,

> the Servant-Leader is servant *first*....It begins with the natural feeling that one wants to serve, to serve *first*. Then conscious choice brings one to aspire to lead....The best test [of a Servant-Leader], and difficult to administer, is this: Do those served grow as persons? Do they, *while being served*, become healthier, wiser, freer, more autonomous, and more likely themselves to become servants? *And*, what is the effect on the least privileged in society? Will they benefit, or at least not be further harmed?[1]

Not everyone is enamored of this paradoxical notion. Some believe the concept has suffered from the name Greenleaf gave to it; after all, does anyone *really* want to be a servant? The word challenges the heroic view of leadership that dominates corporate culture. One may also wonder if it is possible to strike a functional balance between serving others and leading them while maintaining accountability to the financial bottom line. Greenleaf himself posed the question, "Can the two roles [of servant and leader] be fused in one real person, at all levels of status or calling?"[2]

Many who *have* embraced the fusion of servant and leader say they do so simply because "Servant-Leader" describes who they

1

already are deep down, or because it is the "right thing to do." But there are also valid business reasons.

## Servant Leadership Is Great Business

*Servant Leadership: A Journey into the Nature of Legitimate Power and Greatness*
The title of Robert Greenleaf's first book
(Paulist Press, 1977)

The phenomenally popular business book, *Good to Great: Why Some Companies Make the Leap and Others Don't* offers a striking example of how some leadership experts have wrestled with the paradox inherent in joining "servant" and "leader." When Jim Collins and his research team searched for a term to describe the exemplary performance of the leaders behind the "great" companies profiled in the book, *Servant-Leader* was a serious contender. Some members of the team, however, "violently objected" to its connotations of "servitude" and "weakness."[3] Apparently, *Level 5 Leader* sounded safer, less controversial.

At first we thought, "How unfortunate—if it looks like a duck, walks like a duck, sounds like a duck..." But that was before we conducted our own research into leadership greatness. Our results led us to a startling conclusion, offering relief that Collins and colleagues did not appropriate the name, because servant-led companies are even *better than great!*

We used Collins's metrics to compare the financial performance of his eleven publicly traded "good to great" companies with eleven publicly traded companies that are most frequently cited in the literature as being servant-led. During our ten-year study period ending in 2005, stocks from the five hundred largest public companies averaged a 10.8 percent pretax portfolio return. The eleven companies studied by Collins averaged a 17.5 percent return. However, the servant-led companies' returns averaged 24.2 percent! Bottom line: the servant-led companies produced *far superior* financial results.[4]

Three of the servant-led companies in our study—Southwest Airlines, The Container Store, and Starbucks—are also called *Firms of Endearment* in the book of the same title.

A Firm of Endearment is a company that *endears* itself to stakeholders by bringing the interests of all stakeholder groups (society, partners, investors, customers, and employees) into strategic alignment. No stakeholder group benefits at the expense of any other stakeholder group, and each prospers as the others do. These companies meet the tangible and intangible needs of their stakeholders in ways that delight them and engender affection for and loyalty to the company.[5]

The authors also used Collins's lens of financial performance in order to conduct a comparative study. Their conclusions about the performance of Firms of Endearment were strikingly similar to what we found in our comparison of servant-led companies.

[Firms of Endearment] companies pay their employees very well, provide great value to customers, and have thriving, profitable suppliers. They are also wonderful for investors, returning 1025% over the past 10 years, compared to only 122% for the S&P 500 and 316% for the companies profiled in the bestselling book "Good to Great"—companies selected purely on the basis of their ability to deliver superior returns to investors.[6]

Another popular measure of a company's greatness can be found in Fortune's annual "Top 100 Companies to Work For in America." Of the eleven servant-led companies in our comparison group, five were listed as "Top Companies" in 2005. Two of these are in Fortune's "Top Companies Hall of Fame"—having made the list every year since its inception. None of Collins's "great companies" made the list that year.

But wait, there's more. In subsequent reviews of Fortune's "Top Companies" lists from 2006 to 2014, our focus group of servant-led companies, plus a handful of other like-minded organizations, are represented an average of 7 percent of the time. Again, none of

Collins's "great companies" make the cut. In fact, one of his great companies has since gone out of business and another was slapped with a four hundred million dollar fine for fraudulent practices.

As it turns out, the union of servant and leader is possible. It comes more readily to some—those Greenleaf called "natural Servant-Leaders"—but everyone must work at it, must choose and then act. That goes for organizations too. Our experience has shown that most organizations that have implemented Servant Leadership *because it was the right thing to do* have enjoyed benefits others can only dream about.

The servant-led organizations and the leaders that we write about in this book would be the first to admit to imperfections. Nevertheless, they have done an admirable job of nurturing and rewarding the competencies of leading by serving. We are deeply grateful to them for the time they took to share with us their Servant Leadership lessons.

## The Seven Pillars of Servant Leadership

*Wisdom has built her house, she has hewn her seven pillars.*
—Proverbs 9:1

Robert Greenleaf defined Servant Leadership through his writings and his life. Our definition of a Servant-Leader constellates his key insights and, in some cases, expands upon them:

> A Servant-Leader is a *person of character* who puts people first. He or she is a *skilled communicator*, a *compassionate collaborator* who has *foresight*, is a *systems thinker*, and *leads with moral authority*.

As illustrated on the opposite page, we have organized these major qualities or characteristics of a Servant-Leader into the *Seven Pillars of Servant Leadership*.

The seven pillars are mounted on a solid foundation of organizational culture and strategy. Together, they support and sustain the organization's employees, its customers, clients and stakeholders, and

ultimately, the larger community. The seven pillars image also represents a stylized, inverted pyramid, honoring Greenleaf's notion that the authoritarian, top-down model of organizational leadership is upended with a Servant-Leader at the helm. Greenleaf believed that the designated leaders in an organization—who are smaller in number—should support and serve the greater numbers—those who are "doing the work."

Embedded within each pillar are three core leadership traits or competencies. These competencies, presented in the following table, constitute an essential set of skills that contribute to leadership effectiveness.

| I. | Person of Character | Makes insightful, ethical, and principle-centered decisions. <br> • Maintains Integrity <br> • Demonstrates Humility <br> • Serves a Higher Purpose |
|----|---------------------|----------------------------------------------------------------|

Continued next page

| II. | Puts People First | Helps others meet their highest priority development needs.<br>• Displays a Servant's Heart<br>• Is Mentor-Minded<br>• Shows Care & Concern |
|---|---|---|
| III. | Skilled Communicator | Listens earnestly and speaks effectively.<br>• Demonstrates Empathy<br>• Invites Feedback<br>• Communicates Persuasively |
| IV. | Compassionate Collaborator | Strengthens relationships, supports diversity, and creates a sense of belonging.<br>• Expresses Appreciation<br>• Builds Teams & Communities<br>• Negotiates Conflict |
| V. | Has Foresight | Imagines possibilities, anticipates the future, and proceeds with clarity of purpose.<br>• Visionary<br>• Displays Creativity<br>• Takes Courageous & Decisive Action |
| VI. | Systems Thinker | Thinks and acts strategically, leads change effectively, and balances the whole with the sum of its parts.<br>• Comfortable with Complexity<br>• Demonstrates Adaptability<br>• Considers the "Greater Good" |
| VII. | Leads with Moral Authority | Worthy of respect, inspires trust and confidence, and establishes quality standards for performance.<br>• Accepts & Delegates Responsibility<br>• Shares Power & Control<br>• Creates a Culture of Accountability |

We realize that not every accomplished Servant-Leader demonstrates all twenty-one traits all the time. However, whenever any traits are present in adequate measure, and as they accumulate, they serve to enrich and fortify the Servant-Leader and those who surround him or her.

These competencies can also represent a set of performance appraisal metrics—barometers of professional growth for the continuous evaluation of your leadership strengths and development needs.

## A Little Background

*A dwarf standing on the shoulders of a giant sees the farther of the two.*
                                          —Isaac Newton

You will find no references to pillars in any of Greenleaf's writings. However, those who are familiar with the publications of Larry Spears, former Senior Fellow of the Greenleaf Center for Servant Leadership, recognize many parallels between our "Seven Pillars of Servant Leadership" and his list of the ten characteristics of Servant-Leaders.

Spears became the director of the Greenleaf Center in 1990, shortly before Robert Greenleaf's death. Then, after diligently tending the flame of Servant Leadership and reflecting on Greenleaf's original writings, Spears identified a set of characteristics of Servant-Leaders that he considered of critical importance to their development.

He outlined these traits in various articles, including one titled *On Character and Servant Leadership: Ten Characteristics of Effective, Caring Leaders.*[1] This became the best-known list of Servant-Leader attributes and has been the basis of numerous graduate research studies.

Spear's list of characteristics has served many noble purposes. The inventory still begs a fundamental question, however: How does one become, do, and document these things?

*Seven Pillars of Servant Leadership* is our attempt to address this question. It represents our commitment to advancing the field of Servant Leadership. Now, standing on the shoulders of giants, we have reorganized and elucidated the ten characteristics into a competency-based framework that will enable you to acquire, master, and measure the knowledge, skills, and abilities of a Servant-Leader.

The image of pillars takes Servant Leadership out of its too-common characterization as a "soft" view of leadership. Webster tells us that one of the most common definitions of a pillar is "a firm, upright support for a structure." A working pillar is a weight-bearing unit that can be seen, touched, and measured. Without pillars, the superstructure they support would collapse.

When an individual is called a *pillar*, he or she is seen as a central figure, someone who is mainstay of an organization or society, as described in the phrase, "She is a pillar of the community."

Greek mythology gave rise to another definition of pillars—as gateways, or portals to other parts of the world. As the story goes, while performing one of his "twelve labors," Hercules was charged with acquiring the golden apples that Hera had received as a wedding present. Hercules, in quest of the apples, had been told that he would never get them without the aid of Atlas. Not having much luck convincing Atlas to let him pass, Hercules split a mountain in two with his indestructible mace and opened a narrow strait connecting the Mediterranean and Atlantic oceans. The rocky heights on both sides of the Straits of Gibraltar became known as *The Pillars of Hercules.*

Until explorers like Christopher Columbus and Ferdinand Magellan convinced Europeans otherwise, the Pillars of Hercules represented *non plus ultra*—"nothing farther beyond," the end of the world. This perception (which today still appears, in Latin, on the Spanish flag) made them more like a closed gate than a portal, scaring sailors from venturing into the jaws of monsters that may be dwelling there or, worse, sailing right off the world into nothingness.

Eventually, the Pillars of Hercules became *plus ultra*, an entrance to all things wondrous that lay "farther beyond." The Pillars of Hercules were the last thing intrepid sailors saw as they ventured out of the Mediterranean into unknown waters.

As for the number seven, in biblical times it was used to represent a list's "completeness." That is probably why King Solomon tells us that the house of wisdom is supported by seven pillars. We think he should know.

## Concrete Skills for Leading by Serving First

The Seven Pillars of Servant Leadership are meant to symbolize and integrate these multiple meanings. Each leadership pillar represents a set of concrete, observable competencies that bear weight and provide structure and support to an organization's employees, customers, and wider community. They are not merely lovely, abstract ideas, but wise, hard-nosed, and humane ways of being and behaving, as first articulated by businessman Robert Greenleaf through much empirical observation and deep reflection.

The Seven Pillars of Servant Leadership also represent a portal to *plus ultra*, the "farther beyond" landscape for successfully leading an organization in the twenty-first century. They lure us toward a vision, a voyage of discovery beyond the known world of linear management and isolated heroic leaders into the "flat world" of global business, connectivity, shared leadership, and the kind of community that makes it all worthwhile.

# The Psychology of Change

*We are what we repeatedly do.*                    —Aristotle

We are aware that simply listing twenty-one competencies does nothing to transform them into life-giving juices in active servants. In fact, some may find the list overwhelming ("so much to learn, so little time…"), engendering a sense of despair. Despair, by the way, is an attitude St. Thomas Aquinas called the eighth of the seven deadly sins. For those of you with this mindset, let us replace any looming despair with a helping of hope by heeding the wisdom of Aristotle.

Aristotle believed that moral character is the result of consistently acting on virtues like courage, temperance, and modesty. Every time a choice presents itself, one considers all the variables, determines the best course of action in the situation—what Aristotle calls the Good—and chooses it, day after day, week after week. Eventually, the *process* of analysis and reflection becomes a habit, and so does the *outcome* of choosing Good. Character is a result of the right habits.

The analysis component of decision making is not a problem for most people. We analyze, categorize, and prioritize an issue to within an inch of its life, because that is what is rewarded in most organizations. The *reflection* part of problem solving is more challenging. It often requires taking time away from the matter to gain perspective and to draw upon the wisdom of intuition. This element of the process does not come naturally to most people. It requires some precious time, a slight leap of faith, and some loss of control—something that produces anxiety in many people.

One of Greenleaf's major contributions to business thought was explaining the importance of reflection and intuition. He once taught a course at Dartmouth titled "Intuition in Business Decision Making," and it was always standing room only. One wonders why, since few managers are likely to go to their boss with this conversation:

"Well, Karnes, have you made a decision?"

"Yes sir, I have. We will go with the new marketing campaign."

"How did you decide that?"

"I considered all the numbers, the market research, the branding implications, and then…"

"Then you decided, right?"

"No, then I walked away from the problem, slept on it, and ultimately let my intuition have its say. That's when I knew this was the right thing to do.

"Oh, brother! We're basing a multimillion dollar marketing campaign on your hunches? We'd better call Jones in to help you out on this one."

Mr. Karnes was simply demonstrating some of the key principles of Foresight. He developed this habit over time by consistently following the process described in Pillar V. Psychologists know that one must repeatedly practice a new behavior consistently over time before it becomes an ingrained habit.

Analyze, reflect, choose, measure, and reflect on outcomes. That is how we begin to build virtues *and* skills. It is an essential prerequisite to evolving the competencies that support the impulse to serve, and to serve first. And it certainly beats despair!

Recent research into how adults learn, change, and grow can also guide us in the application and transformation of new knowledge, skills, and abilities. For example, Jim Prochaska's groundbreaking work on behavior change, described in *Changing for Good*, informs us that people who become successful at kicking bad habits "for good," such as smoking, drinking, and overeating, have done so because they followed a specific sequential change process.[8] The *Development Pipeline*™ used by Korn Ferry (James's current employer) describes the necessary and sufficient conditions that must be met in order for someone to acquire and maintain a new competency.[9]

## Your Servant Leadership Journey

Our version of a successful Servant-Leader change process incorporates these and other evidence-based best practices in a seven-step process that is reflected in questions you are invited to "Ask Yourself" in each chapter. These are not idle or trivial questions. They are designed to help you address the conditions necessary for long-lasting personal change so that you may begin to lead by serving first with focused, concrete, and forward-looking actions.

### *First, "Ask Yourself"—The Personal Journey*

1. *Identify and reflect upon what needs changing.*
   What are my strengths as a leader? As a servant? As a Servant-Leader? Where do I have room to grow?

2. *Express a desire to change.*
   Am I willing to invest the effort required to change my behavior? Do I have the time?

3. *Find and claim incentives to change.*
   What will be the return on my investment? What are the payoffs for changing?

4. *Gain access to knowledge and skills associated with the target behavior.*
   Where and how will I obtain additional, ongoing opportunities to learn the knowledge and skill of leading by serving—along with completing this book, of course!

5. *Practice, practice, practice.*
   Do I have real-world, real-time opportunities to try out new Servant-Leader behaviors?

6. *Feedback on efforts to change.*
   How will I hold myself accountable to make the changes I desire? How will I know when the new behavior is "wired in?" Am I willing to ask others for feedback about my efforts to develop and grow as a Servant-Leader?

7. *Meet Greenleaf's "Best Test" about how others grow as a result of your actions.*
   Does my new habit meet the best test of a Servant-Leader? How am I contributing to the "greater good" of my organization? My family? My society?

As you determine which of the seven pillars and twenty-one traits you desire to strengthen, please commit some time and energy to answering the questions we provide. Doing so will increase the likelihood that you will meet the necessary conditions for enduring behavior change. Otherwise, despite your best intentions, you may fall short of your Servant-Leader goals.

## *Then, "Ask Others"—The Institutional Journey*

To our knowledge, every successful attempt to implement Servant Leadership in an organization began with small-group conversations. Some groups involved only the top leadership team, but most of them included people from all levels of the organization. The chapter "Implementing the Seven Pillars of Servant Leadership" offers questions you can ask others in a small group. Before gathering, each member would read the same chapter and reflect on the "Ask Yourself" questions. That provides a common base for the questions to ask others. The ensuing dialogue will likely surface a number of interpersonal and systemic issues that could serve as the basis for an action plan to build a servant-led culture.

Like the "Ask Yourself" individual questions, these group questions are based on research about what it takes to implement long-term change in corporate culture. They are arranged in five categories:

1. *Discovery*
   Are we moving in the direction of becoming a servant-led organization? Where do we do things well? Where do we have room to grow?

2. *Desire and Incentives to Change*
   Are we willing to invest the effort required to change our culture? What are the payoffs for doing so? What are the consequences for not doing so?

3. *Learning*
   What resources can we tap to learn more about the changes we wish to make? How can we learn from colleagues who already practice aspects of Servant Leadership? How can we share our learning on a wider basis?

4. *Practice*
   Can we identify specific opportunities to begin trying out new Servant-Leader behaviors right now? Will our current culture reward the practice of Servant Leadership?

5. *Feedback and Evaluation—The Best Test*
   How will we hold ourselves accountable to make the changes we desire? Are we willing to ask others for feedback about our efforts to develop and grow as a servant-led company? How do we stack up against Greenleaf's "Best Test" for Servant Leadership?

As you can see, the Seven Pillars of Servant Leadership cannot be implemented with a few memos and pep talks. Their effective application requires a dedicated effort of study, skill practice, feedback, and reflection about your deepest values. "Everything begins with the individual," said Robert Greenleaf. Whether you are a CEO or an administrative assistant, a district manager or a driver,

Servant Leadership starts with *you*. Only then can it become embedded into your organization's operations, climate, and culture.

In the pages that follow, every Pillar is defined by its core competencies and supported by stories and skill-building exercises. Our goal is to make theory, reflection, and action part of the seamless fabric of Servant Leadership in your life and organization.

Ultimately, we hope to transform the way you live, love, and lead.

# PILLAR I

# Person of Character

*All leadership development is character development.*
—Stephen Covey

A Servant-Leader makes insightful, ethical, and principle-centered decisions.

- Is honest, trustworthy, authentic, and humble.
- Leads by conscience, not by ego.
- Is filled with a depth of spirit and enthusiasm.
- Is committed to the desire to serve something beyond oneself.

## Core Competencies

1. Maintains Integrity
2. Demonstrates Humility
3. Serves a Higher Purpose

## Our Moral Compass

*Let your conscience be your guide.*        —Jiminy Cricket

Jenny could not get to sleep. She knew what she had done was wrong, but everyone in the department was celebrating her cleverness. Using a consultant's detailed project proposal as the framework for their worldwide training initiative was a stroke of genius, they told her. It would save the company hundreds of dollars in development costs, and thousands more in deliverables.

Although Jenny became squeamish each time she called the consultant and asked him for "just a little more detail, another sample lesson plan," she knew he would eagerly comply. Matt made no secret of the fact that he was amazed "his little 'ole consulting firm" made the list of finalists to work with a global retail giant on a project that was worth twice the amount of his firm's total revenue the year before.

Today was the day she had been dreading—the day to call Matt with the bad news. She had her script ready. "Matt, I hate to have to tell you this, but we have decided to go in a different direction. Your ideas were fantastic and you were very easy to work with. However, we chose someone with more international training experience."

And if he wanted to know who they selected, she was all set to respond, "I'm sorry, but I am not at liberty to say."

Unfortunately, she had not anticipated his tears.

And now, she could not sleep. She tossed and turned as her mind raced like the engine of a stock car turning hot laps. Over and over, she heard his quivering voice in her head, "But I put my heart and soul into that proposal. I gave you everything you asked for!"

Is Jenny a person of character? How could she be, having pulled off such a diabolical scheme? And yet, her conscience will not let her rest. Jenny has knowingly violated a set of core values that have, in the past, served as her barometers of right and wrong. You might argue that a person of character would never consider such deceit. But good people are capable of doing bad things. We all make mistakes.

Should the litmus test of character be a sterling record of right choices and ethical decisions? Or is character defined by the ability to allow one's conscience—whenever it decides to kick in—to monitor one's behavior and move the person to act courageously to make necessary corrections?

Jenny found some relief that night after her guilt-ridden conscience surfaced intentions to make amends to Matt by compensating him for his time and effort. Alas, we sadly report that Jenny (not her real name) did not in the end let her conscience be her guide.

She did not act on her good intentions. A handsome bonus from her department head helped rationalize her previous actions. "All's fair in love and business," she told herself, knowing full well that is not quite how the adage goes.

A Servant-Leader lives, loves, and leads by *conscience*—the inward moral sense of what is right and what is wrong. According to Stephen Covey, that one quality is what sets Servant-Leaders apart from all others. It is the difference between leadership that works and leadership—like Servant Leadership—that *endures*.[1]

Other leadership writers have also suggested that a person of character is one whose inner compass stays oriented to "True North," where enduring, universal values and virtues can guide behavior. Listen to Bill George, former CEO of medical device giant Medtronic. He and his colleagues interviewed 125 ethically grounded leaders with diverse backgrounds, from multiple arenas.

> True North is the internal compass that guides you success-fully through life. It represents who you are as a human being at your deepest level. It is your orienting point—your fixed point in a spinning world—that helps you stay on track as a leader. Your True North is based on what is most impor-tant to you, your most cherished values, your passions and motivations, the sources of satisfaction in your life.[2]

That sounds like true wisdom, but which compass should you use to locate True North? Some use the compass of the law or com-pany policy. Others rely on religious scriptures, tradition, philoso-phy, or plain common sense. This challenge comes into sharper relief when we look more closely at the metaphor of True North.

Most people believe a compass always points to true north. Pilots know better. True north is a straight line between you and the North Pole, which is located at the tip of the axis the earth spins round. However, a compass actually points to *magnetic* north, and in the Western hemisphere, magnetic north is actually *south* of the geographic North Pole. The angular difference between the two is called Variation.

For example: if you are using a compass to navigate your plane or boat around Chicago, there is no Variation between True and

Magnetic north because you are on a line that runs right through Magnetic North and True North. If, however, you are flying or boating around Long Island, you need to add fourteen degrees to the compass indication to correct for the Variance. So, to travel ninety degrees (true west), you would set a magnetic course for one hundred four degrees (west by southwest). To make things even more complicated, Magnetic North is a wandering rogue. It moves depending on the ever-changing geomagnetic flux patterns.

So let's bring the metaphor back home. The personal, business, and social worlds you move in are littered with Variations that seek to deflect your compass from True North to a displaced North. If you set your compass by the dominant values portrayed in a reality television series that follows the lives of wealthy women, you might believe that paying $1,500 for a pair of shoes is normal, that wealth is the most important measure of success, and that wildly dysfunctional children are commonplace. If you were like so many "Christian" Germans in 1938, all compasses would point to the Magnetic North of anti-Semitism and the moral virtue of white, Aryan people over all others. Lest we be too judgmental, during the same period, anti-Semitism and racism were also rampant in America. If you were Jenny in a corporate environment where the Good is defined by the Profit, your compass would point to the rightness of behaving toward Matt exactly as she did.

A homing device that points to True North is buried in human consciousness, like the magnetically polarized cells found in the brains of migrating birds. We can, however, like Jenny, choose to ignore that guidance.

An authentic Servant-Leader nurtures enough self-awareness to know the difference between True North and Magnetic North. She takes frequent note of the Variance between the two. Her strength of character enables her to doggedly resist a variety of forces—culturally conditioned values, others' needs and expectations, the seduction of ego—that are pressuring her to deviate from her true leadership course. When her internal compass alerts her to the need for a corrective action, the true Servant-Leader within her would act with courage and determination to quickly get back on course.

## Ask Yourself

- Is my moral compass aligned with True North?

- What subtle Variations—values and behaviors—attract my moral compass away from True North the way a magnet attracts steel?

- How can I reposition myself so that what I do is congruent with what I know I should do? Are there sufficient reasons for me to even try?

## Understanding Character

*There never was a good knife made of bad steel.*
—Benjamin Franklin

Developmental biologists suggest that we are born with certain elements of character, such as cognitive ability and temperament. On the other hand, developmental psychologists believe that character develops throughout one's life, that it can be shaped and molded through various moral teachings and positive life experiences. We are of the mind that character is made up of a little of each.

The dictionary describes character as "the qualities that define who we are." The word comes from the Greek word *charak*, meaning "engraved" or "inscribed." Imagine then, that our character is etched within us as the essence of ourselves, the deep-seated qualities and attributes that embody who we truly are. Or, in the words of the pioneering psychologist William James, "The particular mental or moral attitude that makes one feel most deeply and intensely active and alive…a voice inside which speaks and says, 'This is the real me.'"[3]

People of character who operate in a principle-centered fashion and use highly developed moral reasoning as the basis for ethical decision making are sometimes also referred to as virtuous. According to Aristotle, the father of virtue theory, a virtue is a "good habit" that seeks to balance extremes and is a steadfast and settled disposition toward choosing Good. He saw good character as the life of right conduct—right conduct in relation to other persons and in relation to oneself.[4] The virtuous life includes self-oriented values—such as self-control and moderation—and other-oriented values—such as generosity and compassion. The two virtues related to self and other are connected. In other words, we need to be in control of ourselves (our passions and appetites) in order to do right by others. Contemporary philosopher Michael Novak sums up all of this nicely: "Character is a compatible mix of all those virtues identified by religious traditions, literary stories, the sages, and persons of common sense down through history."[5] No one, he points out, has all the virtues, and everyone has some deficits. Persons of much admired character may in fact differ considerably from one another.

What bearing does all this have on the quality and effectiveness of leadership? Plenty, as it turns out. Many business experts believe that leadership competence is based primarily upon character rather than technique.[6] Leaders who are seen as persons of character are more likely to generate loyalty, creativity, and productivity among company employees.[7] In fact, research at Harvard University indicates that 85 percent of a leader's performance depends upon personal character.[8] Bottom-line, servant-led companies with a strong corporate culture based on a foundation of shared values and principles outperform other companies by a huge margin.[9]

## *A Person of Character*

Can character such as this be taught? Thomas Lickona, author of *Educating for Character*, makes a compelling case that it can. He offers an interesting way of thinking about character that suggests an appropriate method for teaching values and virtues:

> Character consists of *operative values*, values in action. We progress in our character as a value becomes a virtue, a reliable inner disposition to respond to situations in a morally good way. Character as so conceived has three interrelated parts: moral knowing, moral feeling, and moral behavior.

*Good character consists of knowing the good, desiring the good, and doing the good*—habits of the mind, habits of the heart, and habits of action.[10]

Joseph Badaracco also believes that character can be taught or "built." He has developed a process to help leaders transform values and beliefs into calculated action, through the experience of what he calls *defining moments*. He distinguishes between ethical decision making—choosing between an option we know to be right and another we know to be wrong—and a defining moment, which challenges us to choose between two courses of action we believe are *both* right.

We form our character in defining moments because we commit to irreversible courses of action that shape our personal and professional identities. We reveal something new about us to ourselves and others because defining moments uncover something that had been hidden or crystallizes something that had been only partially known. And we test ourselves, because we discover whether we will live up to our personal ideals or only pay them lip service.[11]

Many defining moments are private. Their effects may never be witnessed by others. However, when they are witnessed by others, they become a "moment of truth" (MOT), the point of contact with a leader's character, as revealed in his or her actions.

This MOT concept has its roots in the world of marketing and branding. It is attributed to Jan Carlzon, the former president of Scandinavian Airlines (SAS). In his 1986 book of the same title, he explains that in one year, ten million SAS customers come into contact with an average of five SAS employees. "Thus," he said,

SAS is "created" in the minds of our customers fifty million times a year, fifteen seconds at a time. These fifty million "moments of truth"...are the moments when we must prove that SAS is their best alternative....We have to place responsibility for ideas, decisions, and actions with the people who are SAS during those fifteen seconds: ticket agents, flight attendants, baggage handlers, and all the other frontline employees.[12]

A moment of truth occurs whenever a customer encounters a company's brand, products, services, or employees. A positive MOT will likely result in a purchase, a satisfied customer, repeat business, referrals, and good will. A negative MOT creates a dissatisfied customer, a tarnished brand, a bad reputation, or a lost opportunity to gain a customer.

Moments of truth resulting from positive contacts with a leader increase credibility, trust, influence, loyalty, and authority. Alternatively, even one negative moment of truth associated with a leader's decisions or actions damages credibility, reduces trust, strains relationships, and may compromise the leader's effectiveness.

## *Defining Moments in Action*

As a longtime entrepreneur and small business owner, I (James) have experienced my fair share of the typical tradeoffs associated with self-employment. Many a time, such as during a long, thankless day, or when nursing another cash-flow headache, I consoled myself with one of my favorite ditties: "I would rather work sixteen hours a day for myself, than eight hours a day for someone else!"

Nevertheless, early in my career as a psychologist and a new parent, one of my espoused values was to maintain a proper balance between work and family. I vowed to be a more active, available parent to my children than my father was to me. Unfortunately, a growing number of negative MOTs with my wife over my lopsided work schedule suggested otherwise. I remember one particularly painful admonishment: "Put your money where your mouth is, Dr. Dad," as she pointed out to me that, once again, I was only paying lip service to my desire to live an integrated life.

The turning point in my struggle for balance began quite unexpectedly one morning at the breakfast table. It turned into a significant defining moment in my character formation, and has guided my behavior ever since.

"Daddy, Daddy!" screamed my five-year-old daughter Rachel at the breakfast table as she frantically plumbed the depths of a half-eaten bowl of Cheerios with her spoon. "I lost my tooth!" Sure enough, there in the lower left corner of her smile was a gap where her first "wiggly tooth" had been.

I immediately began a painstaking search that included straining the bowl's remaining contents through a colander. But alas, her missing tooth was literally missing.

"Oh, Daddy, now the tooth fairy won't come," she lamented. "And what about Miss Piggy and Granny Irene?"

I tried my best to reassure her. I agreed that her new bank ("Miss Piggy") was indeed overdue its next feeding. "But don't worry honey, you'll have lots of other loose teeth," I lamely replied, as I rummaged awkwardly through my empty pockets for coins.

As for breaking the news to her great-grandmother who had labored over a handcrafted miniature tooth-fairy pillow, complete with lacy fringes and a special little pouch, "Oh I'm sure Granny Irene will understand," was the best I could do.

Rachel burst into tears and ran sobbing from the room. Further attempts to comfort her were futile. I was crestfallen.

Eventually, we managed to complete our morning routine. I dropped my despondent kindergartener at school and headed for the office.

I desperately needed to spend the bulk of that morning finishing a consulting proposal in time for an important presentation that afternoon, but I could not concentrate. I was haunted by the parting image of my downcast little girl shuffling into school.

Normally, I would have just compartmentalized my feelings and gotten on with the task at hand. It had always been an effective technique for minimizing negative spillover between family and work. However, this situation was different. I did not realize it at the time, but I had come face to face with an ethical dilemma, a defining moment: Finish my project and move on with my day or respond to my paternal instincts to "save the day" for my daughter? I chose to table the proposal and focus first on the tooth. "After all," I rationalized, "how much time can it take to procure a little tooth fairy bait?"

After a brief bout of phone tag with our dentist, I learned that I was after a lower left bicuspid. "No, sorry. I don't happen to have any spare teeth laying around," he chuckled. I naïvely thought that it might be that easy. He referred me to a dental lab.

A quick stroll through the yellow pages and four phone calls later, I connected with a sympathetic dental technician, a father of five. He agreed to donate said tooth and leave it for me at the front desk. As luck would have it, his lab was on the way to my afternoon meeting.

Relieved and excited, I returned to my project. The time remaining required cutting a few corners, but the finished product would have to do. I arrived in time for the meeting with my prospective client with "Rachel's tooth" in tow.

That night at dinner, I could hardly contain my glee when the table talk inevitably turned to the tooth fairy's aborted visit. My wife Dawne and I took turns at parental consolation.

After the meal, I began to clean up. I retrieved Rachel's cereal bowl from the sink and unobtrusively placed the tooth in the bottom. I doused it with a splash of milk and tossed in a few Cheerios. "Rachel, Rachel, you'll never believe what I found in the bottom of your cereal bowl. It looks like your tooth!" I brought the bowl to Rachel and ceremoniously scooped the tooth onto a spoon. There it stood in all its glory, the top of the tooth protruding ever so slightly, looking like the tip of a miniature iceberg adrift in a milky sea.

Hoping that she would not remember how I had absolutely pulverized the contents of that bowl in our morning search, I retrieved the tooth and solemnly offered it to her. The expression on her face was priceless; no amount of new business revenue could compare.

After a barrage of hugs and kisses, she fetched her tooth-fairy pillow, tucked the wayward tooth into the little pouch and placed it under her pillow for safekeeping until the appointed time. The puzzled look on my wife's face gave way to an expression of understanding and admiration.

## Ask Yourself

- What are two of the most important defining moments that have helped shape my character?

- What stories could others tell about their moments of truth with me and my leadership actions?

- Think of an action you took that created a negative moment of truth. What could you have done differently? Can you still make amends for previous negative moments of truth?

There are many "values in action" that help form and define the character of a Servant-Leader. We shall focus on three.

## 1. Maintaining Integrity

For over twenty-five years, researchers James Kouzes and Barry Posner asked more than seventy-five thousand business and government executives from around the globe what they most admired in their leaders. The results are always the same: "Honesty has been selected more often than any other leadership characteristic; overall, it emerges as the single most important ingredient in the leader-constituent relationship."[13]

Other studies are strikingly similar. But honesty must be more than a strategy or a behavior of blurting out whatever one thinks or feels. It is part of being *authentic*, which requires inner work. After five years of research into the subject, Rob Goffee and Gareth Jones concluded that to be authentic, leaders must know themselves and others, use personal histories to establish common ground, and choose carefully which authentic parts of the self to reveal, and in which situations. They claim authenticity is more a matter of subtlety than uncontrolled expression. "If a leader is playing a role that isn't a true expression of his authentic self," they write, "followers will sooner or later feel like they've been tricked."[14]

Honest, ethical, forthright, upright, trustworthy, credible—no matter what it's called, Servant-Leaders maintain integrity. Everyone seems to want a leader who is perceived to be ethical and credible.

### *Integrity in Action*

Seth (not his real name) was a highly successful attorney, founder, and CEO of an influential lobbying firm in a major metropolitan city. I (James) was retained by him to help plan and facilitate his leadership succession, in anticipation of an early retirement.

During the initial stage of the engagement, I tagged along to meetings with his clients and to the capitol as he visited with legislators and attended various committee meetings. At the time, I was unfamiliar with his "industry" and these field trips allowed me to watch him in action. I must admit that when I started this project, I carried with me some untested assumptions about the world of hired guns, political *quid pro quo*, and closed-door deal making.

However, as I got to know my client and watched him work, I was surprised and impressed with how he conducted himself. He was a man of principle, humble in spite of his considerable wealth and power. He listened attentively, disagreed respectfully, and did not shy away from direct and heated exchanges. Here is one example of how he revealed his integrity to me.

Seth was in the process of trying to secure a six-figure account with a healthcare organization that was up against a much larger competitor for the right to build a new medical complex in one of the fastest growing areas southeast of the city. He was reasonably confident that he had a strong shot, given his track record in healthcare and his thirty-year friendship with the district's popular state senator, whose vote of endorsement would likely tip the scales in favor of his prospective client.

To Seth's and my great surprise, not only did he not receive the contract, he was treated rather rudely by one of the prospective client's senior executives. However, as a person of character he was quite gracious in his response. He ultimately assured them that their decision would not be used to influence his senator friend to side with the competitor.

Sure enough, when Seth and the senator met later that day, Seth was reserved and diplomatic in describing the details of the meeting and offered no impressions or recommendations that intimated his poor treatment. I have to assume that he kept his commitment, given that the contract was eventually awarded to the company that had spurned him.

## Ask Yourself

- Here are a few simple things that Servant-Leaders do to maintain integrity: return phone calls, follow up on details, keep promises, and admit mistakes. What about me? What are three actions I am willing to take immediately to strengthen the habit of maintaining integrity?

- Do I act as graciously as Seth in defeat? If not, what can I do about it?

## 2. Demonstrates Humility

Humility is another character trait that contributes to leadership effectiveness. According to Jim Collins in *Good to Great*, leaders who combined personal humility with a fierce resolve to produce results (i.e., "professional will") were depicted as having attained leadership greatness.[15] He recounts multiple stories of leaders of "brand-name" companies who are little known to the public and who pass Collins's test of humility as a quality that differentiates good leaders from great leaders.

What *is* humility? The word, like the term *Servant-Leader*, holds inherent paradox. Leaders who demonstrate humility can increase their potential to influence others, yet a person who works at appearing humble has already blown his cover.[16] Martin Luther knew this when he said, "No one knows less about humility than he who is truly humble."[17] Roman Catholics are familiar with the idea that a man who actively campaigns to be the next pope does not, by definition, deserve it. Until the twentieth century, American presidential candidates were expected to at least give an outward appearance of humility, staying in the background while others sang their praises.

Today, humility has a bad name in a culture where Donald Trump is celebrated as a "hero" worth emulating. "Brasher," the screen name for a contributor to an Internet chat room, neatly summarized a common attitude by writing, "Why on earth would anyone want to diminish the value of who they are? I take pride in who I am. Humility is for people with poor self-esteem." Another chat room member asked what "Brasher" did for a living and learned that "Brasher" was unemployed. Maybe "Brasher" needs to be even brasher—or get a job someplace where patience, growth, and positive change are not rewarded.

Patience, growth, and positive change: Where is the connection to humility?

Someone without humility is usually impatient. Why should he waste time listening to another opinion? After all, like "Brasher," he believes only in himself. Someone who is impatient is a lousy listener. And a lousy listener is no Servant-Leader.

There is more. Because humility cracks us open to possibilities beyond our own skulls, a humble leader is likely to make better decisions, based on broader, more diverse information and analysis. Lutheran Pastor Johan Hinderlie writes that "the Servant-Leader lives by 'second thoughts.' When things go wrong, the first thought is to defend oneself, look for blame, and react out of old patterns. If, however, we are open to change, if we invite a transformation in thinking and being that the Greeks called *metanoia*, we will wait for second thoughts."[18] The word *metanoia* comes from two words: *meta*, meaning "change" or "higher" or "beyond," and *noia* (from *nóos*), meaning "mind." A humble person has the patience to wait for the higher layer of wisdom that comes from second thoughts. He or she is open to positive change in each small, luminous moment of life.

People who embody humility do not overevaluate themselves—that would be grandiosity—or underevaluate themselves—that would be false humility. They keep their talents and accomplishments in perspective, remain other-focused and moderate, and allow themselves to be influenced by the input and feedback of others. They are self-confident but unassuming, always accountable to followers.

That may sound like a list of saintly qualities, but it simply means we should have a proper opinion of ourselves, just like our grandmothers told us. By contrast, too many people who are caught in the shallower currents of the "be all you can be" self-improvement movement see humility as an impossible limitation.

Perhaps it is a limitation—to acting on spur-of-the-moment impulses rather than deeply felt intuitions, a limitation to the kind of boasting and posturing more appropriate for an unformed teenager than an adult leader. Humility *certainly* helps limit the development of a toxic, defensive, in-your-face leader into one who draws upon the strength of others.

Wong and Page see authoritarian hierarchy and egotistic pride as the two forces that oppose Servant Leadership. They wonder why so many Christian leaders hold on to hierarchy, but their answer can apply to all leaders: "Basically, leaders' distrust in Servant Leadership stems from their own insecurity and egotism. They do not have the confidence that others will follow them, if they cannot exercise coercive power indiscriminately."[19] "Pride is a deep-seated problem, originating from our basic need for personal significance and worthiness, and authoritarian hierarchy implies the illegitimate use of power."[20] Their presence in an individual, by definition, spells the absence of a Servant-Leader.

The practice of Servant Leadership as embodied in the trait of humility requires courage of intentional vulnerability and voluntary surrender of one's ego for the sake of others and the organization. Of course no one can do this overnight. Some never begin the journey, while precious few stay with it to completion. However, the *journey* is the key for those seekers known as Servant-Leaders.

The first step is a courageous one: *intentionally make yourself vulnerable to the possibility that you are not right all the time.* This is doable. Try it, see what happens. Ask yourself and your colleagues, "Is this the right thing to do? Is it the wise thing to do?"

National Public Radio correspondent Nina Totenberg tells the story of a conversation with a United States senator who had successfully executed a controversial power play. He boasted that he and his party had the right to take the action they did. She asked, "But Senator, is it a *wise* thing to do?" The question had never occurred to him. It should occur to every Servant-Leader. "Am I right? Is this the right thing to do? Is it the *wise* thing to do?" If you begin to ask these questions *as a habit*, you will notice a change in the responses toward you, a shift in the landscape inside your heart and gut. You—and those around you—will begin to reap the benefits of your emerging humility.

## Ask Yourself

- Am I right?
- What is my second thought?
- Am I doing the wise thing?
- Will this action meet the conditions of Greenleaf's "Best Test?"

## 3. Serves a Higher Purpose

In describing the concept of leading by serving first, Robert Greenleaf articulated two fundamental dimensions of leadership. The first, and best known, is the *desire to serve*. The second is the *desire to serve something beyond or greater than oneself*—what he called a "higher purpose."

Joseph Jaworski, author of *Synchronicity: The Inner Path of Leadership*, has written with passion and depth about the essential need for individuals and organizations to discover and fulfill their unique, higher purpose. "With Greenleaf, I have come to believe that if we are willing to take that most difficult journey toward self-discovery and lifelong learning, we will lead lives filled with meaning and adventure. Moreover, we will gain the capacity to create and shape the future for ourselves and our organizations in ways we can hardly imagine."[21]

In the words of organizational guru Charles Handy, "The companies that survive are the ones that work out what they uniquely can give to the world—not just growth or money but their excellence, their respect for others, or their ability to make people happy."[22]

### *Searching for Significance*

Why am I here? What is my mission in life? How can I make a difference? Each of us must wrestle with these basic yet profound questions as we search for our life's purpose, meaning, and significance.

From the philosopher Socrates, who claimed, "An unexamined life is not worth living," to World War II psychiatrist and Auschwitz survivor Victor Frankl's classic *Man's Search for Meaning*, to contemporary pastor Rick Warren, author of the extraordinarily popular *The Purpose Driven Life*—we have been encouraged to discover and serve our destiny.

So, how do we begin?

One way is to put ourselves at the ultimate *end* of our life, looking back on how we lived it. What are others saying about us? How are we being remembered? Is the world we touched a better place because of our having been in it?

One way I (James) help business executives discover and articulate their higher purpose is to suggest they compose a personal epitaph, a brief inscription suitable for a headstone. You can imagine how much soul searching and angst this task engenders! I know, because I decided to compose my own epitaph, as an illustration. After all, if I expected clients to accept this challenge, I felt compelled to offer a creative—and hopefully illustrative—personal example.

I reflected long and hard on the meaning of my life's journey. I inventoried my strengths, weaknesses, talents, and failures. I asked myself a number of probing questions. Why was I the first fifth-grader at St. Timothy's allowed to serve as an altar boy, when everyone else started in the sixth? How did I become the only seventeen-year-old volunteer at a twenty-four–hour crisis hotline when the minimum age was eighteen? What qualified me as a high school senior to lead a drug rescue team composed of physicians, nurses, and paramedics at outdoor rock concerts? Why, on April 19, 1995, did I happen to be flying to, of all places, Oklahoma City, and wind up on the Red Cross disaster relief team the first weekend after the bombing? How did I get to become an "authority" on Servant Leadership? I saw a theme starting to crystallize, like watching the winter frost creeping along a frozen window: I am a "natural-born servant."

After many hours of contemplation, I decided to table the task. Then, as often happens in the creative process, soon after I gave up trying, the answer came to me in an unexpected fashion. The following Sunday's Gospel message was taken from the twenty-fifth chapter of Matthew, the parable of the talents. There on my lap, in the church bulletin, my epitaph was revealed in the title of the sermon: "Well done, good and faithful servant." That was it!

## *Discovering Your Calling*

What about you? Have you discovered where you should be spending the rich moments of your emerging Servant-Leader life? If not, how will you live out—and help others to find—their higher purpose?

That depends upon whether you recognize your *genius*—which is the name Romans gave to one's individual area of innate passion and understanding—or your *daimon*, the Greek word describing an inborn direction of fulfillment that is different for each person. For example, the *daimon* of an acorn is to grow into a mighty oak tree. The *daimon* of a caterpillar is to transform into a lovely butterfly.

We prefer the word *calling*. Every person has a *calling*—a passionate lure to the highest level of fulfillment—and a calling is a lure, not a mandate. You can ignore it, or accept it but refuse to act on it, but you will never shake it. You can discover your calling by paying attention to the things you love—the people, ideas, projects, or organizations that have sparks around them. Some people seem to know their calling from an early age, but for many of us it emerges after a period of dissatisfaction, followed by reflection and the discovery of new possibilities that seem intuitively right.

Consider the story of Martha and Mike Port. In 1988, when they were both forty years old, Martha was an insurance underwriter and Mike was a community organizer, but they were dissatisfied with their scattered lives and began to reflect on their true calling. They knew they wanted to work together, but more importantly, they wanted to invest their lives in something that served a higher purpose, an enterprise that made a difference for people.

They prayed that God would show them the right path and waited for guidance.

A few weeks later, Martha ran across a United Nations report that estimated more than two billion people in the world could not afford the fuel necessary to prepare food or boil water to make it safe. In several African countries, women were walking up to ten miles every day to find wood for fuel, and the forests were disappearing.

The Ports realized that most of these people lived in areas of the planet that had the most sunshine. The UN Report mentioned solar cookers as a solution, but existing designs were expensive and not very efficient. They thought they could do better. They had found their calling in solar ovens.

Mike and Martha quit their jobs and lived on retirement income for several years while they formed the nonprofit Solar Ovens Society. They put together a board that shared their values, and created an organization that could get things done. Soon, retired 3M engineers and others who caught the breathtaking implications of their vision volunteered to help. Together, they designed a simple, cheap, portable, and efficient solar oven that could be manufactured in developing countries. Today, you can see various models of the Solar Oven at www.solarovens.org.

This unassuming, middle-class Minneapolis couple is changing the world by saving lives, preserving forests, and maybe even preventing one or two revolutions in countries like Kenya, where the government banned the cutting of wood for fuel in 2006.

Martha and Mike Port did not start with such grandiose goals: they started with themselves, asking what it meant to act as servants, discovering their calling, and acting on it.

## Ask Yourself

Do you believe you have found your calling? Ask yourself these questions for clues to your higher purpose.

- Where do I find joy?

- What am I passionate about?

- What am I really good at?

- What have my failures taught me about my proper calling?

- What surprising feedback have I had from others about what I could be doing to make a difference?

- What will be my epitaph?

# PILLAR II

# Puts People First

A Servant-Leader helps others meet their highest priority development needs.

- Seeks first to serve, then aspires to lead.
- Self-interest is deeply connected to the needs and interests of others.
- Serves in a manner that allows those served to grow as persons.
- Expresses genuine care and concern for others.

## Core Competencies

1. Displays a Servant's Heart
2. Is Mentor-Minded
3. Shows Care & Concern

## People before Profits

"Our company is our people!" "Our people are our biggest assets!" "We put people first!" Some organizations act on these mantras. Others simply spout them as slogans. What about you? Do you put people first in your personal and professional life? It is not always easy.

In the course of researching a book on ethics for insurance professionals, I (Don) spoke with scores of insurance agents and asked

34

them about their ethical challenges. One person, whom I'll call Mark, described a situation that, as it turned out, was fairly common. Mark's company introduced a new interest-sensitive policy that offered a generous commission to agents. To sweeten the deal, the company provided an all-expense paid trip to Hawaii for agents and their spouses, provided they sold a certain number of policies by a deadline. Once his wife heard about this opportunity, she became Mark's number-one cheerleader. One morning she woke him up by banging on a pot, saying, "Aloha honey! Time to get out of bed and sell, sell, sell!" And he did, moving enough product to put him within two policies of meeting the goal with two weeks to go.

After doing a thorough analysis of one prospect's needs, Mark realized that the kind of policy that counted for the Hawaii trip was not right for her. She, in fact, needed a simple term policy, the cheapest product with the least commission to the seller. On the other hand, Mark had a great rapport with her and sensed that he could make the sale anyway. What would he choose—ethical responsibility or sandy beaches; the client's needs or personal profits?

Mark told me that he agonized over this dilemma so much that he asked for an extra day to get back to his prospect. He knew what was right for her but wondered if it was also "right" for his company, his income or for that matter, even his marriage.

When he met the prospect the next day, he came clean, told her about the policy promotion, laughed about how excited his wife was, and explained how the new policy might meet her needs a few years down the road but that he could not in good conscience recommend it to her now. She bought the term policy but was so impressed by his honesty that she referred him to several friends who bought the incentive policy, just in time for Mark to make his quota for Hawaii.

Not every story has this fairytale ending. Mark could have just as easily lost out on the trip to Hawaii. But he did the right thing. His defining moment of putting the person before the profit—even before short-term company interests—it turned out well.

Ironically, the practice of putting people before profits makes an organization even more profitable. We've already referred to our data on servant-led companies and their "better than great" financial performance. Additional research conducted by *In Search*

*of Excellence* coauthor Robert Waterman, Stanford University's organizational guru, Jeffrey Pfeffer, and others, also show that "people first" companies outperform all competitors.[1]

Apparently, organizations that say "people are our most important asset" and mean it, have a significant competitive advantage.

## Called to Serve, Inspired to Lead

Robert Greenleaf wrote that a great leader is first experienced as a servant to others and that this simple fact is central to the leader's greatness. In other words, *true leadership emerges from one whose primary motivation is a deep desire to serve!* This is different from "helping others" in the common usage of that phrase. There is nothing wrong with "helping," but that generally means we possess knowledge or skills that we pass along to others. We help them balance a checkbook or clean the house or learn enough to pass an exam. The emphasis is on what we know, and what we can do. When we act as *servant* to others, we are concerned with the full range of *their* knowledge, skills, emotional and behavioral dynamics. We often "help" best by talking but "serve" best by listening; "help" by actions but "serve" by actions *and* simple presence. "While many effective leadership models show concern for their followers," writes leadership researcher Kathleen Patterson and her colleagues, "the overriding focus of the Servant-Leader is on service to their followers [versus] greater concern for getting followers to engage in and support organizational objectives."[2]

Like the authors of this book, Servant-Leaders frequently describe their desire to serve others as a "calling." In fact, John Barbuto Jr. and Daniel Wheeler at the University of Nebraska–Lincoln have added "calling" to Spears's established list of ten characteristics of Servant-Leaders. They believe a calling to serve is a deeply rooted, values-based impulse, "a desire to make a difference for other people…to impact others' lives…willing to sacrifice self-interests for the sake of others."[3]

Some may say that kind of call is a genetically based leftover from early human history when service to one's tribe was a matter of survival. However, many identify it as religious. Robert Greenleaf simply said the source of the impulse to serve was from "mystery." To think of one as a servant in today's highly competitive, consumer-based culture is counter to prevailing wisdom, but the imprint of the call still resides in the quiet places of the heart.

## *Doing Good Feels Good*

Scientists may have discovered physiological correlates of the "mystery" Greenleaf linked to our deepest impulse to serve. When Jorge Moll and his team of researchers at the National Institutes of Health monitored the brain activity of subjects participating in a charitable giving experiment, they found that an act of altruism affects the same parts of the brain stimulated by sex, drugs, and money, causing a biological "warm glow."[4] Therefore, we hereby make this claim: "Serving others is sexy!"

However, is servanthood "natural?" Many evolutionary biologists believe altruism is based on one of two unconscious motives: (1) to help those with whom we share genes or community ties (our "tribe") in order to assure our own survival, or (2) the desire to get something in return.

Psychoanalyst Dr. Joseph Weiss disagrees. His theory of motivation suggests that altruism may be based on an unconscious need to help others rather than an unconscious selfishness.[5] Much of modern psychotherapy focuses on patients "getting in touch" with non-conscious feelings of anger and shame from parents and sexual events, but Dr. Weiss has found that just as often people feel guilty because they have suppressed the unconscious *altruism* that has been with them since earliest memories. "The focus on anger may be one of the more damaging aspects of traditional psychoanalytically-based psychotherapy," says Dr. Lynn O'Conner, a follower of Dr. Weiss's research. "This is particularly true [to the extent that] people's psychological problems are derived from self-sacrifice driven by their unconscious altruism."[6] He goes on to say that too much conscious self-sacrifice can also be maladaptive. Who among us has not known a person who sacrificed so much as a caregiver that she neglected her own needs and eventually could not function as a helper, much less a whole person?

Following the impulse to serve could be an antidote to the excesses and inhuman dysfunctions of modern culture. However, it is not automatic—one must then choose to lead as servant, to risk mistakes and achievements.

For Greenleaf, acting upon the impulse to serve does *not* mean one is a "service provider," a martyr or a slave, but one who consciously nurtures the mature growth of self, other people, institutions, and communities—the objective of which is to stimulate thought and action for building a better, more caring society.

In other words, we reveal what we believe by what we do. We can talk about serving, but until we put on the apron and get our hands on the dirty dishes, it all remains just talk. *Acting* on what we believe by what we do is at the heart of Servant Leadership.

## Ask Yourself

- Would I make the same decision that Mark made about coming clean with his client?

- Do I feel the natural desire to serve in my body as well as in my mind? Where is it located? Can I access it in times of stress when I need to touch this part of my deepest self?

# 1. Displaying a Servant's Heart

> *Leadership is not an affair of the head. Leadership is an affair of the heart.*
> —Kouzes & Posner

In our travels as leadership consultants, we have encountered scores of talented, compassionate Servant-Leaders. It was difficult to decide which examples from our lengthy list might best illustrate how one leads with a servant's heart.

Should we write about Mike Chiles, cofounder of Heatway in Springfield, Missouri, and holder of patents for radiant heating systems, who chose to profit share millions of dollars with his employees when he could have pocketed the money himself? Or should we report on Johan Hinderlie, executive director of Mount Carmel Ministries in Alexandria, Minnesota, who, during his off-season, travels around the country—and sometimes overseas—to preside at employee baptisms, weddings, and funerals? What about Colleen Barrett of Dallas, Texas, whose rise from secretary to CEO is legend among employees at Southwest Airlines, as is her reputation for kindness and caring along the way?

We wanted to write about them *all*.

In the end, we decided to tell a story about a Servant-Leader much closer to home—to James's home, that is.

James would like to tell you about his father.

Dr. James W. Sipe Sr. (1929–88) was a family-practice physician and cofounder of the Coon Rapids Clinic, located a few suburbs north of Minneapolis/St. Paul. Dad and his partner, Dr. Matt Plascha, parlayed a two-person medical practice in a rundown office building behind a bowling alley into a large multispecialty medical center with satellite clinics throughout the Twin Cities north suburban tier.

Although my father rose to great prominence in the community, he always remained humble and never strayed from his love of medicine and his patients. To this day I can hear him say, with ample modesty and reverence, "Please don't mention it, I'm just a simple country doctor," his reply to anyone who gushed with praise for his healing. He continued to make house calls and give patients our home telephone number, long after the advent of the HMO.

When I was around eight or nine years old, after I stopped believing in Santa Claus, I discovered that my dad had established an annual tradition of playing Santa for some of his more "needy" patients. Each year around the week before Christmas, he came home from work and, with my mom's help, got all gussied up as Saint Nick. (Over time, he acquired a theater-grade costume and hired a professional makeup artist!) Then, he piled all the goodies into his old Lincoln Continental and made his nightly rounds, aided by a list that his nurse Jan had readied for him that day.

I recall the day my dad informed me that I was now old enough to play Santa's helper. He asked if I would like to be his "elf" and help pass out the assortment of toys and treats contained in his jam-packed, red sack. Would I ever!

I can still vividly picture the looks of amusement on the faces of those children, the tearful expressions of love and gratitude from parents who could barely make ends meet. Time and again, I witnessed firsthand my father beaming with pride and joy through his fake salt and pepper beard as his servant's heart poured out its unconditional compassion and benevolence.

Kahlil Gibran, author of *The Prophet* got it right: "The joy of giving *is* its own reward."

I enjoyed a few years of participation in this touching holiday tradition, even though my career as an elf was short-lived. It wasn't long before I realized that tights, makeup, and male pubescence did not mix so well.

Shortly before my father died, he passed along all his Santa possessions to me. What an incredible gift that was! What an unspeakable honor. Imagine how I felt the first time I donned that plush, worn suit and became Santa Claus for my three-year-old daughter Rachel and her day-care chums at the Rainbow House.

Dad's Santa legacy lived on in my family until my two children stopped believing. Then I offered the suit to my next oldest sibling Paul, so he could take his turn in our father's footsteps.

## Ask Yourself

- How do I find, claim, and cultivate my servant's heart?
- Am I passing on the legacy of servanthood to my family, my friends, and coworkers?

## 2. Being Mentor Minded

Robert Greenleaf said some controversial things about the topic of helping others grow as persons. He suggested one should have "unlimited liability" for others—a phrase that makes lawyers shudder. Yet it simply refers to an attitude of *love*. He also said that Servant-Leaders should take care that others' highest-priority needs are met. This is love in action. Still, a Servant-Leader is neither a martyr nor a codependent in implementing the growth of others.

He or she is a tough-minded, compassionate, and a wise *partner* in growth—including his or her own growth and development.

When discussing mentoring, Greenleaf advocated a shift from the point of view of *doing* something *to* people to *permitting* something to happen to them. He suggested that mentors not pour their wisdom into their mentees to show them "the way things really are." This would rob mentees of the opportunity to develop their own wisdom. "Give them responsibility," said Greenleaf.

Help them get a feeling of what mature growth involves and assume some responsibility for their own growth. Give them the freedom to take responsible risks. We discover more about ourselves through error than through success. Only the person who can take risks and tolerate the errors has a chance to achieve their freedom to become himself or herself.[7]

This advice sounds similar to the truism in parent education: "Prepare the child for the path, not the path for the child." We have often seen this wisdom at work with family-owned businesses. There comes a time in the life cycle of every successful family business when planning for the succession of leadership to the next generation is paramount. Some of the wisest owners have encouraged their children to work *outside* the family company for a while in order to find their own leadership voice. Some even make this a *requirement* before a family member can take over the reins of leadership. We have only anecdotal experience to make this claim. However, we have found that these protégés are more qualified to run the family business than children who have the business handed to them.

Do you see the difference between leaving one's business to a child who has been groomed to administer *your* achievement versus a progeny who is his own person, capable of dealing creatively and courageously with the problems he will face in your absence? The first example is ego based. The second is servant based.

Robert Greenleaf understood the difference. For him, a mentor should be more like a master teacher whose goal is the growth of the protégé rather than a trainer whose goal is to impart "how-to" tips on meeting organizational objectives and winning at office politics. Not that there is anything wrong with the latter, but the former is what Servant-Leaders focus on.

I (Don) have been honored to have Dr. Ann McGee-Cooper as a mentor. Ann learned from the master—Robert Greenleaf—who was one of her own mentors. Today, Ann is one of the top Servant Leadership authors and consultants in the world, but she was a natural Servant-Leader before she ever met Robert Greenleaf.

Ann has always been an unfailing Servant-Leader to me—supportive, loving, insightful, and openly transparent. When I called her during traumatic periods through the years, she listened carefully, and did not judge or tell me what to do. Typically, she asked questions, shared her own learnings from similar experience, and left me with even larger issues to consider. She would not allow me to wallow in the swamp of "Ain't-it-awful," endlessly repeating the latest outrages in my life.

I remember one conversation in which I shared a difficult situation. After some silent reflection, Ann said, "Don, you might want to think about whether you sabotage your own success. If that's true, where does it come from?" I was stunned. My first impulse was to say, "Oh no, Ann, I'm not doing that!" But then I realized that she had nailed me. On the surface, her suggestion had nothing to do with the details of the situation I had shared but, in fact, it spoke to the real dynamics.

When I succeeded on projects, Ann shared my successes. She taught me how to celebrate, but also how to be accountable. In the early years, I produced her media materials, including audio tapes of her inspiring speeches. One day I received an upsetting call. She had not received the latest order on time, putting her in a bad situation with a client. She wanted me to know the effects of my failure to deliver. She cared enough about me to allow me to understand the consequences of my actions.

I always wanted to give something back to Ann, so I shared every new book that captured my imagination, every interesting quote or insight. She let me riff on ideas like a jazz musician improvising on unusual chords, even when I was off pitch, and then jumped in with her own connections and inventions.

Ann always believed in me enough to not tell me what to do, to support me in my growth as a person. She was a consummate Servant-Leader mentor.

## Ask Yourself

- Is my mentoring about me or the person I am mentoring?
- Do I get ego "goodies" out of being the expert?
- Am I evolved enough to allow others to find their own ways, even when they are different from my ways?

## 3. Shows Care and Concern

"Caring" is the primary concept in the Tires Plus mission statement. That might explain why Tom Gegax, founder and former CEO of Tires Plus, takes issue with those who would downplay caring in the workplace as squishy or weak.

"Some people deride caring as tantamount to being soft, or even encouraging low standards," he says. "This is a misguided concern. When the situation calls for it, caring [also] calls for tough love—meeting inappropriate behavior with firm, yet loving discipline. As with any caring feedback, separating the behavior from the person is key: the person is lovable; the behavior is not."[8]

Expressing care and concern goes beyond "being nice." It even goes beyond one's personality style. Genuine care and concern are expressed through *actions*. One way to show concern for employees is to provide opportunities for them to meet their highest priority needs—for safety, security, belonging, esteem, purpose and meaning, for self-actualization, and fulfillment.[9]

Author James Autry once heard the CEO of the Meredith Corporation make a most amazing claim: when it comes to the work of self-renewal, the most important thing is *love*. Autry described a company manager who modeled love in his marketing department—love for his employees, for the products they created, and for their customers. The outcome was that revenue climbed from $160 million to $500 million. Autry believed it was due to a transformation in the way the manager led with love.[10]

The word *love* still sounds strange in the context of *business*. It normally floats around *church* settings. However, here the emphasis is not on sentimentality but on acting intentionally in ways that support the health, wisdom, freedom, and autonomy of persons, with the motive of meeting *their* most critical needs rather than our narrow ego needs. Blessed Mother Teresa was known as one of her generation's most loving persons through her commitment to the poorest of the poor in Calcutta. During an interview, a TV anchorman said, "I would not do what you are doing for a million dollars." Mother Teresa answered, "Neither would I!" Love, *not* money, was the power that shaped her and kept her caring for the people she found dying on the streets.

Research bears this out. In the last paragraph of their monumental study of leadership, Kouzes and Posner wrote, "Of all the things that sustain a leader over time, love is the most lasting. The best-kept secret of successful leaders is love: staying in love with leading, with the people who do the work, with what their organizations produce, and with those who honor the organization by using its work."[11]

The Beatles famously sang "All You Need is Love," but that is not quite right. You, we, all of us need active love beyond sentiment—love expressed through presence with others, made real by decisions that put people first; love that incarnates by holding oneself and others accountable. Love that is mentor minded, delighting in the healthy growth of others even if it branches off the path we prefer for them. That is how servants love. That is how Servant-Leaders lead.

## Ask Yourself

- What are three new and specific actions I could take tomorrow to show care and concern?

- How would I analyze my "return on investment" if the investment was love rather than money?

# Skilled Communicator

*A true natural servant automatically responds to any problem by listening first.* —Robert Greenleaf

A Servant-Leader listens earnestly and speaks effectively.

- Seeks first to understand, then to be understood.

- Listens receptively to others, demonstrating genuine interest, warmth, and respect.

- Listens honestly and deeply to oneself and invites feedback from others.

- Influences others with assertiveness and persuasion rather than power and position.

## Core Competencies

1. Demonstrates Empathy

2. Invites Feedback

3. Communicates Persuasively

## Frank and Earnest Communication

We'd like to introduce you to Frank N. Earnest. Frank is a composite of a number of aspiring Servant-Leaders we've trained and coached over the years.

Frank is approximately forty years old, married with children. He's a midlevel manager in a midsized company, with five to seven employees who report directly to him. He's considered by coworkers, family, and friends to be smart, decent, hardworking, and caring. If you were at the company water cooler when the topic of conversation rolled around to Frank, you might hear, "I'm not sure Frank totally bought into our rationale for an immediate, department-wide database software upgrade, but he's a pretty open-minded guy—I think he gave us a fair hearing." Or, "Sometimes I think Frank tries a little too hard. He should chill out more." Or, "I know Frank's heart is in the right place, but if he doesn't tell Sylvia to shut up about her grandkids and focus on the phones, I'm going to scream!"

Frank is an ideal candidate for leadership development. His employer considers him a fine manager with good instincts—a candidate for promotion.

Frank was receptive to being coached. He described himself as inquisitive and eager to learn. He also saw his development opportunity for what it truly was—a potent statement by his employer about his value to the organization. He knew the company would not invest ten to fifteen thousand dollars over the next six months if it didn't consider him a significant contributor, with potential for even greater responsibilities.

Coaching Frank through the assessment and discovery process revealed a representative set of leadership strengths and development needs: principle centered, compassionate, strategic, occasionally indecisive, conflict adverse, somewhat self-critical, ambitious, and mildly anxious.

Maybe you're thinking, "I know a guy like Frank." Or, "Frank would make a great employee." Or, "You know, I wouldn't mind working for Frank." You might even conclude, "Hey, Frank sounds a little bit like me!" A solid individual, a capable manager.

Frank was not surprised by our findings. He knew he had room to grow—as a decision maker, a supervisor, a listener, a leader. He was an enthusiastic, creative participant in the crafting of his coaching plan.

Here's a sampling of Frank's development objectives:

1.1 Strengthen your active listening and assertive speaking skills according to the guidelines described in the ABC's of Communication.

    1.2 Demonstrate the ability to confront a coworker's unacceptable behavior in a direct, firm, and fair manner and provide specific suggestions for performance improvement and accountability.

2.1 Identify your conflict management style via the *Conflict Roost Inventory* and create corresponding action steps for improvement.

    2.2 List the three most common triggers of your conflict avoidant behavior and devise one preemptive strategy and one coping strategy for each.

3.1 Facilitate a meeting of team members to introduce them to the techniques outlined in Objectives 1.1 and 2.1, invite feedback, and solicit their commitment to help you apply them.

    3.2 Conduct an exercise with the group to help each member identify their respective strengths and weaknesses as speakers and listeners.

Twice a month we met with Frank to provide direction and support, review his progress against plan objectives, ask pertinent questions, and offer whatever real-world, real-time advice about current or emergent circumstances Frank required. As time went on, Frank flourished. Through trial, error, success, feedback, and support, Frank not only accomplished his coaching plan objectives, but also acquired new skills and competencies. This was evidenced by observation, feedback from others, and the use of new behaviors both inside and outside the workplace.

"I tried out some of the listening and conflict stuff we've been working on during a heated conversation with my wife last night," Frank proudly reported at one of our regular coaching meetings. "Instead of me ending up on the couch—as often happens—we stayed in bed together, if you know what I mean." The gleam in Frank's eye was luminescent.

"That's great Frank," we replied. "No extra charge."

## Great Leaders Are Great Communicators

We should all be experts in communication. After all, every day we send and receive thousands of verbal and nonverbal messages filled with ideas, emotions, and desires. Communication is how we connect with and influence other people. It is the glue that holds our relationships together—at work, at home, and in the community. Why then study something we seem to already know how to do?

Not so fast! Experts say that *skillful* communication is the foundation of effective leadership—but notice the key word here is *skillful*, which means listening to understand others and expressing one's thoughts, feelings, and needs with genuineness, respect, and clarity.[1] In our quiet, honest moments, most of us must admit that we fall short of that standard. All too often we would rather talk than listen, make quick judgments or convince others of our "rightness" rather than patiently seek understanding.

"Excuse me, Susan, is this a good time to run something by you?"

"Yeah, sure, Sally," her boss replied without missing a beat on the keyboard, eyes glued to the screen. "What is it?"

"I think I figured out why the server has been so temperamental lately." Sally was beaming with pride. "I can fix it, but I'll have to take it offline for about an hour."

"Darn it, Sally, I'm swamped right now and this memo is two hours overdue." Susan stopped typing and turned to Sally with a look of frustration and fatigue. "Can't it wait?"

"Of course," she said. "I just thought you'd like to know. I was planning on staying late to work on it after everyone left for the day."

"Oh, sure…thanks, Sally," Susan replied sheepishly. "That's a great idea. And be sure you have Eddie's cell number handy, in case you need an IT rescue."

Sound familiar? We admit that we have been on *both* sides of conversations like this.

Susan is not a bad person or a lousy boss. She is nowhere near as inconsiderate as this brief interchange portrays. Instead, one might say she was a distracted or inactive listener, one who might occasionally take her bright, well-meaning employee too much for granted.

Notice the missed opportunity to strengthen a bond, affirm a job well done, and reinforce initiative and creativity. Susan failed to notice Sally's facial expression of pride and satisfaction. She did not hear the subtly expressed need for recognition. And she demonstrated absolutely no curiosity about the problem, nor about what Eddie in IT would later describe as Sally's "brilliant" solution.

Skillful, ethical communication offers significant benefits for leaders and followers:

- Empathic listeners who seek first to understand communicate respect, warmth, and unconditional positive regard. The speaker feels attended to, cared about, affirmed—the emotional building blocks of trusting, dependable, and productive working relationships.

- Effective communicators are more likely to see results from clear, realistic expectations because they know how to persuasively delegate responsibility, provide adequate encouragement and support, and offer firm, fair reminders of accountability.

- The workplaces of seasoned communicators will enjoy more constructive conflict resolution because the leaders have learned to rationally detach from their own internal emotional turbulence and focus the conflicted energy of others on creative, collaborative solutions to the problems.

- Teams enjoy healthier emotional give and take when effective communicators are conversant in the vocabulary of feelings and model the forthright sharing of a full range of feelings—joy, sadness, fear, anger, and guilt.

- Coworkers stay more oriented to their shared mission when seasoned communicators help make sense of life's experiences by using symbols, metaphors, and stories— creating islands of shared meaning and connectedness in the sea of individual diversity.

- Effective communication is a primary way of serving others while lifting up the vision of the organization. Exceptional communicators inspire others to stretch their thinking, clarify their values, and take constructive action.

Ultimately, these benefits and the competencies of an effective communicator that make them possible, allow one to use *persuasion*, the Servant-Leader's preferred mode of employing power. One who truly persuades is open to being in the process, and never confuses persuasion with manipulation or coercion.

## Communication Skills Are Relationship Skills

Leaders can learn from the experience of psychotherapists, who are highly trained as communicators. Gerard Egan, author of *The Skilled Helper*—currently the most widely used counseling text in the world—refers to these skills as the "facilitative dimensions" of high-level human relating.[2] They include the following:

1. Empathy (deep, accurate understanding)

2. Warmth (kindness, respect)

3. Genuineness (openness, authenticity)

4. Concreteness (specific, direct)

5. Initiative (solution oriented, risk taking)

6. Immediacy (mutual, intimate, "here-and-now" sharing)

7. Self-disclosure (appropriate sharing of self)

8. Confrontation (challenging others to grow)

9. Self-exploration (self-reflection, inviting feedback)

These competencies are sometimes referred to as "people skills." You may have heard others remark, "He is a real people person," or more recently, "I'll bet she has a pretty high EQ" (emotional intelligence).

# Ask Yourself

- How are your people skills? The following survey will help you determine how you measure up.

# How Are YOUR People Skills?

Listed below are a number of behaviors that are essential to high-level human relating. Rate yourself on these behaviors, using the following scale.

| 1 = Poor   2 = Fair   3 = Good   4 = Very Good   5 = Excellent | |
|---|---|
| _____ Empathy | I see the world through the eyes of others; it is easy for me to put myself in other people's shoes. Understanding their point of view is important to me. I listen well to both verbal and nonverbal cues. I reflect back my awareness and understanding of their thoughts, feelings, and desires with clarity and respect. |
| _____ Warmth | I express that I am "for" others in a variety of ways, that I respect and care about them. I accept others for who they are, even though I do not always necessarily approve of what they do. I am a supportive and positive person. |
| _____ Genuineness | I am real and authentic in my interactions. I do not hide behind roles or facades; others usually know where I stand. I am comfortable being myself. |
| _____ Concreteness | I am not vague when I speak to others; I do not speak in generalities nor do I beat around the bush. I deal with concrete experience and behavior when I talk. I am direct and specific. |
| _____ Initiative | In my relationships I would rather act than just react. I confront problems directly. I am solution-oriented and optimistic. I do not blame others. |

Continued next page

Continued

| 1 = Poor    2 = Fair    3 = Good    4 = Very Good    5 = Excellent | |
|---|---|
| _____ Immediacy | I deal openly and directly with my relationship to others. I engage in "you-me" talk in the "here-and-now." I am willing to take risks to promote mutual, intimate sharing. I am open to feedback. |
| _____ Self-disclosure | I let others know the "person inside" whenever appropriate. I am willing to share my thoughts, feelings, likes, dislikes, regrets, ambitions, and dreams. I am not intrusive; I maintain adequate interpersonal boundaries. I use self-disclosure to help establish sound relationships with others. |
| _____ Confrontation | I challenge others responsibly and with care. I invite others to examine discrepancies in their thoughts, feelings, intentions, and behaviors. I use confrontation as a way of getting involved with others, helping them to grow, and never to punish. |
| _____ Self-exploration | I examine my lifestyle and behavior and want others to help me do the same. I desire to learn how I affect others. I respond to feedback as nondefensively as possible. I am open to changing my behavior. |

**Scoring:** If you scored between 38 and 45, you are a people skills genius! If your score is between 27 and 37, you win the congeniality award. If you scored between 18 and 26 you can check "mildly personable" on your next personality test. However, if your score falls between 5 and 17, please read on: you have some serious work to do.

It can take years to become proficient in all nine areas, but what you are about to learn will allow you to operate as a more skillful communicator *immediately*. The remainder of this chapter bundles the nine facilitative dimensions with specific communication skills that support three core competencies: (1) Demonstrating Empathy, (2) Inviting Feedback, and (3) Communicating Persuasively.

# 1. Demonstrating Empathy

*Walk a mile in my moccasins.* —Native American Proverb

If communication is the joint that holds relationships together, empathy is the connective tissue. It is what enables us to establish bonds of trust and caring with our colleagues and customers, to meet them with our hearts as well as our minds, and to influence them to faithfully follow our lead.

Being empathic, as the saying goes, requires us to "put ourselves in other people's shoes." Skillful, empathic Servant-Leaders are comfortable walking in moccasins, flip-flops, clogs, or high-heeled pumps. They demonstrate a level of caring and appreciation that unconditionally affirms others—whoever they are, whatever their circumstances, allowing each person to feel understood and appreciated.

## *Empathy in Action*

When asked to describe how he put empathy into action in the workplace, Ken Melrose, retired CEO and chairman of Twin Cities-based Toro Company, proudly shares a story he calls the "Windom Dare."

Windom, population 4,500, is a picture-book, rural farming community in southwest Minnesota. A view of the town's main street, with its stately historic courthouse and the nearby Des Moines River, is classic Norman Rockwell. Along with the customary small-town businesses—a bakery, café, and a bar or two—Windom includes a Toro manufacturing plant, by far the city's largest employer.

Melrose tells of a time in the 1980s when the Windom workers wanted to slow down the assembly lines in order to pay greater attention to the quality of the lawn mowing and snow blowing equipment they manufacture. On a visit to the plant, about 150 miles south of Toro's headquarters, Ken heard the complaints from the plant's union head, Emil Horkey, while walking the assembly lines. Melrose saw an opportunity for empathy, and goaded him a bit by saying, "Emil, even our management up in Minneapolis could make quality products at these line rates."

Of course, Emil took this criticism as a dare and challenged the white-collar corporate types to come down to the facility and "prove it." "Our people showed up and after a brief orientation," said Melrose "began working the lines at 80 percent of the normal speed." During the first hour, the Minneapolis managers were constantly hitting the buttons to stop the lines, so the plant manager had to reduce the line rate further, to 60 percent of normal. Even at this rate, it was difficult to keep the lines running, due to the novices' inability to keep up. And all the while, as the corporate managers worked furiously to maintain the pace, the Windom plant people chattered back and forth about their lives, their kids, and community activities—replete with mentions of church, little league, fundraising, family problems, and illnesses.

During the "postmortem" at the end of the day with everyone, the officers spoke in amazement how the Windom folks could keep up the small talk while the Minneapolis contingent were frantically trying to do their multiple operations. It was obvious to them that the Windom folks could do their jobs with much greater proficiency than they could. However, what was even more enlightening to the management team members was the realization that these individuals lived daily lives that were very similar to their own.

Melrose credits this encounter as a significant element in forging the company's new culture—a culture that embraced empathy as a key cultural component. Managers from Minneapolis started thinking about "those hourly workers" in Windom as real people, with similar life challenges, heartaches, and blessings. As a result of the "Windom Dare," Toro began to send out corporate and divisional managers to visit and work in all the Toro plants. These events still occur to this day.

## Empathy Defined

Our working definition of *empathy* is "being keenly aware of another's thoughts, feelings, and needs associated with an experience, and explicitly expressing to them a deep and caring understanding of their experience."

Carl Rogers, father of the humanistic psychology movement, spoke with clarity and passion about the power of empathy, especially the significance of being fully present and "with" another:

Being fully present means entering the private perceptual world of the other and becoming thoroughly at home in it. It involves being sensitive, moment by moment, to the changing felt meanings which flow in this other person, to the fear or rage or tenderness or confusion or whatever he or she is experiencing. It means temporarily living in the other's life, moving about in it delicately without making judgments. For empathy, presence must precede practice.[3]

## *Hardwired for Empathy*

A growing body of research in the emerging field of social neuroscience suggests that human beings are more naturally capable of making deep connections than scientists and helping professionals ever imagined—that we may be "hardwired" for empathy.

In a paper entitled "The Roots of Empathy," Vittorio Gallese hypothesized that "sensations and emotions displayed by others can be implicitly understood, through a mirror-matching mechanism in the brain."[4] This insight came as a result of research by his team who studied grasping behaviors in monkeys. They attached electrodes to the monkeys' brains to observe precisely which neurons fired when a monkey grabbed a raisin. Later, during a break, one of the researchers reached for a raisin. His fellow researchers coincidentally noticed something extraordinary on the monitor: neurons in the monkey's brain also fired—*the exact same neurons* that had fired earlier when the monkey grasped a raisin!

The team was astonished: nothing like this had ever been seen before. Their serendipitous finding was the first clue to the existence of what scientists now call "mirror neurons," so named because they appear to actually reflect the activity of another's brain cells. This was a genuine brain-to-brain connection. In an instant, the definition of interconnectedness, the notion of empathy, changed forever.

Subsequent neuroimaging research in humans suggests that we, too, may have a similar mirror-neuron system that allows us to deeply "get" the experience of others. It seems that we were created to resonate with one another at profound emotional levels.

Daniel Goleman also makes this point in his book *Social Intelligence: The New Science of Human Relationships*. It's not just that our strong emotions are "contagious." Empathizing with others, whether in sorrow or joy, can activate the same circuits in our brains as in theirs.[5]

We are now learning that empathy is not solely a feature of human beings and primates. In a 2011 experiment reported in *Science*, researchers at the University of Chicago discovered that a rat will release a fellow rat from a cage if given the opportunity, even if there was no ostensible payoff to the rat for doing so. In fact, if given access to a small pile of chocolate chips, the free rat would usually save at least one chip for his released compatriot.[6]

These are exciting findings. They mean that empathy is a natural, higher-order biological process, not a fuzzy, touchy-feely New Age idea. Nature will help us succeed as empathic listeners as long as we dedicate ourselves to understanding and serving others. Consider a line from the popular peace prayer that is attributed to St. Francis of Assisi: "O, Divine Master, grant that I may not so much seek to be consoled as to console, to be understood as to understand."[7]

## Ask Yourself

- Do I usually feel empathy for others or am I too busy? When I do feel empathy, how do I show it?

- How could empathy improve a specific, difficult situation in my workplace?

- Am I willing to center myself to bring my full presence to a conversation so I can "be fully at home in it?" How can I do that? Some ideas include the following: take three deep breaths, remove distractions, shift into a heightened awareness of the other's body posture, use language and emotional nuances.

# Servant-Leader Listening

The best way to connect in empathy is to *listen*, to listen with full presence and attention. Robert Greenleaf said listening is the premier skill of a Servant-Leader.

> I have a bias which suggests that only a true natural servant automatically responds to any problem by listening *first*. When he is a leader, this disposition causes him to be *seen* as servant first. This suggests that a nonservant who wants to be a servant might become a *natural* servant through a long arduous discipline of learning to listen, a discipline sufficiently sustained that the automatic response to any problem is to listen first.[8]

A quick Google search will convince you that the whole world wants to learn how to listen better. In less than a second, you can find references to *active listening, strategic listening, compassionate listening, reflective listening*, and many other approaches. Habit Five of Stephen Covey's *Seven Habits of Highly Effective People* includes information on *empathic listening*. Six Sigma, a popular quality control process, begins with listening to the customer, and also validates the positive outcomes of listening to employees.

Many of the ideas in these approaches were presaged by Greenleaf, but too often the popular lists of tips and techniques remind one of the short comedy routine Steve Martin gave on how to become a millionaire: "First, get a million dollars." Often, the listening advice is, "First, listen. Then, prove you are listening. While you're at it, show empathy."

When Robert Greenleaf decided to teach a course in listening to AT&T managers, he titled it "Talking With People." From long experience, he knew that most people were not interested in learning how to listen, an activity they thought was passive and intuitively obvious anyway. Managers wanted to learn how to get their own ideas out in ways that compelled others to *listen to them*, and to do what they said. Greenleaf did not rush in with evangelical fervor and condemn this attitude. He said, in effect, "Okay. That's a good place to start. We'll just go from there and see what happens."

Sometimes master teachers lure learners down paths they may never have entered if they had been clearly labeled. Such was the case with Greenleaf's listening course. If he had said, "Here is some useful learning about deep personal growth and awareness," or even, "We are offering a course about listening," AT&T may never have allowed him to teach it, and few would have signed up if he had. Greenleaf rooted his strategy in a deep understanding of the defenses of the human psyche, and he employed it for the growth of people. He meant it when he wrote, "An organization exists for the person as much as the person exists for the organization," and he believed that one of the most powerful things an organization could do for the growth of persons was to nurture their listening skills and capacities.

Greenleaf also advised Servant-Leaders to combine listening to others with regular periods of self-reflection; that is, getting in touch with one's inner voice and seeking to understand what one's body, mind, and spirit are communicating.

"Don't assume, because you are intelligent, able, and well-motivated, that you are open to communication, that you know how to listen," said Greenleaf.[9] Servant-Leader listening is *demanding*. Not everyone is ready for the commitment. It requires listening to one's self first and nurturing an emerging complexity of integration. It demands heightened awareness, openness to transformation, and a willingness to supplement—and transcend—personal ego with an interest in and desire to understand others. A Servant-Leader listener consistently practices the behaviors that communicate *presence*, like asking clarifying questions and reflecting ideas, feelings, and emotions. Finally, it demands a capacity to accept human imperfections.

Greenleaf referred to this practice as "receptive listening."

Consider the analogy of acting. Many actors know "how to act." They can hit their marks and emote a range of behaviors designed to reveal character. Great actors *inhabit* the roles they play. They become their characters by rooting them in authentic inner experience. Likewise, great listeners generally know the rules of listening, but then go beyond them by *becoming* listeners.

The servant as leader always empathizes, always accepts the person but sometimes refuses to accept some of the person's effort or performance as good enough. If each person is worthy of being accepted, it follows that the first task for a listener is to be silent while the other is speaking, to attend to what is being said with the same kind of sensitivity and openness one might cultivate while praying or meditating.

*Silence is an art.* The renowned Austrian classical pianist Arthur Schnabel said, "The notes I handle no better than many pianists. But the pauses between the notes—ah, that is where the art resides."[10] If we are speaking, we are not listening with undefended receptivity. "Many attempts to communicate are nullified by saying too much," wrote Greenleaf, and that applies to listeners as well as speakers.[11]

Sometimes it is difficult to be quiet long enough to understand the speaker because we either agree or disagree. If we agree, we want the speaker to know so right away. This saves time, but it also cuts off the richness of the communication, especially the sharing of feelings. If we disagree, we want to jump in and fix things. Show the error of the speaker's ways! This attitude is based on grandiosity, the notion that *we* have the truth—or at least the best answer. At its deepest level, grandiosity is also a spiritual issue, and Saint Thomas Aquinas gave this advice on the subject: "We must love them both, those whose opinions we share and those whose opinions we reject. For both have labored in the search of truth, and both have helped us find it."[12]

## Communication as Easy as the ABCs

Many people confuse the passive process of *hearing* with the active process of listening. Steve Goodier, author of a delightful free newsletter (www.lifesupportsystem.com), shares a cute story about the difference between hearing and listening.

A man realized that he needed to purchase a hearing aid, but he was unwilling to spend much money. "How much do they run?" he asked the clerk.

"That depends," said the salesman. "They run from $2.00 to $2,000."

"Let's see the $2.00 model," he said.

The clerk put the device around the man's neck. "You just stick this button in your ear and run this little wire down to your shirt pocket," he instructed.

"How does it work?" the customer asked.

"For $2.00—it doesn't work," the salesman replied. "But when people see it on you, they'll talk louder!"

In other words, listening does not happen solely with our ears. Active, deep, or reflective listening requires one's whole body and mind—and sometimes one's soul—in order to experience and demonstrate the kind of empathy that helps the speaker feel clearly heard and deeply understood.

Active listeners not only listen to the speaker's words, but also watch for and listen to the speaker's important nonverbal cues—body language, gestures, facial expressions, tone of voice. Their body language demonstrates that they are paying careful attention to the speaker, choosing to be intimately involved with the speaker's experience at that very moment. Let's just call it "being with."

Active listening also involves checking out one's understanding of the speaker's message. Just like a mirror, you "reflect back" to the speaker what you've heard to let the speaker know if you have received the message as he or she intended.

Let's put this together in a simple package you can easily remember and immediately use, called "The ABCs of Communication": Act interested. Be encouraging. Clarify.

If the ABCs are the *only* technique you put into practice from this chapter, your effectiveness as a communicator will soar!

## *Act Interested*

When someone wants to talk to you, stop what you are doing and pay attention even if you are rushed, overwhelmed, or do not like what you are hearing. Display a "posture of involvement": turn and face the other person squarely, lean slightly forward, maintaining a comfortable distance. Look directly at the speaker's face, making appropriate eye contact and adopting a pleasant or neutral facial expression. Use your body language to let the speaker know that you are interested in her and in what she is saying. Relax and continue to listen.

Some people worry about "acting interested" when they really are *not* interested, but that attitude discounts the power of the philosophy of "as if." When we act *as if* we are interested, soon we *will* be interested. When we begin making eye contact and acting *as if* we are present to another, soon we *will* be present.[13]

I (Don) once worked with the head of a Fortune 500 company who moved desk papers to the side when a colleague came in to talk, a powerful symbolic statement that he was available. Turning one's body toward the speaker and establishing direct eye contact are behaviors that are both strategic and ritualistic. They transmit the message, "I am here, now, and I am ready to listen to you."

Imagine what a difference these intentional adjustments would have made in the earlier exchange between Sally and her boss Susan. What if, when Sally darkened her door, Susan stopped typing, spun her chair in Sally's direction and engaged her with eye contact and a pleasant face?

## Be Encouraging

Effective listening requires overcoming one's natural tendency to analyze or judge what the speaker is saying. Keep listening, for now. Avoid the temptation to evaluate the other person's statements from your own point of view. Do not interrupt or hurry up. Instead, offer the speaker words of encouragement. "I see…that's interesting…then what?…you don't say!" Be *positive*; invite the speaker to express what is in the heart and on the mind. Communication experts call this "facilitative responding."

The appropriate use of simple phrases invites the speaker to continue sharing and reminds her that you are still interested and actively listening. Also, ask brief, appropriate open-ended questions to draw the speaker out and to help you punctuate and organize the information.

"That's great Sally," affirmed Susan. "Tell me more about your fix for that finicky computer."

## Clarify

In order to help the speaker feel truly listened to and fully understood, periodically summarize what you've heard and, in your own words, reflect back to him your understanding of his point of view. The speaker can then determine if you have received the message as he intended. And, if you're off message, he has an opportunity to "set you straight."

When Sally finished her explanation, Susan could have replied, "You should be proud of yourself for figuring this out, and for your initiative. By the way, thanks for offering to stay after work."

Act interested, Be encouraging, and Clarify—a simple yet powerful technique for showing empathy. Now let's enlarge the ABCs technique and review an approach that further expands on the act of clarifying—the XYZs.

The letters *X*, *Y*, and *Z* come at the end of the alphabet and the XYZ technique comes at the end of the conversation. It can also be used as a way of summarizing key points during the conversation. Here's how it works:

Let's imagine you are the speaker and I am the listener. After you've shared your message, I might express empathic understanding using the XYZ formula: "Let me see if I have this straight: You feel X, because of Y, and you want Z. Did I get that right?"

If I did not get it right, I ask for more clarification and keep paraphrasing until you agree that I understand exactly what you feel, why you feel it, and what you want to happen next.

## Listening as a Grand Adventure

The ABCs of listening and responding help a leader check the accuracy of assumptions and perceptions. If a speaker knows you care enough to get it right, chances are the dialogue will continue. Remember, though, that most people are perceptive. Unless you use the ABCs and XYZs as part of a process of empathy and authentic caring, they will see your technique as wooden, insincere, or shallow manipulation.

Instead, think of yourself as an adventurer into the mysteries of the human experiment with listening as a key tool. "Openness to communication is the tendency to view everything heard or seen (or sensed in any way) with unqualified wonder and interest," wrote Greenleaf. "Later, for purposes of analysis or action, one may form a value judgment about what he or she saw and heard. However, the initial attitude and response would always be: 'This is interesting. I wonder what the meaning is—what is being said to me?'"[14]

Wonder, curiosity, and human growth are as important to Servant-Leader listeners as skill sets. We learn *how* to listen for reasons that range from the personal to the practical and professional. We become listeners to make it all worthwhile.

## Ask Yourself

- Am I willing to test the ABCs and XYZs of communication today at work and at home?

- Do I get nervous when no one is speaking? How can I improve my comfort with silence?

- Am I a skilled communicator? Take a few moments to complete the following survey to help you determine where your listening and speaking skills might need a little attention.

## Are You A Skilled Communicator?

How often do you use the skills of effective communication?

| Listening Skills | Hardly Ever | Once in a While | Usually |
|---|:---:|:---:|:---:|
| • My body and face show that I am involved in the conversation and interested in what the speaker is saying. | ❑ | ❑ | ❑ |
| • I do not interrupt or hurry up the speaker. | ❑ | ❑ | ❑ |
| • I ask appropriate, open questions to draw the speaker out. | ❑ | ❑ | ❑ |
| • Using my own words, I clarify my understanding of the speaker's message by reflecting back his or her thoughts and feelings. | ❑ | ❑ | ❑ |

Continued next page

Continued

| | Hardly Ever | Once in a While | Usually |
|---|---|---|---|
| • I do not judge, criticize, analyze or try to fix the speaker. | ❑ | ❑ | ❑ |
| • I respond to feedback as nondefensively as possible. | ❑ | ❑ | ❑ |
| **Speaking Skills** | | | |
| • I express my thoughts, feelings and desires clearly and directly. | ❑ | ❑ | ❑ |
| • I take responsibility for my own feelings and behavior. | ❑ | ❑ | ❑ |
| • I stand up for myself when I believe that someone is taking advantage of me. | ❑ | ❑ | ❑ |
| • I tell others about how their behavior affects me without punishing them. | ❑ | ❑ | ❑ |
| • I make choices about when to speak up and when to hold back. | ❑ | ❑ | ❑ |

## 2. Inviting Feedback

*Our critics are our friends because they do show us our faults.*
—Thomas Jefferson

Others can see faults in us better than we can see them in ourselves. That is why we all need feedback. The poet Robert Burns once wrote,

Oh would some Power the giver give us
To see ourselves as others see us!
It would from many a blunder free us,
And foolish notion.[15]

Leaders often say they "welcome feedback." Maybe they do, or maybe they just say that because it makes them *appear* to be more open. It might seem like a stretch to regard feedback as a "gift," especially when the gift package is unwrapped and it contains an inventory of one's faults and missteps. The truth is *all feedback is good* if we see it as an opportunity to improve.

We recall our work with Mitchell (not his real name), a member of a metropolitan city council who had recently been elected its president. He sought coaching to become a more effective meeting facilitator.

Although Mitchell had an adequate command of the basics of *Robert's Rules of Order*, whenever he felt compelled to passionately weigh in on an issue, he lost his focus, along with control of the meeting. At times, his colleagues on the council gently reminded him to get the meeting back on track. Unfortunately, he interpreted these attempts as criticism of his abilities and vociferously defended his right to his opinion.

During subsequent coaching sessions, Mitchell was helped to recognize his defensive filters. He admitted to the difficulty he was having separating his emotional involvement with an issue from the obligation to maintain the meeting's structure and order. He decided that in the future he would use these comments as a "focus barometer" to help him maintain control. He also recognized that his peers were acting in good faith, trying to help him adjust to his new role with occasional reminders to temper the timing and tone of his comments. Once Mitchell was able to let go of his defensive posture and *really listen* to feedback from colleagues, he became a much more effective and efficient meeting moderator.

## *Guidelines for Receiving Feedback*

If you want to know how you are doing, you have to accept the responsibility of finding out. By inviting feedback you have a chance to measure how you are doing on progress toward attaining your goals. When receiving feedback, you should strive to be

1. *Open.* Listen without interruption, objections, or defensiveness.

2. *Responsive.* Be willing to hear the speaker out without turning the table. Ask questions for clarification.

3. *Thoughtful.* Seek to understand the effects and consequences of your behavior.

4. *Calm.* Be relaxed, breathe. Assume a comfortable body posture. Be aware of your own emotional reactions.

5. *Explicit.* Make it clear what kind of feedback you are seeking, and why it is important to you. Offer a structure for the feedback—questions, rating scales, stories.

6. *Quiet.* Refrain from making or preparing to make a response. Do not be distracted by the need to explain, defend, or fix.

7. *Clear with your commitment.* Describe how you have benefited from the feedback and what specific steps you will take toward improvement.

8. *Accepting.* Be open to assuming their good will.

9. *Clarifying.* Make sure you are clear about what they are seeing, saying, and recommending.[16]

A story from the fast-paced world of sales and customer service proves that following these feedback guidelines can make a huge difference, both personally and financially.

Dr. Ann McGee-Cooper tells the story of her work with a chemical supply company that wanted to boost the productivity of its sales force. After investigation, Ann learned that every salesperson had at least one grumpy customer whom they dreaded visiting. It seemed these people always had a complaint about some product or the label or even the color of the packaging! Salespeople said they lost energy the day before visiting the grumps just thinking about it, and were still recovering the day after. Ann also noticed that the company's R&D, sales, and marketing departments worked in their own silos and seldom collaborated. She began to connect the dots.

First, she suggested that the salespeople consider *any* complaint an opportunity to improve. "Right!" they said. However, then Ann explained that the complaining customers were trying to give feedback that would cost a fortune to unearth in a research study. If one buyer had problems with the way the product was packaged, others probably did too, only, instead of giving feedback, many of those others probably just stopped buying the product. This "problem" was a potential goldmine!

Ann introduced the sales representatives and customer service people to guidelines for receiving feedback. They had fun learning the principles of empathic listening, like attending carefully to all levels of communication without defensiveness, probing for further information, and checking out their understandings of what the customer said. They decided to promise complainers that their "suggestions for improvement" would be fully considered by the company and to mail thank you notes to customers after each meeting.

The new strategy worked for everyone: customers, sales representatives, and the company. Customers were delighted that the company was now open, responsive, thoughtful, and calm in hearing suggestions. The company learned about issues it had never considered, and departments began stepping out of their silos to solve problems. For example, a "complainer" mentioned that one of their wax products was packaged in a drum that resembled their bleach drum, and the two were sometimes confused. The company became a hero to customers by changing the color of a drum! Another customer suggested a faucet be installed at the bottom of a drum so his people did not need to lift the heavy item to pour product out of the top spout. The R&D department eagerly listened to other suggestions that led to reformulated and improved products.

Sales people now looked forward to speaking to their former "complainers" and began seeing them as "consultants." Sales became the front end of R&D, the marketing department had new benefits to sell, and the entire organization moved from a fragmented operation to an integrated team, all because of feedback.

## Assertiveness

Before we review the guidelines for *giving* feedback, let's look at how the communication skill of assertiveness helps make our feedback to others palatable and motivating.

Assertive speaking is a method of initiating a message and expressing oneself to communicate accurately thoughts, feelings, expectations, and needs. It's a way to define one's own space, set appropriate boundaries, and to inform others respectfully how their behaviors affect you. Acting assertively enables you to speak your mind, share what's on your heart, and even plumb the depths of your soul.

In brief, *responsible assertiveness is a way to take charge of one's life.* Dr. Robert Bolton, in his classic book *People Skills: How to Assert Yourself, Listen to Others, and Resolve Conflicts*[17] encourages the practice of composing "assertion messages" to promote effective self-disclosure, need gratification, and even self-preservation.

Following are our guidelines for composing an assertion message. You will notice that they are based on knowing yourself *first*, before communicating a message.

## 1. Name the Feeling

Knowing how you *really* feel can sometimes be difficult. Are you feeling mad, sad, glad, afraid, ashamed, or guilty? Some feelings are easier to recognize than others. Work on increasing your feelings vocabulary. Look at the vocabulary list of feelings below to appreciate the multitudes of emotional nuance.

## "How Am I Feeling Today?"

| Glad | Mad | Sad | Bad | Afraid |
|---|---|---|---|---|
| Happy | Angry | Depressed | Guilty | Anxious |
| Elated | Upset | Blue | Ashamed | Fearful |
| Ecstatic | Furious | Down | Worthless | Frightened |
| Tickled | Peeved | Lonely | Exhausted | Cautious |
| Delighted | Frustrated | Morose | Embarrassed | Jealous |

## 2. Claim the Feeling

Your feelings are *your* feelings. Other people do not cause you to feel the way you do. *You* decide how you feel and how to act. You are in control of your life. Take responsibility for your thoughts, feelings, and behavior. Remember Communication ABCs. Use "I" statements instead of "you" statements when telling others about how you feel: "I feel upset when meetings are not started on time" rather than, "You are wasting my time, let's get this meeting going!"

## 3. Frame the Feeling

The direct expression of feelings provides us with emotional relief and keeps us connected to others. However, feelings are best communicated within a context or frame of reference. Even though other people do not *cause* our feelings, their behavior does *affect* us. Explaining how you feel about another person's behavior allows you to protect your rights and interests. It gives the other person a chance to examine her behavior and change it. You might say things like, "I feel hurt when you talk to me that way" or, "I get frustrated and angry when you don't meet your deadlines."

## 4. Make a Request

We all have needs and wants. Love, money, happiness, achievement, adventure, and security are just a few of our many human desires. Even though you may assume your colleagues and family know what is important to you, only *you* know what your needs and wants are. Therefore, tell others what helps or pleases you.

Some people are cautious about expressing their own needs. It does not seem like the kind of thing a Servant-Leader might do. However, the fact is that relationships are strengthened when individuals work together to identify and gratify each other's reasonable desires. Be *clear* and *realistic* with your expectations.

Assertive speaking uses the same dynamics of empathic responding. Only now, you are claiming, naming, and framing *your own* thoughts, feelings, and desires: "I feel X, because of Y; I want Z."

There is an important difference between the way Servant-Leaders practice assertiveness and the way it is usually taught in workshops. Servant-Leaders are conscious of these questions: "To what end am I being assertive? Is it to assert my will? Is it to build or protect my ego? Promote a greater good? Serve the growth needs of others?"

When in doubt, consult Greenleaf's Best Test for a Servant-Leader: "Are those being served, *while they are being served*, healthier, wiser, freer, more autonomous, and more likely themselves to become servants? And, what is the effect on the least privileged in society? Are they helped, or at least not further harmed?"[18]

## =Guidelines for Giving Feedback

Now that we have reviewed the parameters for being responsibly assertive, let us put it together in the context of giving feedback to others.

Feedback should be

1. *Timely*. The more immediate the feedback, the more relevant and helpful it will be.

2. *Supportive*. Given in the spirit of care, encouragement, and advice toward improvement, and delivered with sensitivity to the needs of the other person.

3. *Nonjudgmental*. Focus on behavior and performance, not on personality characteristics.

4. *Specific*. Emphasize facts, evidence, and behavior, not intuition or impressions. Be brief and to the point.

5. *Well-paced*. It should be given in moderate doses, thoughtful rather than impulsive.

6. *Directive*. Feedback should focus on behavior that can be changed and contain suggestions for alternate ways of doing things.

7. *Presented with a request for clarification*. Get feedback on your feedback. It should allow for ongoing dialogue.

8. *Offered by permission*. Ask the other person if he or she is open to feedback.

Let us look at what can happen when these guidelines for giving feedback are not taken into account.

Scott's boss rapped lightly on his closed office door and without waiting for a reply, swung it ajar, strode in, and plopped into the side chair by his desk.

"Sorry to interrupt," said Howard, sounding anything but. "I need to talk to you about something. Do you remember the meeting with the sales department last week where Murray spilled coffee on his BlackBerry®?" (*Did Howard ask permission to give feedback? He may be thinking, "I don't need permission, I am the boss!" Was he timely? No. The incident happened a week ago.)*

"Yes, of course. Murray still owes me a handkerchief." A knot was forming in Scott's belly.

"I thought they agreed to furnish us with the specs for the new catalogue by now. Have you seen them?" Howard's tone of voice and facial expression betrayed the fact that he knew full well Scott had received them.

"Just so happens, that is what I'm working on right now," said Scott as he gestured toward his computer. "I discovered a few minor omissions that need taking care of. I will probably have it on your desk first thing tomorrow."

"Well that's what I wanted to talk to you about." Howard stood up.

"Oh boy, here it comes," thought Scott. He braced himself.

"Why didn't you let me know when they came in? I just made a fool of myself in front of the VP of sales! You know how much I value being informed. You sure have been forgetful around here lately." *(Was Howard supportive? Hardly. Nonjudgmental? Well-paced? We think not.)*

Scott knew when he was being shamed. At least he had learned that much in those costly therapy sessions during his divorce.

"I'm sorry, Howard. It won't happen again."

"Right!" Howard spun on his heels and strode away.

What is wrong with this picture? *Pretty much everything.* Howard did not follow any of the eight guidelines for giving feedback.

By contrast, let us take a lesson from our friend Frank Earnest, as he carries out coaching Objective 1.1, to give an employee corrective feedback about her excessive use of personal time on the job.

"Good morning, Sylvia. I see that your grandkids sent more artwork. You must be so proud!"

"Oh hi, Frank. Yes, thanks. The little darlings are so precious. I just found out that Nathaniel did his first potty on the toilet this weekend. Marcia sent me the cutest pictures." She typed furiously on her keyboard and beckoned to Frank. "Check this one out, he looks as if he's about to—"

"Excuse me a minute, Sylvia" interrupted Frank, in the most gentle and diplomatic tone he could muster. "I need to speak with you about something. Is this a good time?" *(Frank asks permission.)* Sylvia turned away from her monitor. "Sure thing, Frank. What about?"

"A couple of team members have come to me recently with concerns about your performance. Apparently, they are upset about the amount of time you've been spending on nonbusiness matters, such as personal phone calls and internet scrapbooking. I'm hearing complaints that some things have fallen through the cracks." *(Gives specific information directly, without judgment.)*

Sylvia shifted uncomfortably in her chair. "But, Frank," she started to protest.

He calmly yet resolutely continued. "Sylvia, this is difficult to talk about. However, I would appreciate it if you would hear me out before you respond. Are you OK with that?" *(Frank is direct.)*

"Sure, Frank."

Frank went on to provide Sylvia with additional details surrounding her lapses. He politely listened to her side of the story, using the ABCs of empathic listening. When she was finished, Frank gave her a brief list of performance expectations for remediation with a three-month timeline. *(Provides specific direction in a supportive manner.)*

Can you not only see but feel the difference between the approaches of Frank and Howard? Frank followed the guidelines for giving feedback.[19]

# Ask Yourself

- Am I comfortable naming and framing feelings? If not, how can I become better at it? (A hint: begin with an enlarged vocabulary of feelings, using the list in this chapter.) Expressing feelings can be as uncomfortable for some women as for some men, but piles of research indicate that women are generally better at it.

- What are my strengths in giving and receiving feedback?

- Am I open to hearing from colleagues about the areas where I can improve? Do I have the courage to do an informal 360 degree evaluation of my competency in this area, using the behavioral competencies in this chapter?

- Do I feel comfortable being assertive in communication?

- Can I find a learning partner who will help me track my accountability in improving Servant-Leader communications?

## 3. Communicating Persuasively

The term *leadership* does not have one official, scientific, or generally accepted definition. Nevertheless, virtually all descriptions of leadership share the view that it involves the process of *influence*.

Aristotle's *Rhetoric* is probably one of the most important and widely regarded works on influence and persuasion ever published. In it, he detailed three strategies to persuade others to accept the speaker's point of view:

- *Ethos*—ethical, credible appeal.

- *Pathos*—emotional appeal.

- *Logos*—logical, rational appeal.

In the classical sense then, a key to becoming a persuasive communicator is to build one's message upon each of these fundamental appeals. Of the three, Aristotle said that *ethos—who we are—*is the most important factor in persuasion.

Robert Greenleaf had a different take on persuasion than you will find in most college textbooks. He believed that persuasion

involves arriving at a feeling of rightness about a belief or action through one's own intuitive sense....The act of persuasion, thus defined, would help order the logic and favor the intuitive step. However, the person persuaded must take that intuitive step alone, untrammeled by coercive or manipulative stratagems of any kind.[20]

Persuasion is the *preferred* mode of using power for a Servant-Leader. Greenleaf argued that most leaders do not understand how ill-equipped they are to practice this kind of persuasion, because they frequently pull out the coercive tools when things do not go their way. "Did you ever try to persuade someone with a baseball bat behind your back?" he asked. We refer you to Greenleaf's classic essay *The Servant as Leader* for more information on practicing persuasion. For now, let us focus on how to be a better *storyteller*, and why it matters so much to your leadership influence.[21]

## Storytelling Moves People

*One aspect of leadership that is routinely overlooked is the extent to which it is a performance art.*

—Warren Bennis

Jack Cranfield is convinced of the power of stories to inspire and influence. Canfield is the originator of the *Chicken Soup for the Soul* series, referred to by *Time Magazine* as the "publishing phenomenon of the decade." Unless your name is Rip Van Winkle, you have heard of, read from, or are in possession of one or more of these books. When this book was first published, Barnes and Noble listed 176 *Chicken Soup* titles with inspiration for the souls of prisoners, dieters, expectant mothers, veterans, nurses, sports fans, and pet lovers, among others. As of this writing, we were able to account for over 250 titles. In fact, over one hundred million of these books have been sold worldwide. Any wonder then that effective Servant-Leaders are adept at telling stories.

Let us listen in on Robert McKee, "the world's best-known and most respected screenwriting lecturer, award-winning writer and director," in a recent conversation with the *Harvard Business Review*:

> All good stories deal with the conflict between subjective expectations and an uncooperative objective reality. They show a protagonist wrestling with antagonizing forces, not a rosy picture of results meeting expectations—which no one ends up believing anyway.

Consider the CEO of a biotech start-up that has discovered a chemical compound to prevent heart attacks. He could make a pitch to investors by offering up market projections, the business plan, and upbeat, hypothetical scenarios. Or he could captivate them by telling the story of his father, who died of a heart attack, and of the CEO's subsequent struggle against various antagonists—nature, the FDA, potential rivals—to bring to market the effective, low-cost test that might have prevented his father's death.

Good storytellers are not necessarily good leaders, but they do share certain traits. Both are self-aware and both are skeptics who realize that all people and all institutions wear masks. Compelling stories can be found behind those masks.[22]

Abraham Lincoln was a terrific storyteller. One day he met with several congressmen who could not decide on a piece of legislation that Lincoln wanted passed. Instead of threatening them, Lincoln told the story of a mule that was positioned between two piles of hay. He could not decide which one to eat so he stayed in the middle and eventually starved to death. (This philosophical argument is known as "Buridan's Ass.") The point was made with humor and grace: Lincoln wanted a decision, one way or another. Stories encode the values of a person and an organization.

Southwest Airlines and Nordstrom's have story-rich cultures that celebrate the actions of employees who go to outrageous lengths to satisfy customers. Leaders of every great, enduring company tell stories from the organization's early days that say more about vision and values than a dozen statements drafted by committees. Inside Eli Lilly & Company they still take pride in the organization's decision to not fire a single employee during the Depression. Scientists with doctorates might have swept basements, but they kept their jobs.

Anthropologists have a saying: "Whoever tells the stories defines the culture." If you want to shape a servant-led culture, begin by telling stories of serving that inform, entertain, and, most of all, inspire.

## Ask Yourself

- Can I tell stories that demonstrate my personal values?

- Am I able to tell them with openness, humor, and self-deprecation?

- Do I have stories that back up my organization's professed vision and values?

- Could I begin to accumulate and share stories of serving?

## A Lifelong Journey

Like water falling on rocks and dissolving hard minerals, calm, persistent listening and direct, respectful sharing of the self can break down barriers to communication and slowly transform people. Servant-Leaders know that skillful communication is not something we learn once and forget. It is the very stuff of life. It takes conscious effort to improve listening skills, to remove barriers to communication and let our natural empathy do its magic. Learning the techniques of listening, responsible assertiveness, giving and receiving feedback, and telling great stories will improve your life at home, at work, and in the community. It is all part of the package of choosing to lead by serving first.

# PILLAR IV

# Compassionate Collaborator

*None of us is perfect by ourselves.*          —Robert Greenleaf

A Servant-Leader strengthens relationships, supports diversity, and creates a culture of collaboration.

- Invites and rewards the contributions of others.
- Pays attention to the quality of work life and strives to build caring, collaborative teams and communities.
- Relates well to people of diverse backgrounds and interests and values individual differences.
- Manages disagreements respectfully, fairly, and constructively.

## Core Competencies

1. Expresses Appreciation

2. Builds Teams and Communities

3. Negotiates Conflict

   Together
   Everyone
   Achieves
   More

The concurrent workshop at the Fourteenth Annual International Conference of the Greenleaf Center for Servant Leadership was packed full. Ten of us were jammed around a table suitable for eight. Ann McGee-Cooper and Duane Trammell had just completed a lively icebreaker to kick off their session, "Teaching Servant Leadership: Methods and Materials." Ann and Duane, always gracious in sharing their work, gave us permission to share one of the terrific exercises from the session.

"You are all no doubt familiar with the concept of IQ as a way to measure cognitive capacity and intellect," said Ann. "Some of you are also aware of Daniel Goleman's work on emotional intelligence and the EQ, a measure of emotional and social competence. Today, we would like to introduce the concept of 'team intelligence.' We have created a teamwork simulation to provide you with an opportunity to experience the power and synergy of collaboration."

We were instructed to gather around one of the "Synergy Box" stations in a corner of the room. There, on the table, was a shoe box containing twenty objects. We were allotted a few minutes to examine the items in silence. When we returned to our seats, we were asked to record as much stuff as we could remember on our scorecards. Points were awarded based on the accuracy and specificity of our lists. For example, I (James) wrote "a plastic bag of seeds," so I got one point. However, if I had written, "a Ziploc bag containing about an ounce of anise seeds," I would have received the maximum five points. I ultimately remembered thirteen of the twenty objects, in various levels of detail, for a total of thirty-nine points.

Now for the *synergy* part. The final step in the activity was to join forces at our table, comparing notes and collectively filling in any missing details. As a result, our team intelligence score reached seventy-nine points, close to the "winning" team's score of eighty-four. Hence, the acronym for team: "Together Everyone Achieves More." It also describes the benefit of collaboration.[1]

## Culture of Collaboration

If collaboration is so all-fired effective, why do we see so very little of it in America? I (Don) began to ponder that question a few years ago after an international trip. I was deeply honored when I was asked to speak at the first Asian Conference on Servant Leadership in Singapore. There, I learned that Sally Chew, Low Guat, and the other impressive Servant-Leaders who had invited me were getting their message out through original programs offered in collaboration with Singapore's leaders in youth programs, education, finance, and even police and security forces. "Wow," I thought. "These folks can teach us something about working together to get things done."

I flew home by way of Japan where Dan, my oldest son, had been living and teaching for five years. It was cherry blossom season, and we joined hundreds of Japanese in a public park, sitting on blankets and watching lovely pink petals float to the ground. Dan told me that the brief, two-week period for cherry blossoms represents the impermanence of life on an island where, historically, earthquakes and tsunamis could extinguish life at any instant. All shared the same peril. As he showed me around, he explained the rituals that bind that society—bowing, removing shoes, following rules that would keep one from dishonoring one's self, family, or country. "*Harmony* is the guiding value in Japan," Dan explained. "That's why my Japanese friends are so good at working together." I found the same sense of harmony when we visited one of Dan's friends, a Buddhist priest who lived with his family on the grounds of the temple he served. He was not only a priest but also a master of the Japanese tea ceremony. As I sat in the simple hut he constructed especially for tea ceremonies and looked out at the impeccably designed garden that surrounded it, I experienced in my gut something I had learned long ago—even Japanese aesthetics promote harmony. The viewer is invited to identify with the thing being viewed, to experience beauty by transcending the West's traditional subject-object dichotomy.

And then I came home. What a difference!

Within a week, I found myself as part of a group pondering a major issue that would take more time and study than we could afford. Someone suggested appointing a committee to hash it out and come back with possible solutions. Then, one of those members who preferred strong, individual action over messy group processes interjected, "Hey, you all know what a camel is, don't you? A horse designed by committee!" Everyone laughed and then sighed, probably believing in their hearts that he was right.

I suspect a Japanese group would have been puzzled by the comment, but it made perfect sense to an American audience raised on the guiding ethic of rugged individuality rather than harmony. It is foolish to argue that one approach is always better than the other. Both have their glories and their shadows. Besides, American history is replete with stories of how people collaborated for the greater good, while Japan also reveres its historical heroes who acted with individual genius. Yet, maybe America's go-it-alone heroic mythology gets in the way of compassionate collaboration. Perhaps it should be balanced with more collaborative models sparked by the sight of Amish people gathering for a barn raising, the memory of how Sacagawea and other Native Americans collaborated with the Lewis and Clark Corps of Discovery to assure their survival, or the amazing online collaboration that occurs every day between people who have never met in person.

For Servant-Leaders, the trick is to collaborate by honoring each individual contribution *and* molding them into solutions that serve the common good. As a thought experiment, let's return to the committee member's comment that a camel is a horse designed by committee. Imagine how that collaboration might work successfully...

"The Evolution Committee" has gathered with the assigned goal of designing a horse. Members of the committee include experts in geography, ecology, animal and cellular biology, weather, hydrology, nutrition, mechanical design, cultural anthropology, and a dozen or so other specialties—a diverse gathering of people who normally would not interact with each other. The appointed chair of the committee figures everyone else is smarter in each specialty than she is, so her job is to be "first among equals" and make sure every member can contribute fully to the final horse.

The first issue is to define the problem, understand the context. Where will this horse live? What is it expected to do? What challenges must it overcome to be successful? As it turns out, this horse is expected to operate in deserts and transport people and goods. Okay. What next?

Study deserts and their challenges. Then, brainstorm ways to match the beast to the burden of surviving and thriving in its environment. Geologists point out that an animal big enough to carry people will need lots of water, and there is little to be found in the desert. That gets biologists going to design ways to efficiently store water in body cells, as well as food stored in fat humps. Ecologists figure ways to measure the horse's impact on the environment, and social scientists wonder about its interaction with human life and culture. Engineers have fun drawing up detailed specifications. Everyone does his or her own thing. Then they consolidate all they know.

The "desert horse," as they now call this animal, is an impressive creature. It can drink twenty-seven gallons of water in ten minutes and go for ten days on the supply. It is big enough to carry one-thousand-pound loads for its human partners, provide milk for their sustenance, and lots of dung to fuel their fires. During sandstorms, dense hairs protect the desert horse's ears, while long eyelashes and a third eyelid guard the eyes, and contracting muscles protect the nostrils by closing nearly shut. The weather expert had surprised everyone by pointing out that deserts can be hot *and* cold, so the cellular biologists provided the desert horse a thick coat for overall insulation and a giant callous on its belly for protection from the hot sand while it rests. The creature also has long legs to distance its body from the hot desert surface while it stands, courtesy of a proud structural engineer.[2]

The horse of the desert has bad breath and likes to spit, but that doesn't seem important for its ultimate mission.

Then someone mentions a rumor that other animals called "horses" live in different environments, and they look different from this horse of the desert. "So what?" asks the chair of the Evolution Committee. "We got our job done. It doesn't matter *what* they call it."

Imagine that kind of collaboration on *your* next committee assignment. Every member contributes fully, guided by the final mission, unhampered by preconceived notions of how the result should look or what it should be called. The "Evolution Committee" gives us a model for pure collaboration that responds to stark realities by drawing on the knowledge and inventive genius of each individual.

Collaboration, from the Latin roots *com* and *laborare*, means to "co-labor" or simply "to work together." However, true collaboration is not so simple, as Crislip and Larson point out in their book, *Collaborative Leadership*:

> Collaboration is a mutually beneficial relationship between two or more parties who work toward common goals by sharing responsibility, authority, and accountability for

achieving results. Collaboration is more than simply sharing knowledge and information (communication) and more than a relationship that helps each party achieve its own goals (cooperation and coordination). The purpose of collaboration is to create a shared vision and joint strategies to address concerns that go beyond the purview of any particular party.[3]

Crislip and Larson are right—*true* collaboration is successful only to the extent that individuals forego the need for personal glory to create a shared vision and joint strategies. Servant-Leaders go beyond the notion of being an effective facilitator or team builder to the larger view of a collaborative culture that is intentionally designed and nurtured throughout the entire enterprise. The Servant-Leader understands how to organize individuals into teams, teams into communities, communities into culture, so that they all contribute meaningfully to the success of the whole organization. To help individuals consistently think and act collaboratively—and on behalf of something greater than themselves—requires a shared belief in the power of team over individual effort, in an atmosphere where people are willing to teach to and learn from each other.

A collaborative culture includes the following:

- Trust and respect in everyday situations
- Egalitarian attitudes among members at all ranks
- Power based on expertise and accountability
- Shared leadership where all members take initiative
- Commitment to the success of other members, rather than just one's own success
- Valuing of truth and truth telling
- Commitment to continuous improvement of the whole organization
- Active learning
- Personal responsibility

## A Culture of Collaboration in Action

A collaborative culture evolves when these values are embedded into the rhythms and routines of everyday practices.

That is the how the leadership team operates at Heraeus Vadnais, Inc., a St. Paul, Minnesota, manufacturer of special alloy medical devices. Ask Anja White, chief operating officer, about the company's collaborative decision-making process, and her comments deserve a full hearing.

> In all of our decisions, we strive to reach a consensus about "doing the right thing." However, often "the right thing" may be different for me, the customer, or the manager on the line. Therefore, our definition of consensus decision-making means that while some of us may disagree with the ultimate decision, we agree to support the decision and not undermine it. At the conclusion of any decision-making discussion, we want all parties to leave the room claiming "we" made the decision to do this together, rather than having any manager leave saying, "they decided this, but if it had been up to me, I would have done it differently."
>
> We do this by engaging in a dialogue around the tension between the needs of our five stakeholders: employees, customers, suppliers, shareholders, and the community.
>
> For example, before we were acquired by our multinational German parent organization, we had a self-funded health insurance plan. As expenses continued to increase, we faced the question of whether to pass on some of these costs and, if so, how much.
>
> We examined how various options would affect each shareholder group: raising prices to our customers, squeezing our suppliers for cost reductions, finding a lower-cost plan that provided leaner benefits than the current one, letting the shareholder share the cost through reduced dividends, raising premium costs and/or laying off employees, creating hardships and straining the goodwill of our community.
>
> A spirited discussion ensued. Some managers on the team felt strongly that under no circumstances should we burden

our employees with these costs. Traditionally, employees paid a nominal amount each month for this benefit and fully expected this practice to continue. Others felt strongly that it was irresponsible for the organization not to have a higher cost-sharing philosophy. And so it went.

Ultimately, we raised the premium, quite significantly for our measure. We also implemented variations of other options to dilute any one stakeholder's net financial burden. Most importantly, we all believed our decision was righteous, that our process was clean and just. This enabled us to better articulate and stand behind the rationale for our decision.[4]

*Engaging in a dialogue around the tension between the needs of our five stakeholders*...sounds like Heraeus Vadnais also qualifies as a Firm of Endearment!

For more on how an exemplary organization uses collaboration, see the chapter in this book titled, "The Seven Pillars in Action."

## Ask Yourself

- Do I really believe collaboration can be more effective than powerful individual action?

- What would I need to change in my thinking to begin considering collaboration as a first option?

- Specifically, what have I lost by not collaborating those times when I could have?

- Am I willing to check out at least three websites or books on the subject of collaboration in the next week?

## 1. Express Appreciation

Everyone appreciates appreciation. Research shows that a majority of employees value continuous positive feedback and appreciation more than any other workplace perk, including compensation. Network professionals involved in a 1999 Lucent Worldwide

Services survey said that working for a company that maintains strong cultural values is of equal importance to receiving monetary recognition for achievement.[5]

Better yet, when a company's corporate culture values enterprise-wide employee recognition and praise (a "positive culture"), it translates directly to the bottom line—big time. Kotter and Heskett conducted an eleven-year research study summarized in their book *Corporate Culture and Performance*. They found that companies that maintained a positive and collaborative cultural influence over customers, stockholders, and employees did better economically than companies that did not maintain similar positive cultural traits. This translated into an increase in revenues by an average of 682 percent, an expansion of the workforce by an average of 282 percent, and growth in company stock prices by an average of 901 percent.[6] Big, big time!

Unfortunately, there is a significant gap between how employees are currently recognized in the workplace and how they actually want to be recognized. In a recent national survey conducted by Robert Half International, "limited praise and recognition" was ranked as the primary reason why employees leave their jobs today, ahead of compensation, limited authority, and personality conflicts. Other studies show instant recognition and verbal and written praise for good performance were powerful incentives.

Tips on how you can help your employees feel valued include the following:

- Offer employee reward options
- Identify what is meaningful to your employees
- Keep recognition programs fresh
- Train managers on recognition best practices
- Recognize all levels of employees
- Give recognition consistently
- Develop a peer-recognition program

We have offered a few guidelines for giving feedback in the previous Pillar III chapter. Here are some additional tips on giving praise.

1. *Praise with a Purpose*. The purpose of praise is to reinforce positive performance, increase morale, motivation, and productivity. Praise is not the same as a compliment. Telling an employee you like her new glasses is a compliment. Telling her you appreciate her contribution to helping you stay organized and on schedule is effective praise.

2. *Be Specific*. "Good job, way to go, all right dude!" may be welcome recognition. Better yet, "What an awesome procedure you developed for minimizing customer service call wait time!" Be brief and to the point.

3. *Consider the Receiver*. The example above suggests that the purveyor of appreciation is speaking using a "generation-sensitive" vocabulary. It helps to be aware of the personality and feelings of the receiver of your recognition. Sam might appreciate a quiet hallway conversation. Sarah may prefer a banner and balloons.

4. *Be Sincere*. Make sure your praise is heartfelt, proportionate, and timely. Most people can spot a phony or a brownnoser.

5. *Do it Often*. Do not wait for the momentous occasions. Celebrate small successes—frequently, consistently, and conscientiously. Expressing appreciation is one way a Servant-Leader acts on his commitment to the growth of others. It is also good business.

## Ask Yourself

- How did I feel the last time someone expressed heartfelt appreciation to me?

- If I want to pass that feeling on, who are three people I can honestly express appreciation to today, following the five guidelines?

## 2. Build Teams and Communities

The last seventy years have produced libraries of research about teams—how to build, start, manage, and support teams and team members, how to keep teams "on task," and more. This has been augmented by even more data on the dynamics of groups that aims at transforming individuals rather than completing a shared team task. In any organization, teams come and go, but they are all charged with delivering products, suggesting policy, solving problems, or projecting future needs.

Robert Greenleaf was an expert on leadership in groups. He believed that Servant-Leaders should understand that any given group will have multiple leaders who serve different roles. Here are the more important leadership roles he outlined:[7]

- *Mediator*. Intervenes in disputes and forms a basis for resolution so the work of the group can go on. Greenleaf saw this as "usually a subtle and inconspicuous role, but one of inestimable value."

- *Consensus finder*. The rare person who is patient enough to try a different "language" to state the consensus idea with which all can agree.

- *Critic*. One who finds logical flaws or sometimes states what others do not want to admit, like, "Hey, this isn't working!" A destructive critic can hurt more than help, but one should still see the critic as a leader with gifts to contribute to the group.

- *Meliorator*. The person who is willing to allow his or her love for others to show, and who seeks good feelings. "With as many abrasive people as there are around," said Greenleaf, "nothing would move without the meliorators."

- *Keeper of the conscience*. Those who "hold the work of the group solidly within a context of values and belief that all accept as necessary for the work they want to do."

- *Process watcher*. One who observes the overall group process and leadership roles and takes quiet action to address any malfunctions or deficiencies.

- *Titular head*. The appointed chairperson or chief, necessary because team members need to understand who decides routine matters, who holds group members to agreed-upon protocols, and who speaks for the group to the wider world.

Greenleaf's analysis of team leadership roles is more radical than it may appear. First, notice that several of the leadership roles he considers important, like critic and process watcher, are the bane of most traditional-minded leaders who value tight control and who frequently describe those pesky critics as a "pain-in-the-you-know-what!" With that attitude, the leader and the entire team will miss valuable contributions to their joint work.

Second, the role we usually associate with "team leader" is only one out of seven leadership roles. In fact, Greenleaf says that "*if all the other roles are well cared for, the titular head may be a quite nominal role.*"[8]

Third, this view of team leadership invites each member to take on a leadership role consistent with her experiences, skills, temperaments, and interests. If all of the roles are carried out well, Greenleaf says the group "may seem to be leaderless. But, in fact, such a group or team may be the most intensely led of all."[9]

In addition to the role of compassionate collaborator, a Servant-Leader helps group members develop the skills to identify and eliminate any barriers to group's success and helps them solve any interpersonal problems that may prevent the group from maintaining high-quality interactions or diminish group cohesiveness.

Clearly, this view of team leadership is not for those who want to use a group role to satisfy ego. It is for Servant-Leaders who value the best outcomes over personal gain and acclaim: in short, leaders with moral authority.

## *Guidelines for Group Effectiveness*

Wendall Walls wrote, "Collaboration is not the handing out of paintbrushes so others can paint your fence. It is not an example of 'many hands make light work,' nor is it an example of 'too many cooks spoil the broth.' It is hard work. It is worthwhile work. It is worthwhile work, because it makes good things happen."[10]

How will you know if yours is a high-quality, high-performing team? By measuring its performance against a set of standards, like the following:

1. *Goal Setting*. To increase the level of commitment toward the successful accomplishment of group goals, the goals should be cooperatively developed, relevant to the needs of the team (and the organization), and clearly understood.

2. *Communication*. Respectful, direct, clear, and accurate two-way communication is the basis of all group functioning and interaction. Open expression of thoughts, feelings, and needs is expected and rewarded. Communication is not clear and accurate if the group avoids conflict.

3. *Participation*. Participation and leadership are equally distributed among all group members. Everyone accepts the responsibility to meet goals, respect each other, and perform. The leader makes sure that the talents and resources of each group member are being optimally utilized.

4. *Decision Making*. Consensus is the most valuable approach to making decisions in a group, especially decisions with great import. However, decision-making procedures need to be flexible, and must be matched with the situation. Different methods may be used at different times. Regardless, each group member is allowed ample opportunity to weigh in on every decision.

5. *Problem Solving*. Controversy, tension, and conflict are inevitable in all groups and should therefore be expected, even encouraged. This is a lesson Quakers learned during nearly four hundred years of evolving and practicing the rules for consensus decision making. Conflicts must be aired and addressed in a way that encourages a solution everyone can live with.

6. *Interpersonal Effectiveness*. Group members value emotional intelligence, self-confidence, emotional maturity, and authenticity.

7. *Cohesiveness*. Members enjoy being in the group and feeling safe. Because of mutual positive regard, inclusiveness, high morale, and *esprit de corps*, they are willing to take risks. They feel free to fail.[11]

These principles all came together dramatically in an unlikely venue—the Ferrari racing team.

Say the word *Ferrari* to a car enthusiast and you will get a swoon. The marquee's glorious designs and legendary successes on racetracks—especially the Formula One (F1) circuit—make the hearts of gearheads beat fast. But it was not always so.

In 1968, Fiat bought 90 percent of Ferrari's road car business and 50 percent of its racing division—called Scuderia Ferrari— from founder Enzo Ferrari. Until then, Ferrari was known as the flashy, passionate Italian manufacturer with a string of unprecedented racing wins, but after its merger with Fiat, the Scuderia Ferrari racing group slowly lost ground, for many reasons. First, Enzo Ferrari retained control of racing activities and his inherent conservatism and autocratic style hampered healthy collaboration, as did internal bickering and political intrigue. Engineering was usually a year behind the times: one year, a magnificent engine was installed into a poorly designed chassis, and two years later the engine was unworthy of its brilliant chassis. Drivers with high promise turned in mediocre performances or, like Gilles Villeneuve, died in accidents.

And plain old bad luck intervened.

In 1990, Gerhard Berger, a Ferrari employee, quipped, "Stand outside the Ferrari factory and you wonder why they don't win every race. Stand inside the factory and you wonder how they manage to win any races."[12]

That changed in 1996 when Ferrari hired German world champion driver Michael Schumacher and gave him a free hand to assemble a world-class "dream team" to turn around Ferrari's fortunes. Schumacher first snagged the English technical genius Ross Brawn, the man behind Schumacher's wins for Germany. He convinced Rory Byrne to scuttle plans to tool around the globe in a sailing boat and become his chief engineer. Jean Todt, who had come to Ferrari from Peugeot three years earlier, was invited to bring his organizing genius to the team. Most importantly, however, the dream team changed the culture inside Ferrari. *Every* employee was indispensable! A janitor was as important as the chief designer. This was not rhetoric, but fact, and was reflected in policies that invited everyone to be part of a passionate team.

Years later, technical chief Ross Brawn remembered the Ferrari team's decision-making process:

> Every last detail is critical....You cannot be weak in the tangibles, like the design of the car, and you cannot be weak in the intangibles....Whatever you felt you could achieve you've then got to go out and find another 10 per cent.... We all knew that we had to do it and we knew the other guys were doing it, so that if you were not doing it, you would be letting your side down. It was great to be a part of the mind-set; a group where we were all giving absolutely everything.[13]

Every employee felt important—was important—and their passion, collaboration, and dedication showed results. Schumacher was runner up for the World Championship the next two years and went on to drive Ferrari cars to five consecutive Driver World Championships and six consecutive Constructors Championships. Neither feat had ever been accomplished before.

## Ask Yourself

- Which of Greenleaf's group roles do I normally take on? Which should I try out more often?

- Would I feel secure in a group with seamless, shared leadership, or do I prefer a group with a strong leader? How often do I try to impose my preference for group leadership style on others who may not agree? What would a Servant-Leader do?

- How does my current team stack up against the seven standards for a high-performing team? If I am not currently on a team, how did my last team measure up?

- Am I willing to teach the seven standards to other members of my team at our next meeting?

## 3. Negotiate Conflict

Men, women, and children; black, white, red, yellow, brown; some live in the country, others live uptown; a Catholic, a Buddhist, a Protestant, a Jew. Sasha orders a beef kabob, Drew gets vegetable stew. Just imagine all of the ways that people differ. Our world contains an incredible assortment of individuals, families, and communities. "Variety is the spice of life!" is a cliché—because it is *true*.

Fortunately, our differences need not keep us apart. As we live and work with others, as we play and pray together, we become aware of the many ways in which we are alike. We realize how friendship, laughter, love, and a common purpose can bring us closer. We learn to value our diversity.

And yet, our differences sometimes cause us to disagree. Julie wants to consolidate the purchasing department; Jerry suggests expanding it. Eli lends a coworker his stapler; Lamont thinks it's a gift. Each day we experience at least one disagreement, argument, or misunderstanding. Conflict is an unavoidable fact of life!

Whether conflict works for you or against you depends on how you choose to deal with it. Positive approaches to conflict can help you protect your interests, freeing you to take action and solve problems. On the other hand, conflict can be mishandled. It can storm out of control and cause harm to you and others.

Compassionate collaboration will not happen if you hold on to the old ways of handling conflict based on "I win, you lose!" Let's explore alternatives, and begin with an understanding of how you tend to manage conflict.

## *How Do You Act in Conflicts?*

We learn about managing anger and conflict during childhood. At one extreme, children are taught that anger and conflict are not okay. They may end up stuffing their anger and avoiding confrontation. At the other extreme, kids see anger and conflict handled aggressively and violently. They may have been encouraged to use force to solve their problems.

Other children fall somewhere in between these extremes. They have been shown healthier and more productive outlets for their anger and frustration.

How do *you* act in conflicts? What were you taught about anger and confrontation? Do you try to win an argument at any cost, even if it means straining a relationship or losing a friend? Or do you easily give in, afraid that if you stand up for yourself, the other person might not like you? Do you see a conflict as a shared situation and search for solutions that both of you can accept? Or do you pretend that the problem does not exist?

The refusal to admit to disagreements can be as destructive as aggressive confrontation. We have been in group meetings with clients where no one in the room would admit to conflicts, even when the boss was not present. In one case, the employees admitted that they thought it "wasn't nice" to bring up problems. In another, they finally admitted that they were afraid they would pay a price for stating anything that could be interpreted as challenging power. Yet even the Quakers, who practically invented consensus decision making, stress that consensus will not work unless every person surfaces disagreements so they can be dealt with honestly.

On the graph "What is Your Conflict Style?" on the next page, locate where you tend to "roost."[14] Be honest! If you want blunt honesty, ask someone where they see you roosting. By following the two axes of "relationships" and "results," you can see that geese are most successful at getting results because they have both a high "results" and a high "relationship" factor.

Even geese can blow it if they get mad at each other and refuse to cooperate. All of us birds occasionally need to go back to basics and remember how to manage our anger when it arises.

# What Is Your Conflict Style?

*Locate Your Roost*

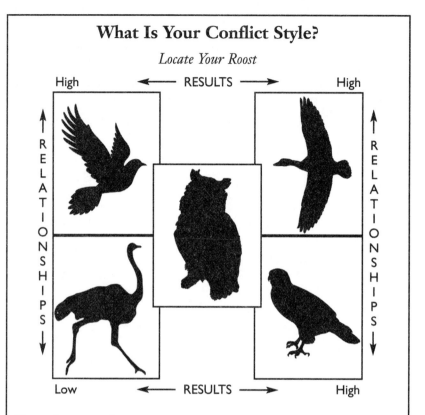

## Doves Accommodate
Doves smooth over conflict in order to avoid ruffled feathers. They worry that conflict might cause hurt feelings or ruin a relationship.

## Ostriches Avoid
Ostriches do not like conflict. They prefer to bury their heads in the sand or to run away from the problem.

## Geese Collaborate
Geese value cooperation and closeness. They fly together so that all the birds in the flock reach their goal safely together.

## Hawks Compete
Hawks manipulate, threaten, or attack those with whom they disagree. They fight to win.

## Owls Compromise
Owls believe it's wise to compromise. The seek fair and peaceful solutions to conflicts.

## *Managing Your Anger*

Anger can get in the way of Servant-Leader responses, like listening with presence and using persuasion rather than coercion, yet anger is a natural and acceptable feeling experienced by every human being. While we are learning advanced competencies of Servant-Leaders, let us also review the basics of an emotion that can spoil your day and cause others to wonder how much you really believe this Servant Leadership stuff.

Anger provided our ancestors with a useful tool for survival in a dangerous environment. The powerful physical and emotional energy of anger bolstered courage to defend loved ones from an enemy attack. It helped speed escape from a hostile beast.

Today, just as in times past, whenever you perceive a threat to your well-being—whether from a cruel boss or a sarcastic coworker—anger energizes you and prepares you to stand up to the problem or to withdraw from it expediently.

Even though we all get angry, not everyone expresses angry feelings in quite the same way. Whether your anger is helpful or harmful depends upon what you decide to do with it. The positive use of your anger energy can help you protect yourself, allowing you to take action and solve problems. On the other hand, negative expressions of your anger may storm out of control and can cause damage to you and others.

If angry feelings are not handled properly, they can eventually show up in harmful ways. THE CHILL DRILL®, explained later, helps you take control of your anger and channel it positively. This useful, effective anger management technique helps you calm your body's anger energy and lets you focus your mind on positive thoughts and constructive solutions.

## *Controlling Your Anger*

Some people mistakenly believe that angry feelings are caused by people, situations, or events outside of themselves. They may exclaim, "You make me so angry!" or, "She really hurt my feelings!" Your angry feelings are *not* caused by other people or events, but rather are caused by your own thoughts *about* other people or events. Angry responses are determined by how you choose to interpret a situation.

For example, let us say a coworker keeps criticizing the way you keep your work space. Lisa hates it when this happens. She thinks, "I wish she'd stop picking on me all the time, all she ever does is nag."

This is called an *anger trigger thought*. Lisa has chosen to respond to her coworker's criticism with anger. As a result, her negative interpretation causes her to become even more defensive and upset. And, if she's not careful, Lisa might lash out at her colleague and say something to make matters worse.

On the other hand, Lisa could choose to hear her colleague out. Remaining calm, Lisa might tell herself, "I hate being yelled at, but she's right, my work space does look like a tornado went through it." Instead of getting angry, Lisa chooses to reply, "You're right, it wouldn't hurt me to tidy up my space a bit."

## *Knowing Your Anger Warning Signs*

When you experience a problem in your life—whether it's a minor hassle or a major threat—your body reacts in predictable ways.

Your breathing changes and your heart races to pump extra oxygen to your brain for quicker thinking, and to your muscles for extra strength. You may feel a rush of adrenaline, a powerful chemical that stimulates and energizes your whole body. Certain muscles become tense, preparing you for action: the face frowns, the jaw tightens, and fists begin to clench. Your body's temperature also changes. You may begin to sweat or shiver.

These are just a few of your body's anger warning signs. They signal to you that something is wrong and needs correcting, just like the warning lights on a car's dashboard. These physical changes are important cues that notify you to take control of your anger before it takes control of you.

Introducing THE CHILL DRILL®,[15] an instant calming technique for controlling the automatic responses of fight or flight or freeze that are grounded in extensive neurological and physiological research. Learn it for yourself and teach it to your children.

To use THE CHILL DRILL®, you must first learn to recognize your own anger warning signals.

## Ask Yourself

What are *my* anger warning signs?

Anger Trigger Thoughts:_____

Body Warning Signs: _____

These are your special cues to begin THE CHILL DRILL®. For example, Miguel knows he's getting angry when his cheeks start getting warm (body sign) and when he says to himself "this isn't fair" (trigger thought).

### *Calm Your Body's Anger Energy*

1. CHILL: When you first become aware of your anger warning signs, *tell yourself to "CHILL."* Thinking "Chill" is your cue to pay attention to what is happening in your body and mind so you can begin to calm and control yourself. "Chill" also reminds you that you have choices about how to respond to your anger.

2. BLOW (Breathe): When you are faced with a disturbing, tense, or scary situation, your breathing changes: you may briefly hold your breath, or your breathing may become rapid and shallow.

   Thinking "Chill" is your cue to *take a balloon breath*, to breathe as if you were blowing up a balloon. Blowing up a balloon requires strong, steady breaths as you inhale through your nose, and uses the muscles in your stomach as you exhale through your mouth. This is also called an "abdominal breath" or a "cleansing" breath. This is the most effective way to release the buildup of carbon dioxide in the brain, which contributes to growing feelings of anxiety.

   After a few balloon breaths, return to normal breathing.

3. [Relax your] FACE: The look on your face shows other people how you *really* feel, more so than your body language,

tone of voice, or even the words you say. As your anger grows, your face may give off negative or hostile messages that could make the situation worse. Relax your facial muscles. *Try to make a positive face.* The two muscles that control your smile are connected to the pleasure centers in your left cortex and to the vagus nerve, which controls your heart rate. A relaxed, positive face signals your brain's facial nerve to release the chemical acetocholine, which jump-starts your body's natural calming abilities.

Use a mirror to practice changing your face from an angry expression to a positive or neutral one. It will feel silly at first, but eventually you will be able to do it naturally, on command. Keep this positive look as you continue THE CHILL DRILL®.

4. [Get some] SPACE: We all have a personal comfort zone, an invisible boundary around ourselves. When someone steps over that imaginary line and enters our personal space, it can feel quite unpleasant, especially during a conflict. This is what it means to "get in someone's face," or to be "too close for comfort."

When you are angry, it is important to give yourself and others enough space to maintain that comfort zone. Take a step back and place your body in a balanced position. Remain in an open and relaxed posture to be sure that you do not look threatening. Your body should be saying that you are willing to work out your differences.

Getting space also addresses the need to mentally step back, to take some time to reflect on constructive action steps. Reflection will produce insights that may allow you to successfully resolve the challenge that stimulated your fight/flight response in the first place.

## *Focus Your Mind on Positive Action*

1. CLAIM your Anger: Angry feelings are *not* caused by people, situations, or events outside yourself. Blaming others for "causing" you to feel the way you do prevents you from taking control of your own anger. Instead, take responsibility

for your thoughts, feelings, and reactions and for any part of your behavior that may have contributed to the problem. Pay attention to your second thoughts.

2. NAME the Hurt: Angry feelings often protect you from the emotional pain caused by feeling hurt. For example, anger can defend you against the feelings of fear, shame, loneliness, and frustration. *Identify your hurt feelings*. Recall the list of vocabulary words in the previous chapter.

   What are you *really* feeling under your anger? Search for ways to soothe your discomfort. As you push back against the brain's limbic system, which is fueling your anger, your frontal lobes—where you do your creative problem solving—are more capable of finding a constructive solution to your problem.

3. TAME your Anger: Think about what else you can do to take the edge off your anger. Gain distance from the situation to get a different perspective. Consider things that make you calm—take a long walk, count slowly to ten, say a prayer. Contain your anger. For example, practice abdominal breathing by thinking about blowing up a balloon with all your anger. When the balloon is full, mentally let it go and watch it drift away.

4. PLAN: Anger lets us know that something is wrong and needs correcting. Anger warns us of threats, danger, and pain. Therefore, when you become angry, determine what you can do to relieve your hurt and angry feelings. *Focus on solutions*. Make a plan and then take positive actions. Know when you need to ask others for help.

### *Principled Negotiation as Collaboration*

In 1979, the Harvard Law School established the Harvard Negotiation Project. In 1991, HNP director Roger Fisher coauthored *Getting To YES: Negotiating Agreement Without Giving In*.[16] It included principles like: Don't Bargain Over Positions, Separate People from the Problem, Insist on Objective Criteria, What If They Won't Play?, and an idea considered novel at the time by seasoned negotiators, Best Alternatives to a Negotiated Agreement. The book, based on a traditional paradigm of winning and losing, was a best-seller. However, Fisher realized that something was missing—emotions. In 2003, he corrected that by coauthoring another book: *Beyond Reason: Using Emotions as You Negotiate.*[17] This book advises negotiators to be aware of five core concerns that stimulate emotions in their counterparts—the need for appreciation, affiliation, autonomy, status, and role. By inviting hard-core negotiators to get out of their own skins and understand the emotional needs of others, the Harvard experts are dangerously close to teaching that negotiation is a mature form of collaboration!

We contend that at its best, even negotiation is really a kind of collaboration for a common goal.

## *Peace R.U.L.E.S!™ Negotiation Guidelines*[18]

Some techniques for bargaining and resolving conflicts simply work better than others, especially for Servant-Leaders. If you observe the following Peace R.U.L.E.S!™ guidelines, you are much more likely to reach a respectful and satisfying agreement with the other person.

- **R**emain Calm.

    Pick the right time and place for your negotiation. Make sure that you feel ready to approach the other person calmly and respectfully, and are able to engage in a sensible discussion of the problem.

    Practice THE CHILL DRILL® to control your body's anger energy and to focus your mind on positive solutions. Agree to a timeout signal beforehand, in case either of you becomes too upset to maintain a respectful, productive conversation.

- **U**nto Others as Yourself.

    Remember the Golden Rule: "Do unto others as you would have them do unto you." Treat the other person as you would like to be treated. Avoid hostility, put-downs, or threats. *Attack the problem, not the person.* Do not blame. Instead, take responsibility for your part in the conflict.

- Listen to Understand.

  When you are angry, it is difficult simply to listen to the other person. You are probably more concerned with convincing him of your side of the story than you are with listening to his view. Remember to apply the key principles of Servant-Leader listening: respond to the problem by listening *first* and practice empathy through reflective listening. The most important skill in the negotiation process is the ability to see the problem situation as the other side sees it.

- Expect Success.

  Successful negotiators enter the conflict resolution process with positive attitudes and expectations. They clearly communicate their intention to cooperate and their expectation that fair and satisfactory win/win solutions can be found. When you express feelings of warmth and optimism, you help the other side feel less defensive and more receptive to your point of view.

- Seek Outside Support (S.O.S.).

  Sometimes a conflict is so big or deep a solution seems hopeless. Ask someone to help you work through your thoughts and feelings. A caring, objective third party skilled in mediation can make a big difference.

## *Peace Plan: Steps to Making Peace*

Once you have identified a mutually agreeable set of negotiation guidelines, use the following format to discover a mutually agreeable solution to the conflict.

1. *Agree to Rules*: Review and discuss Peace R.U.L.E.S!™ together, with the help of a third party if necessary. The exact wording of the rules is not important. What *is* important is that you both agree upon and stick to the conditions of your negotiation.

2. *Share Your Views*: Every misunderstanding has at least two points of view. To reach a mutually satisfying settlement, you

must define your conflict in a way that both of you can accept. After Peace R.U.L.E.S!™ have been established, one person describes her perception of the problem. Each party takes turns sharing facts and feelings. Using the skills of active listening and assertive speaking, try to understand the conflict from the other person's perspective. Put yourself in her shoes. Some mediators suggest that you reverse your roles and attempt to argue the other person's case. This is made easier by actually switching chairs and viewing the situation from "where the other person sits."

3. *Discuss Solutions*: You are now ready to identify a solution to the conflict. Each of you takes turns coming up with as many alternatives as possible. Neither side comments on whether an idea is good or bad. Every suggestion is listed. Get creative, even outrageous! It really helps if both of you sit on the same side of the table to "face the problem" together, having in front of you some kind of writing surface for listing your suggestions.

4. *Agree and Choose*: After you come up with as many solutions as possible, evaluate the merits of each. Mark the options that you both agree might succeed. If necessary, search for a compromise position. Finally, select one alternative as the solution that you both are willing to follow. Make a commitment to one another to comply with that solution.

If after all this, you have not reached an agreeable settlement, you both may choose to "agree to disagree" and move on with a pledge of peaceful coexistence.

You can see that acting as a compassionate collaborator does not mean one agrees with everything that others say or sweeps issues under the rug. It *does* mean modifying the traditional dog-eat-dog rules about acting for sole glory, negotiating for victory for one side only, and manipulating to gain power. Compassionate collaboration is not always an easy path, but it is the noblest choice for a Servant-Leader.

# Ask Yourself

- Do I like my conflict "roost," especially when I realize that this is also how I probably face conflicts with family and significant others? Do I want to be a goose enough to make some changes?

- What negative results have I experienced by acting like a dove, hawk, or ostrich? What positive results could I experience by handling conflict like a goose?

- While I think of something that makes me really angry, I'll try THE CHILL DRILL® sequence of Chill, Blow, Face, Space. What is the difference in my body sensation and attitude after THE CHILL DRILL®?

- Just for kicks, am I willing to try the Peace R.U.L.E.S!™ Negotiation Rules and Peace Plan at my next opportunity to negotiate? Will these ideas work with my family? Am I willing to try them out tonight?

- Honestly, is it worth my effort to see negotiation as a tool for collaboration, or do I enjoy the power-play game of traditional negotiation too much to give it up?

# PILLAR V

# Foresight

*No one is ever as shocked and surprised as when the inevitable occurs.* —Paul Baran

A Servant-Leader imagines possibilities, anticipates the future, and proceeds with clarity of purpose.

- Views foresight as the central ethic of leadership.
- Knows how to access intuition.
- Can articulate and inspire a shared vision.
- Uses creativity as a strategic tool.
- Is a discerning, decisive, and courageous decision maker.

## Core Competencies

1. Visionary
2. Displays Creativity
3. Takes Courageous, Decisive Action

## Foresight beyond Projection

The gray December sky was spitting sleet as I (Don) drove to my job on the campus of Viterbo University in La Crosse, Wisconsin. I parked the car, pointed my head into the wind, and walked quickly, taking refuge along the way under the canopy of the Fine Arts Center. I was so relieved to be out of the stinging sleet that I stopped a moment to give a silent prayer of thanks for the people who had the foresight to put an overhang by the entrance of that wonderful facility. Then I realized that the Fine Arts Center, opened in 1970, was the largest building on the campus of this small religious university. It was built when the school was miniscule compared to today. How did that happen?

I was new at Viterbo so I asked around and learned that the Franciscan Sisters of Perpetual Adoration (FSPA) who founded Viterbo were as smart and visionary and faithful in using foresight as any international corporation—probably more so. When the good Sisters planned the Viterbo Fine Arts Center, the school was still a woman's college with only a handful of students majoring in the arts. None of the surveys or most optimistic projections predicted the need for a facility so large that fine arts majors and their teachers could wander around all day and not see each other.

However, the FSPA had their divine calculus. First, as Franciscans, they were committed to the expressive and redeeming value of the arts. Second, they knew the Fine Arts Center would attract more robust growth for Viterbo. They could have coined the phrase, "If you build it, they will come." Third, they were dedicated to the La Crosse community and wanted the Center to be available for lectures, community classes, and a full range of activities that would enhance this gem of a city on the Mississippi River. Mostly, though, they prayed, and gradually got the message that this was the right thing to do.

The budget was five million dollars, a pretty penny today but downright daunting in 1968. Sr. Georgia Christensen, one of the FSPA, was completing a doctorate in California when she got word of what her colleagues were up to back in Wisconsin. She remembers being taken aback by the vision of the thing. But it happened. The Fine Arts Center opened in 1970 with two theaters, studios for dance, music, painting, ceramics, and now, even digital media, plus a score of offices. Not a week goes by that the Fine Arts Center is not buzzing with one or more community events, and Viterbo's students are accustomed to seeing lines of school buses from outlying areas dropping off elementary-age children to experience plays and concerts, many of them for the first time.

"The Sisters have never followed traditional wisdom in building their vision," says Elizabeth Brindel of Viterbo's development office. "They've always been out front. They've always had foresight."

Elizabeth's statement made me recall Robert Greenleaf's comment that orders of Catholic Sisters "got" Servant Leadership before anyone else. They live the life of servanthood—wise as serpents (because historically they have needed wisdom to get things done in a male-dominated organization), and gentle as doves. They are well-educated and strategic, and usually practice some form of consensus decision making. The Sisters' version of "reflection" that Greenleaf urged for Servant-Leaders is prayer; it does not get any deeper than that.

## *What Is Foresight?*

The Sisters teach us that foresight is not strategic planning, positioning, economic forecasting, or simply forecasting. Those are all activities that organizations and governments undertake to make assumptions about the future that, in turn, drive policies. As powerful as these tools are, they are mostly based on analytical models that have their limitations and should not be substituted for foresight. According to Robert Greenleaf, foresight includes but goes beyond traditional planning activities to "have *a sense for the unknowable and be able to foresee the unforeseeable.*"[1]

*Foresight is a practical strategy* for making decisions and leading. In fact, Greenleaf said foresight is the only "lead" a leader has. Think about that. Why do we trust a person to be a leader? Usually it is because he or she appears to see a little further ahead. When this leader says, "Come, follow me," we respond because we trust both the person *and* the leader's vision of the future. In other words, we trust the leader's foresight.

Larry Spears based his definition of foresight on Greenleaf's thinking when he wrote, "[Foresight is] the ability to foresee the likely outcome of a given situation, enabling the Servant-Leader to understand lessons from the past, realities of the present, and likely consequences of a decision for the future. It is deeply rooted in the intuitive mind."[2]

Intuition sounds like a "soft" subject for leaders who must make hard decisions. However, knowing how to access intuition is a prerequisite for developing foresight and, for that matter, fully understanding Servant Leadership. A friend of ours once learned a powerful lesson about the importance of intuition.

Dr. Haley Fox, an artist and psychotherapist, always had an interest in intuition, but she, like most of us, did not always heed her own intuition. That changed one fateful night, with profound consequences. Imagine what you would have done in Haley's place...

It is late summer, 2002, and Haley drives alone in Central Illinois. Unfamiliar with the countryside, but armed with a good map, she looks forward to finding a nice, quiet hotel, a place to think and write. She has determined the best route through careful calculation. She points the car in the direction that logic tells her to go, but something in her gut feels uneasy about where she is headed. She ignores the feeling in favor of the logic.

Mile after mile, while traveling a road her mind *knows* will intersect with the highway that will take her directly to her final destination, another kind of *knowing* emerges, urging Haley to turn back. But the further she travels, the more stubborn she becomes. In time, she sees a sign: "Road Closed Ahead." That should have sent her back—but no, she is sure some other road will help her cut to that highway. None of them do. Eventually, Haley *sees* the highway she seeks, but there seems to be no clear way to get there— except to backtrack fifteen miles and start over.

She tries another road she hopes will offer a shorter route to the highway. *That* road takes her to the edge of nowhere—at the end of a long, narrow, muddy country lane, surrounded by cornfields on three sides and bugs the size of small birds raining against her windshield. She doubts that she even has room to safely turn around. Feeling utterly defeated, she stops the car and drops her forehead to the steering wheel in a gesture of surrender. More than a little worried now—alone with no cell phone and no place to seek help—she whimpers a desperate prayer to the universe. A clear voice comes to her: "This is a cheap lesson, Haley. This is *nothing* compared to what could happen in the future if you do not heed your intuition."

Haley then manages to turn her car around with surprising ease, and retrace her route back to where she first turned off. She arrives at her destination without further delay.

As Haley reflects on the experience during the next few weeks and months, she pays special attention to the way intuition communicates with her so she can better recognize and integrate this wisdom into her life and work.

Fast forward five years to August 1, 2007. Dr. Fox is on her first day at a new job, north of Minneapolis. She is scheduled to leave work at 5:30 in the afternoon, but at 4:30 a colleague asks if he can walk her out, or if she will be staying later. Considering this, she suddenly feels she does indeed need to leave at that very moment. As she walks out to her car, she thinks, "What am I *doing*? I should be making a good impression on my first day. Yet here I am skipping out an hour early! This is so unlike me!"

As she heads south toward home, Haley notices that her car can use some gas. She thinks about stopping, but her intuition calmly insists, "No, you need to continue driving at least until the other side of the river." Haley's scientific training as a clinical psychotherapist makes this seem like an irrational compulsion. Although she feels a bit silly about it, she heeds the message. A few minutes later she feels a gnawing in her stomach and remembers she has not eaten a thing all day. She thinks about stopping for a bite. "No," the calm voice repeats, "You need to continue driving at least until the other side of the river." It makes no logical sense, but she keeps driving.

As she enters a southern suburb of Minneapolis, she suddenly feels less anxious and decides that she may as well drive the final half hour home. The internal dialogue stops.

Once home, Haley turns on the evening news to learn that at 6:05 p.m., precisely the time she would have passed over it, had she left work according to her original plan, the I-35W bridge that spans the Mississippi River collapsed, killing thirteen people and injuring scores of others.

You could say that intuition saved Haley's life, but it would be more precise to say that her faithfulness in *acting* on intuition saved her life. Because of her experience in the cornfield, Haley learned that intuition possesses a sense of otherness that can seem strange to the ego consciousness but communicates a keen sensibility of its own. In this case, cold logic told her to stay at work until quitting time, to stop for gas and food—all perfectly reasonable actions that could have helped to kill her.

Haley paid attention to the wisdom from her heart and gut. That is what the rest of us should do in order to go beyond the important analytical work to evolve foresight.

Incidentally, you can read about the impact the I-35W bridge collapse had on the Minnesota Department of Transportation (MnDOT) in the chapter in this book titled "The Seven Pillars in Action."

Greenleaf believed that foresight was an essential function of Servant-Leaders and went so far as to say that this ability to see just over the horizon is the central *ethic* of leadership.[3]

Why an ethic? Two reasons:

First, getting the future wrong can cause great harm. Consider the chaos that followed the layoffs and closed plants after Detroit automakers focused on selling profitable large vehicles rather than preparing for a future of high gas prices.

Second, those who fail to relate their actions to the future will soon lose their ability to contribute as leaders. Reading the following quote from Greenleaf, we can fairly conclude that foresight is a *survival* strategy for leaders.

> The failure (or refusal) of a leader to foresee may be viewed as a failure, because a serious ethical compromise today (when the usual judgment on ethical inadequacy is made) is sometimes the result of a failure to make the effort at an earlier date to foresee today's events and take the right actions when there was freedom for initiative to act....By this standard, a lot of guilty [leaders] are walking around with an air of innocence that they would not have if society were able always to pin a label "unethical" on the failure to foresee and the conscious failure to act constructively when there was freedom to act.[4]

Daniel Kim, founder of the Society for Organizational Learning, concurs. He suggests that all leaders have an ethical responsibility to perceive and describe "*the significance and nature of events* before they have occurred, to make predictions that can guide their people to a better future."[5] This is different from planning.

Let us look more closely at the traditional models of planning and forecasting to better understand what distinguishes them from foresight.

## *Traditional Approaches to Understanding the Future*

Every approach to planning begins with deep research into the present moment, including analysis of available data, generation of new data, and scans for trends. Then, the trends are projected into the future, remembering that longer-term forecasts are less likely to be accurate.

### *A Logical Way of Planning*

Analyze the present and project it into the future

These straight-line projections are tidy. They help us sleep better at night, knowing that we have a "handle on the future." Yet life has a funny way of surprising us, often dramatically. Imagine the shocks awaiting your airline company if you had just completed a five-year strategic plan on September 10, 2001.

As forecasting became more sophisticated, planners incorporated variables to account for uncertainty, using scenarios and "fuzzy logic." A scenario is a fictional but plausible story about a likely future. Some scenarios are lovely and compelling. Others scare the pants off you, like the thermonuclear war scenarios developed by the Rand Corporation and the Hudson Institute during the Cold War.

*Planning For Alternative Scenarios*

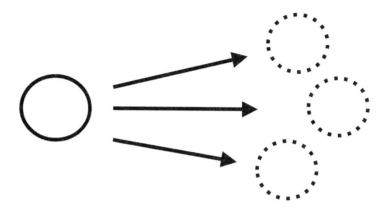

Analyze the present and project it into possible scenarios.

Scenarios are refined by polling experts and often expanded into games, computer simulations, and modeling. All along the way, forecasters conduct historical analyses, use tools of brainstorming and creativity, and finally end up with a vision for a preferred future.[6]

A discipline called futurism has evolved around these tools for forecasting, and anyone who is serious about understanding the future should be familiar with them. However, foresight, as explained by Robert Greenleaf, goes beyond these mostly analytical tools, taking advantage of resources in the head, heart, and gut to access the intuitive mind.

Although some suspect that foresight is the one Servant-Leader characteristic only a few are born with, we believe it is equally available to all. Humans continuously experience the process of foresight because our astonishing brain never stops calculating future possibilities, even while we sleep. The trick is to focus the brain's pattern-generating capacity so it becomes a useful tool for insight and decision making. Fortunately, recent research helps us understand how this works.

## *Foresight's Partners in the Head, Heart, and Gut*

Leaders are trained in the use of analytical tools, but logic can only take us so far, because there is always a gap between what we know and all there is to know. If only we had the resources to augment logical analysis and take us further into understanding a likely future.

As it turns out, we *do* have those resources, and have had them all along. They are hardwired into our human structure. Recent research reveals that the brain includes more than the complex neuron systems in the head and spinal cord. An independent "second brain" called the enteric nervous system resides in the intestines and contains more neurons than the spinal column! A "third brain" in the heart develops in the fetus even before the structures in the head. It contains over forty thousand neurons, more than some key areas of the cranium's brain. The heart is five thousand times more electromagnetically powerful than the brain. It has the capacity to communicate with and exert control over the brain. And, it can remember.

According to psychoneuroimmunologist Dr. Paul Pearsall, writing in *The Heart's Code: Tapping the Wisdom and Power of Our Heart Energy*, the heart stores energy and information that comprise the essence of who we are, and sensitive persons who have received cardiac transplants are capable of revealing the often invisible heart's code of the donor's organs living inside them.[7] His research has uncovered remarkable stories from heart transplant recipients regarding changes in food preferences, dreams, fantasies, and personalities that reflect those of their donors.

One particularly poignant account came from an eight-year-old girl who received the heart of a murdered ten-year-old child. She was brought to the attention of her family's physician after she started screaming at night while dreaming of the man who murdered her donor. The police were called. Using descriptions provided by the little girl, they actually found the murderer. The time, the weapon, the place, the clothes he wore—everything the little heart transplant recipient reported was completely accurate. The murderer was eventually convicted.

There is more: our hearts contain the capacity to communicate *directly* with our brains. Scientists have determined that signals from the gut and the heart travel independently to a filter called the Reticular Activating System (RAS), which sorts through one hundred million impulses per second and allows negative messages through posthaste, because they may represent an immediate threat. Even if they are not life threatening, like a few well-intended words of criticism from the boss, evolution has trained the RAS to treat them negatively because it is better to be safe than sorry. From the RAS, the messages speed to the ancient limbic system, which analyzes the world and our place in it, and finally on to the cerebral cortex, the site of what we call "thinking."

*So in neurological sequence, we do our logical "thinking" last, not first.* If we try to think first with our head, ignoring emotions and gut feelings, we tend to make poorer decisions, because we block useful information from intelligent functions in the heart and intestines. As it turns out, the old clichés about "speaking from the heart" and "a gut feeling" have a basis in physiology.[8]

This science is amazing, but leaders need a practical way to use it. The following process will help you access all available information and wisdom in the head, heart, and gut to generate foresight that goes well beyond forecasting and planning.

## How to Harness Your Power for Foresight

You can learn the steps that make reasonably accurate and useful foresight possible. Some parts of the process may seem unusual, but they work. To get started, consider this picture of past, present, and future.

Imagine a flashlight beam focused on NOW, moving with the action. The beam is most intense at the present moment but also illuminates the past and the future. "'Now' includes all of this," says Robert Greenleaf, "all of history and all of the future. As I view it, it simply gradually intensifies in the degree of illumination as this moment of clock time is approached."[9]

Keeping this image in mind, follow these steps to nurture your foresight.

1. *Analyze the past.* History seldom repeats itself in the details, but frequently does repeat its patterns. Foresight comes from bringing to consciousness the deep patterns your brain already generates. Sigmund Freud realized that only a portion of the brain's

activity is conscious or, using the image of an iceberg, "above the waterline," and while the nonconscious elements may be out of sight, they are never "out of mind." They are always on the job, even when we are asleep or in a daydream mode. Neurologists proved this when they discovered "dark networks" lighting up the brain's circuits even when test subjects were not occupied with a specific task.[10] The finding was a surprise to many traditionally minded researchers.

By analyzing the past—reading history, reflecting on market forces, understanding the models that drove our own previous actions and those of others—we are also feeding the dimension of mental capacity that continues to generate wisdom "below the waterline." Like Dr. Fox, spend some time reflecting upon past experiences where intuition, premonitions, or hunches actually came to pass. Analyze these circumstances to better understand how intuition presents itself to your mind and body.

2. *Learn everything there is to know about the issue at hand.* Accurate foresight depends upon accurate information. Your conclusions are only as good as your facts and assumptions. Use all the forecasting tools of data gathering, analysis, and scenarios. Research, absorb the numbers, talk to colleagues, consult with people at all levels in the organization, and use analytical reasoning as far as it will take you in understanding where the issue is at this moment. You can then make some good guesses about what may lie just around the corner, but realize that intuition can help fill the gap of what you *still do not know* so you have a broader grounding for foresight.

3. *Let the information incubate.* Quit thinking directly about the issue. Do something else for a few days—or weeks. This is not procrastination. It is a strategic choice to get rational processes out of the way so the majority of your brain can chew on solutions in its own sweet time and in its own subtle ways. You may absolutely trust that productive work is being done during the incubation period, even while you sleep. Frederick Kekule, for example, took a break from a long day in his lab and discovered the structure of the benzene ring after dreaming of an image of a snake eating its own tail.

Do not rush things. Anyone who cares passionately about his or her work is susceptible to "the hurries," as Abraham Lincoln used to say. The heart requires silence between beats, the respiratory system needs time between breaths, and a Servant-Leader's practice of foresight requires patience and silence.

4. *Be open for breakthroughs.* Patterns of foresight dawn upon people in different ways. Some experience new possibilities through hunches that certain things may transpire in the near future. Stay with the hunches, the fleeting suggestions, and the ideas that may at first seem incomplete. Others find themselves doodling, only to notice that the image they have drawn contains hints about what could happen in the near future. Robert Greenleaf liked to simply clear his mind, be still, and allow ideas to bubble up as general impressions. Still others make discoveries through dialogue.

This stage reveals several paradoxes. First, *un*like in step two, trying harder does *not* lead to better results. Silence and patience *do*. Second, immersion into the *present* is more likely to reveal hints of the *future*. Be gently present with your senses, your questions, and your awareness.

Glimmers of foresight are not likely to march forth initially in completed bullet points. That is the way of analysis, not intuition, so do not expect refined answers and do not discard images that seem to make no sense at first.

5. *Share your insights with trusted colleagues.* Anyone can be dead certain about something and still be dead wrong, so in the humility of a true Servant-Leader, seek informed feedback. Choose your sharing partner carefully, because new ideas may challenge the status quo and upset people.

There are two reasons to run your insights by others.

First, you may or may not be on target. Perhaps in your enthusiasm you forgot—or chose to ignore—a key piece of research.

Second, if you expect foresight to make a difference in your organization, you will eventually need to persuade others to accept your scenario and translate it into strategic choices and working policies. Early sharing will give you a chance to practice making your case for the future before rolling it out to the wider community.

## *How Far Ahead?*

In 1967, James McSwinney, CEO of the Mead Corporation, declared that "the world is going digital." At the time, his coworkers hardly understood the meaning of the phrase, and those who did were alarmed. Mead was a paper company. If the world went digital, customers would buy less paper. McSwinney, whom Robert Greenleaf once described as a natural Servant-Leader, acted on his foresight by buying a small company working on inkjet technologies and databases. Against all internal and external advice, McSwinney held on to the company, which eventually developed databases called Lexis and Nexis. Today, LexisNexis is the most respected source of digitally based information in the world, and Mead ended up selling *more* paper, not less, because the world did indeed go digital, and those inkjet printers used a lot of paper.

Foresight has its limits, though. Ten- or twenty-year predictions are not likely to be useful for strategic decision making, but a five-, ten-, or twenty-year vision of where you want your organization to be is not only possible but desirable.[11]

## *A Ten-Minute Exercise of Silence*

*Silence*, as Greenleaf uses the term, is not simply the absence of sound; it includes quietness of mind. Striving to achieve quietness is not quietness. As Ezra Bayda says, "You can enter silence not by trying to enter but through the constant soft effort to let life be."[12] With that in mind, try this technique for quieting the mind. Sit with your feet on the floor, hands resting comfortably by your side or on your legs. Close your eyes and take three long, deep breaths. As you inhale, imagine you are breathing in quietness; as you exhale, imagine breathing out your pressing concerns of the moment.

Before long, current thoughts, images, or anxieties will try to intrude. Do not drive them away; simply accept and observe them. Some people find it helpful to imagine putting those distractions on a floating log and watching them drift down a stream.

Next, imagine a place of natural beauty and peace, perhaps a mountain scene, a forest or an ocean view, someplace where you feel safe and content. See, hear, and smell the environment. Expect nothing and force nothing; simply experience what unfolds. Perhaps nothing will happen, or animals will appear or a surprising scene will emerge.

Now empty your mind of everything. No images, no sounds. When you are ready, bring yourself back to the present.

What did you see and hear? How do you feel now? What did you gain from the experience of silence? Is it worth ten minutes a day to repeat this exercise?

Some people achieve silent serenity by reading a scripture or an inspiring quote and sitting with it. Many people who have never valued silence need practice to live into its gifts, and that is fine too.

## Ask Yourself

- Do I really believe that silence can lead to wisdom beyond obvious facts?

- Can I remember a time when I experienced strong intuition? How did that intuition present itself to me?

- How can I discriminate between intuition and personal wants or needs?

- Do I feel resistance to any pieces of the foresight model presented here? If so, can I articulate the reasons why?

## Foresight as Joyful Learning

Peter Senge's 1990 book, *The Fifth Discipline*, spurred an interest in "learning organizations." Leaders who embrace Senge's wisdom about a culture that practices systems thinking and seeks to evolve through continuous learning should understand that foresight is a key part of a learning organization. Foresight is the cutting edge of decision making and learning, and it should be fun!

In 1981, Arie de Geus was named coordinator of group planning for Royal Dutch/Shell, one of the organizations Greenleaf studied and admired. After reflecting on several books by educator John Holt (*How Children Fail* and *How Children Learn*) and studying the theories of Jean Piaget and Seymour Papert that emphasized the connection between play and learning, de Geus realized that fundamental decision-making processes in organizations were really learning processes.

> The real decision-making process is a learning process rather than the application of knowledge. Many at high levels of management are convinced they are there because of what they know and how they represent what they are. Statements [about the value of discovery and experiential learning] were saying you're not there because of what you know. You're there because you're reasonably good at intuitively or otherwise finding your way to a learning process together *with* your colleagues, such that you learn and arrive at new conclusions that are more or less successful.[13]

Humans move through the grand journey of greater awareness by learning from experience, failures, and triumphs. It is all a form of play—even the failures. Perhaps we can recapture the joy that makes an onerous process like planning *fun* by seeing it as discovery.

As a child during the 1950s, I (Don) lived in Last Chance, Colorado, smack in the middle of the barren Great Plains that define the eastern part of that state. During that time we experienced droughts that rivaled those of the Great Depression. After one rare, heavy rainstorm, I was eager to go outside and play, but what I really did out there was *learn*.

I discovered tadpoles swimming in shallow depressions, miles from any water. It had literally rained tadpoles! That's how I learned that strong wind currents could carry frog eggs, or perhaps even tadpoles, and deposit them in faraway places. Within a few days small blossoms sprouted atop cacti; tiny green sagebrush and showy milkweed plants miraculously erupted from the dust, and a vivid carpet of tiny wildflowers covered the fields. I learned about the tenacity of life as it waited patiently for nourishment, about the biodiversity of one of the bleakest landscapes in the country, and where the water came from that fed our well, the one identified by a local dowser (whom we called "the water witcher") with a Y-shaped stick that vibrated and then pointed down to the exact spot to begin drilling. For me, all this was joyful play, delicious discovery, magical mystery.

Remember a similar event from your own childhood and then imagine undertaking foresight with that kind of joy.

Now let's look at foresight through the lenses of *vision, creativity*, and *courage*.

## 1. Being Visionary

When two atomic bombs ended World War II, humanity was shocked to realize that we could erase all human life in a blinding flash. This was a possible future that military and government planners in the United States wanted to avoid. They needed the best brainpower in the world to see past tomorrow and generate better options.

Only ten weeks after Hiroshima, the Rand Corporation, the world's first think tank, was born. Rand—an acronym for "Research and Development"—was created as a spin-off of Douglas Aircraft. Its original mission was to preserve the research capacities developed during the war and apply them to emerging scientific and technological trends so military planners could effectively plan for the future. The Rand Corporation was charged with anticipating the future in order to save humanity. Talk about a compelling vision!

Within seven months, Rand issued its inaugural report titled *Preliminary Design of a World-Circling Spaceship* that predicted the world's first satellite, eleven years before the Soviet Union launched Sputnik. Other Rand reports contributed significantly to digital computing, artificial intelligence, game theory, network theory, mathematical modeling and simulation, the Delphi method, economic and social policy analysis, and many other important discoveries.

One of the smartest things Rand did was employ people from multiple disciplines—psychology, economics, engineering, mathematics—to work on the same problem and apply "systems analysis" as a way of looking at the interconnectedness of trends. All of this was done in an atmosphere of remarkable freedom that allowed individuals to pursue their peculiar interests even while specific projects were delivered to the military.

Paul Baran, a Rand employee in the early days, is held in awe by people who know the history of the Internet. While working at Rand, Baran developed the scheme of distributed networks and packet switching that made the World Wide Web possible. In 1990, Baran remembered Rand as

> by far the most effective research organization I have ever encountered in my life, in part because of this freedom. I might mention that this degree of freedom was not a result of management laziness. Rather it was the result of management wisdom, dedication to intellectual honesty, trust in individuals, and a true understanding of the research process.[14]

Baran left Rand in 1968 to cofound the Institute for the Future, a not-for-profit research group specializing in long-range forecasting, and he proceeded to make dozens of additional contributions to the emerging digital world. He always claimed that Rand's vision of saving humanity was what drove him and his colleagues to scientific breakthroughs.

A Servant-Leader sees where to go (through foresight), paints a compelling picture of the destination (with a vision), and invites others to "come, follow me." Scores of books have been written about the differences between vision statements, mission statements, goals, strategic objectives, enabling objectives, and performance objectives. Let us make it simple.

A great vision

- appeals to what Abraham Lincoln called "our higher angels" by inviting us into a great and worthy shared enterprise,
- paints a picture of a brighter future that connects to our deepest identity,
- excites with unlimited possibilities, and
- lures us forward to action with its compelling power.

"Returning 12 percent per annum in shareholder value" may be a fine goal, but it is not a vision. It does not make the average employee want to jump out of bed in the morning and head for work. A limited, impaired vision can actually be toxic, creating unmotivated workers who spend precious life energy in support of a direction unworthy of their gifts.

Instead of an unenlightened vision of returning 12 percent per annum, imagine the same company with the following vision: "To be the world's beacon as an ethical, inventive community that creates software designed to unleash the creative potential of humans everywhere." That vision provides heroic context for even the most mundane work tasks like filing papers and writing memos. With that vision, *everything counts*. Every activity is a small sparkle that contributes to the larger light the team is generating. Most importantly, how does that second vision make you *feel*? Does it excite those neurons in the heart and gut?

Here is the paradox: if the same company embraces the second vision rather than the first, it will be *more* likely to return 12 percent in shareholder value! It will have loyal employees who take personal ownership in creative contributions that advance the whole enterprise.

Listen to the wisdom of Jack Lowe Jr., CEO of TDIndustries in Dallas, a company voted to *Fortune*'s Hall of Fame for consistently landing on their "100 Best Companies to Work For in America" list. Jack said, "If you follow Servant Leadership to make more money, it won't work, but if you do it because it's the right thing to do, you'll make more money."[15]

## *Seeing Your Organization's Vision*

A worthy vision need not be grandiose, but it *must* be grand. Employees at *all* levels have a stake in their organization's vision, so they should also have a stake in creating a vision that reflects their aspirations. After all, every person yearns for higher meaning in work. Besides, the "latest vision statement" is not likely to excite employees unless they help create it.

Foresight is only possible if an institution and the people within it have the vision to know who they are and where they want to go. As you sit down with colleagues to express or revise a vision, remember that this is not an exercise in semantics. It is the stuff of your very identity.

A soaring vision should answer the following questions:

- "Who are we?" Say it directly, then look for a powerful image that sums it up.

- "Whom do we serve?" Remember that employees, clients, suppliers, and the larger world are not only objects of service, but partners in service.

- "How will we serve them?" A statement—even a breathtaking statement—about the difference the organization will make in the world and in peoples' lives.

Answering these questions takes time. Everything worthwhile does.

Once the vision is in place, a Servant-Leader will refer to it frequently, using it to paint a compelling picture of what it means to work with these people for these ends. A Servant-Leader will constantly reinterpret the vision and not be afraid of refining it. This is all part of being a "visionary leader."

## Ask Yourself

- Am I sick of hearing about vision statements? If so, what can I do to reinvigorate *my own vision* of the power of a vision statement?

- How would I act differently if I lived by a personal vision statement I believe in?

- Instead of beginning with words, can I begin to formulate a personal vision by noticing the passions that consistently lure and excite me?

- Who is a trusted friend who will help me be accountable to my personal vision?

## 2. Displaying Creativity

Those who have studied creative people and the creative process recognize a parallel in the steps that lead to foresight and those that encourage creativity. In fact, one could say that foresight is a more focused application of creativity.

The ancient philosopher Lao-Tse said, "The wise leader knows about pairs of opposites and their interactions. The leader knows how to be creative. In order to lead, the leader learns to follow. In order to prosper, the leader learns to live simply. In both cases, it is the interaction that is creative"[16] and, "in both cases: learn to see things backwards, inside out, and upside down."[17]

To compete in a global economy with rapid-fire innovations and razor-sharp competition, an organization must not only permit but *nurture* creativity. This realization is expressed in popular sayings like "Think out of the box," "Get outside your own silo," and "Look for the third right answer."

Teresa Amabile identifies three criteria for distinguishing more creative contributions from less creative ones:

1. Novelty (it has not been seen or heard before),

2. Relevance (it satisfies the need that originally prompted the contribution),

3. Spontaneity (a "mechanical" formula was not used to come up with the contribution).[18]

You can read some terrific books that will convince you that creativity is within your reach, explain the steps of creative problem solving, and provide useful exercises.[19] Our approach is adapted from the teachings of various creativity mentors.

1. *State the problem* to point everyone in the same direction. Be careful! The real problem could be disguised by symptoms that seem like the problem. For example, the stated problem could be, "We need to find ways to cut expenses!" when the deeper issue may be, "We need to seek ways to be more productive."

2. *Suggest possible solutions.* This is the fun part. Classic brain-storming rules that apply here include the following:

- Suspend judgment. For the moment, forget those prudent comments like, "That will cost too much money," "No one would accept such a thing," and even, "That's crazy!"
- Go for quantity of ideas. Judgment of quality comes later. Elaborate on ideas to increase fluency.
- Change perspective. How would we treat this problem of disposing of scrap manufacturing materials if the castaways were made of gold? How would a flea see this problem? How would we see it if we were floating over it in a dirigible?
- Play with metaphors. What is this problem *like*? Is it like a waterfall, a ski jump, or a lovely meadow with a swamp in the middle? Maybe it's like a valuable trophy that sits atop Mount Everest.

In a sense, we owe the existence of the Internet to the question "What is this like?" Paul Baran, the Rand Corporation employee mentioned earlier, was genuinely frightened at the prospect of nuclear war. He was working on the control system for America's Minuteman missiles and realized that the military's command-control system was vulnerable. The country needed redundancy so that if one center of command was destroyed, others would still be available. He asked himself, "What is this problem like?"

Well, it reminded him of brain research done by a neurologist named Warren McCulloch in the 1940s. McCulloch discovered that if certain parts of the brain are damaged, other parts of the "neural network" would take over. Hmm. A network. What is *that* like? It is a little like a fish net. You could destroy one nexus where the cords are tied together and the net would still work pretty well. With these metaphors in mind, Baran developed a redundant electronic network scheme that had not one, but many control centers. In order to move information around this network, the information had to be digitized and sent as "packets." Each packet would find its own way around the system and be reconstructed into the original message at the destination.

AT&T thought Baran was nuts. They were old-fashioned "analog" folks and could not get excited about an idea that threatened the philosophical and technical basis of their corporation's long history. The world's largest communications company missed out on the beginnings of the digital revolution because they could not think creatively.[20]

So, add this question to your arsenal of creativity tools: *What is this like?*

3. *Evaluate and choose possible solutions.* Cull ideas for quality and connections. Which ones have a germ of possibility? Can you piggyback several ideas to come up with a more complete solution? Now is the time to consider practical matters.

4. *Test the creative solution.* Creative Servant-Leaders are wedded to pragmatic outcomes. Something that sounds great over pizza and soda in the meeting room may not work out in implementation. That's life. It does not mean creative problem solving does not work, just that *this* creative solution did not work. Evaluate results and use them for another creative stab at the problem.

## *A Story of Creativity*

This story has been around creativity circles for some years, but it bears repeating because it illustrates the key traits of creative people. After returning from a hunting trip with his dog one day in 1948, a Swiss electrical engineer named George de Mestral began to pluck the cockleburs stuck to his wool pants and the dog's fur. This was a pesky ritual he had performed many times, but on this day he became curious about what made the burrs hold so tenaciously. He took several of them home to examine under a microscope and noticed that every burr was covered with tiny hooks that held tightly onto the fabric loops in his clothes and the fur strands of his dog.

He smiled as he realized that nature had provided the design for a new kind of fastener. Friends and experts alike laughed when he told them he was going to use little hooks and loops to create a fastener that would rival the zipper, but he persisted with his experiments. Working with a weaver at a textile plant in France, de Mestral's big breakthrough came when he discovered that nylon sewn under an ultraviolet light created small, tough, tight loops. In 1951, he applied for a patent for a fastening invention he called Velcro, a combination of the words *velour* and *crochet*. Within a few years, he was selling over sixty million yards of Velcro® annually.[21]

The inventor of Velcro teaches us that creative people are

- curious,

- observant,

- able to make connections between current ideas and disciplines and pregnant possibilities,

- able to use positive humor,

- willing to endure skepticism about their new ideas, and

- fiercely dedicated to following through.

## *Tips for Inspiring and Managing Creativity*

A Servant-Leader uses creativity in approaching problems and welcomes it in others. The latter task may be the hardest. If your team is ready to move on a policy after long discussion and planning, nothing is more frustrating than a pesky innovator who keeps coming up with new "cool ideas" to start all over. You do not want to frustrate this person's willingness to contribute or sabotage her creativity, but the group does need to move ahead. What can you do?

Here are a few tips for inspiring and managing creativity:

- Even though creativity functions at every stage of problem solving, set general boundaries for each step of the process. "Okay folks, we're going to brainstorm for fifteen minutes. We can listen to a few crazy ideas later, but let's try to get most of them on the table right now."

- Identify and reduce barriers to creativity and the creative process.

- Recognize the tension between creativity and control. They tend to be incompatible. If you need careful control to feel comfortable as a leader, be honest about it and maybe your team can identify creative ways for you to gradually give up your urge to micromanage. They probably have better ideas than you about how to create a new balance. If a creative colleague insists on total freedom with no accountability, the group can also help that person strike an appropriate balance.

- Highly creative people offer exceptional gifts and sometimes pose exceptional management problems. Even though everyone has the capacity to be creative, highly gifted people are often more likely to see "the big picture," to think in conceptual terms rather than in bullet points and to-do lists. Greenleaf said that "conceptual skills allow us to see the big picture, the *where we want to go*. Foresight allows us to map out how we are going to get there by anticipating the various consequences of our actions and then picking the actions that will serve us best."[22] Every organization needs a few "conceptualizers" along with the people Robert Greenleaf called "operationalizers"—those who are good at tracking details with integrity and watchfulness.[23] The trick is to help both kinds of people understand that they need each other. Together, they make the best possible teams.

- The Servant-Leader model encourages creativity *in the right context*. By contrast, a leader who talks a good game of creativity but is impatient with creative ideas and continues to make decisions in safe, predictable ways sends the message, "Don't be creative," and provides little or no context for creative thinking.

The old management saw remains true: "What gets rewarded gets done." If creativity is not rewarded or practiced by a leader, it will not get done.

## Ask Yourself

- Do I see myself as creative even though I am not an artist or musician?

- What is my most vexing problem *like*? How can I change the negative metaphors I associate with it to positive ones?

- Am I too quick to judge "crazy ideas" in myself and others without looking at their creative possibilities?

- What are three ways I can be creative before the end of the day? (They could include such mundane items as taking a different route to work or cooking a novel meal.)

## 3. Taking Courageous, Decisive Action

Robert Greenleaf said that leaders must have an armor of confidence in facing the unknown. Foresight, vision, and creativity lead to decisive action. Here is why:

- A Servant-Leader who has gone through the process of creatively accessing foresight and developing a vision is less likely to jump on the first idea offered. He or she has a picture of the larger forces that must be considered and waits for the second, third, and fourth idea, but then is free to act with more solid assurance that all the bases have been covered.

- A leader with foresight is more likely to heed the Native American guideline to consider the impact of every decision seven generations into the future. With those stakes, an action needs to be decisive.

- By working creatively and collaboratively, a Servant-Leader guards against personal grandiosity. Critics and colleagues act as a check on one's ego. There is less likelihood that a decisive action will originate in ego, or be seen that way by others.

- A community of servants is collectively smarter than any one person. Although there will always be a place for the lonely leader who goes against the grain to do what is right, the chances of actually *getting* it right are increased when like-minded servants participate in the process.

Principled public servants understand that one must be prepared to pay the price for taking courageous, decisive action. After Matthew Welsh became Indiana governor in 1961, he realized that the state needed its first ever sales and income taxes. The Hoosier state had neither, and was in financial trouble. The Indiana General Assembly disagreed, so in 1963, Governor Welsh held them over for a forty-day special session. The issue went down to the wire, resulting in a 24-24 tie vote in the Senate. Only Lieutenant Governor Richard (Dick) Ristine could save the bill. However, unlike Governor Welsh, a lame-duck Democrat who could not succeed himself, Dick Ristine was a Republican with rosy political prospects. His friends (and even his enemies) warned that if he crossed the aisle and voted with the governor, he would effectively end his political career. He believed them, but voted for the tax anyway. Sure enough, in 1964, Mr. Ristine was defeated in the governor's race by a record-breaking plurality, but he had no regrets. He did the right thing.

Your courageous, decisive action may not have such dramatic consequences, but you can count on it generating opposition, for several reasons. First, a leader who takes courageous action becomes a target because he or she is "going out ahead to show the way." Second, a decisive action eliminates possibilities that others may favor, tempting them to grouse and sabotage. If, like Dick Ristine, you first consider all aspects of the situation, including history, current data, and probable impact on the future, you too can move ahead with no regrets, regardless of consequences.

The mathematician and philosopher Alfred North Whitehead said, "The vitality of thought is in adventure. Ideas won't keep. Something must be done about them."[24] Of what use is foresight if it is not acted upon? In truth, anything that requires the doing of something is an opportunity to put foresight, vision, and creativity into action. Exercising courage, being decisive, or demonstrating productive problem-solving abilities rests upon a solid foundation of insight and intuition, combined with a practical set of problem-solving skills.

In the end, foresight, vision, creativity, and principled action become more than tools; they become integrated as part of the deep identity of a Servant-Leader. Because a Servant-Leader is creative and visionary, and is one who sees the world every day with heightened awareness and foresight. It is a great way to live and work.

## Ask Yourself

- What makes me act boldly even when I am not sure of the decision? What keeps me from acting boldly, even after I am as sure as I can be?

- How can I be bold and humble, assertive and collaborative, reflective and proactive?

# Systems Thinker

*When you look at anything or consider anything, look at it as "a whole" as much as you can before you swing on it.*
—Robert Greenleaf

A Servant-Leader thinks and acts strategically, manages change effectively, and balances the whole with the sum of its parts.

- Connects systems thinking with ethical issues.

- Applies the principles of Servant Leadership to systems analysis and decision making.

- Integrates input from all parties in a system to arrive at holistic solutions.

- Demonstrates an awareness of how to lead and manage change.

## Core Competencies

1. Comfortable with Complexity

2. Demonstrates Adaptability

3. Considers the "Greater Good"

## Tools of Systems Thinking

What do the following disciplines, sciences, and philosophies have in common?

- Baldridge National Quality Program
- Total Quality Management
- Six Sigma
- Lean Enterprise
- Appreciative Inquiry
- Chaos Theory and Self-Organizing Systems
- Change Management
- Fuzzy Logic
- Cybernetics
- The Learning Organization
- Family Therapy
- Servant Leadership

In one way or another, they are all expressions of systems thinking, the process that Robert Greenleaf once described as "seeing things whole and finding the language to express it."

When a problem arises in an organization, the natural tendency is to *zoom in* on the person or issue to analyze and fix it. This is a useful strategy, one that is followed by the vast majority of management and scientific processes. Systems thinkers take the next step, however. They also *zoom out* in order to see the problem in the context of the underlying patterns and structures of the whole organization, and the organization's relationship to its community, environment, and country.

Systems thinking can literally save or lose lives, as New Yorkers discovered on September 11, 2001. A few minutes after the South Tower collapsed, observers in police helicopters radioed the news that the North Tower was glowing red about fifteen stories from the top and was also likely to tumble, and soon. That information was not picked up on Fire Department radios, preventing at least some of the 121 firefighters in the North Tower from scrambling to safety before it collapsed around them twenty-one minutes later. This should not have happened. During the response to the first World Trade Center attack in 1993, radios were so ineffective that runners hustled messages back and forth for both the police and fire departments. Even if the radios had worked perfectly, they were not interconnected—that is, they operated on different frequencies. After the first attack, police and fire departments had talked for years about improving radio communications, but turf battles and resistance to change doomed the effort. No one was able to "zoom out" and imagine an aerial picture of a major disaster like 9/11 and employ systems thinking, not only for efficient operation, but also for the greater good.[1]

Before we are too hard on the brave public servants who sacrificed so much, let us admit that every one of us has done the same thing on a smaller scale. We have protected turf, resisted new ideas, and focused on short-term hassles rather than the greater good. The only difference is that the world was not watching us.

Systems thinking is modern but not new. Even the 2,500-year-old text *I Ching* teaches systems thinking by expressing the relationships between people, nature, and spirituality. Modern general systems theory (GST) has its roots in biology. Ludwig Von Bertalanffy, an Austrian biologist, is generally acknowledged to be the father of general systems theory, first described as a theory of the organism in his 1928 book *Modern Theories of Development*.

Later, Von Bertalanffy's 1950 paper "The Theory of Open Systems in Physics and Biology" in *Science* magazine received widespread attention, stimulating an even greater interest in these matters. Shortly thereafter, Professor Jay W. Forrester founded the System Dynamics Program in the Alfred P. Sloan School of Management at MIT in 1956. More recently, Peter Senge's 1990 book *The Fifth Discipline* set off an avalanche of interest in the area.

In recent years some powerful tools have been developed to help make sense of complex organizational systems and find leverage points for changing them. These include process diagrams with balancing and reinforcing loops, stocks, flows, and boundaries. Some organizational processes are so predictable they are called "archetypes." The purpose of this chapter is not to train you in the use of these tools, but we do strongly urge you to look into them. We recommend the writings of Peter Senge, Daniel Kim, and the publications and workshops of Pegasus, an organization devoted to the application of systems thinking in everyday life.[2]

## The Systems Pyramid

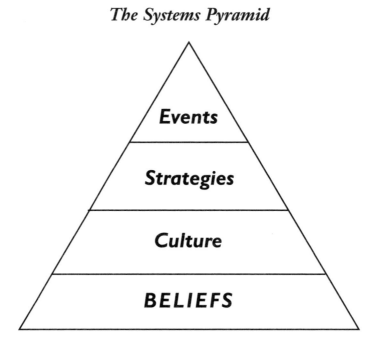

Systems thinkers are fond of the image of a pyramid to illustrate how their discipline gets beneath appearances.

*Events* constitute the top part of the structure that is "above the waterline," in conscious view. These are the situations we see and react to.

*Strategies* are below events, often created in response to events, or to a vision of what should happen.

*Culture* can either support or sabotage strategies, but is certainly more powerful than strategy. Andy Grove, former Chairman of Intel, is credited with saying, "Culture eats strategy for lunch every day of the week."[3] An organization's culture is a constellation of causal connections, relationships, and historical patterns that have been rigidified into policies and assumptions.

*Beliefs* quietly run the show in organizations, just as they do in individuals. An organization organized around the deep belief that doing business is simply waging war in another arena will foster a radically different structure and culture than one organized around the belief that doing business is a noble enterprise that should contribute to the growth of people and serve the wider public.

Culture is often unconscious and deep beliefs are even more so, but these are the areas of greatest leverage.

When an event occurs that poses a problem, all the analytical resources of an organization swoop in to fix things. However, if there is no systemic thinking going on, the fix could make things worse.

Consider this scenario: The latest report shows sales down by an average of 6 percent in the last two quarters. This is an event that announces itself with blinking red lights! What should the company do? Create new strategies that directly address the event, of course! Warn, or even replace, the sales manager. Increase incentives to individual salespeople. Offer discounts to customers. Then to make up the financial loss, the organization might cancel or delay an R&D project, lay off a customer service representative, or take any number of other actions.

A deeper "Strategy" response would be to take a deep breath and try to understand trends over time that have either not been measured or have been ignored. Perhaps sales figures are a result of seasonal effects that started several years earlier, or the company has not paid enough attention to several lean, hungry competitors who are cutting into market share.

A "Culture" response zooms out even further, looking for cause-and-effect relationships, with the most important ones often the best hidden. Perhaps salespeople are not well trained because the culture considers them less important, or they are not in contact with the customer service people who could offer valuable real-life feedback because the structure encourages silos. Maybe R&D needs to develop an updated product, or perhaps they have one but have not told the marketing people, who are still basing their strategy on the older version. Suppose certain departments do not speak to each other because that is the way the founder wanted it fifty years ago when he started the company. The organizational culture supports this separation by allowing—even encouraging—vicious competition and name-calling between the departments. Stranger things have happened.

The "Beliefs" base of the pyramid undergirds and quietly informs everything above it. Perhaps one of the beliefs of this company is that they are in business to sell widgets, period. No need to pay attention to larger environmental concerns, issues in the local community, or how happy people may be in their jobs. Do your job, get your paycheck, sell more widgets! That's what we believe about the function and meaning of business. Got it?

A systems analysis of the reason for declining sales may find multiple causes, but zero in on the surprising conclusion that "sales have gone down because engineering and marketing haven't spoken much in fifty years and one of our core beliefs is counterproductive and we're finally paying the price."

Culture and Beliefs issues are the easiest to overlook, but they offer the best opportunity for sustained change. That's why vision statements and credos are important. They offer a True North that informs—or should inform—every corner of policymaking and ethics and behavior. During the Tylenol poisoning crisis of 1982, Johnson & Johnson executives were guided by a credo written by founder Robert Wood Johnson in the 1940s. The credo stressed the importance of working in the public interest.[4]

Why should we care about the Systems Pyramid or even about systems thinking?

The first reason is profits. Edward Deming suggests that workers are responsible for only 15 percent of the problems in organizations. The overall system is responsible for the other 85 percent, which means that 85 percent of the apparatus that generates products that keep a company in business is at the mercy of systems.

Second, a person who understands how systems work can see her personal role in the whole enterprise, anticipate problems in order to prevent them, and become a designer rather than a victim.

This is not an abstract benefit. One client came to us for help with an expensive problem—high turnover among people in the data entry department. This was a major insurance company, and the smallest mistake in entering financial or policy information could cost thousands, even millions of dollars if the company was sued. We interviewed employees in the department and learned that management had decided individuals should only be given enough information on a "need to know" basis, just enough to do their jobs. Employees had no idea of how their work fitted into the overall flow of paperwork in the organization, much less how important accuracy was to the lives of policy owners just like them. We convinced management to share information about the whole system so that each employee could see the importance of his or her job in the context of the company's mission.

We also taught them the principles of praise described in Pillar IV, convinced them to give out buttons with the slogan "What You Do Counts," print stories of extraordinary service in the in-house newsletter, celebrate victories and, yes, add a few financial incentives. Before-and-after surveys showed a marked increase in morale and performance, most affected by two key variables: (1) the map that helped them understand what their jobs meant to the company and to clients, and (2) expressions of personal appreciation.

The third reason we should care about the Systems Pyramid is because we will never integrate processes that "Put People First" if we only focus on Events. Servant-Leaders need to dig down to the levels of *effective* Strategy, but especially Culture and Beliefs.

The "laws" of systems thinking often seem counterintuitive, in the same way that the solution to the Chinese finger-trap puzzle is counterintuitive; one must push, not pull, to get out of the trap. Even if a person thinks systemically, she may not understand why seemingly desirable inputs result in undesirable outputs. Senge's "Laws of Systems Thinking" offer deeper truths that give context to the practice of systems thinking.[5] Here are eight of them:

- Today's problems come from yesterday's "solutions."

- The harder you push, the harder the system pushes back.

- Behavior grows better before it grows worse.

- The easy way out usually leads back in.

- The cure can be worse than the disease.

- Faster is slower.

- Cause and effect are not closely related in time and space.

- Small changes can produce big results, but the areas of highest leverage are often the least obvious.

Can you think of examples where these laws played out in your organization?

A person could spend years in pleasant academic study of systems thinking, but most of us do not have that luxury. For now, we will focus on how Servant-Leaders use insights from systems disciplines in their quest to build healthier, wiser, freer, and more effective organizations.

## *Robert Greenleaf and Systems Thinking*

Well before systems thinking was an academic area of study, Robert Greenleaf learned about seeing things whole by studying the writings of E. B. White. Greenleaf listed four requirements for Servant-Leaders who wish to think systemically.[6]

First, wholeness requires *moving in the right direction.* "One often does not know the precise goal," wrote Greenleaf, "but one must always be certain of one's direction. The goal will reveal itself in due course."

Second, a Servant-Leader is determined to *see life in all its glorious messiness without all the loose ends tied up in neat, simplistic bows.* Jim Collins and his research team found this same quality in the CEOs profiled in his book *Good to Great.* Our world includes messy dangers that must also be acknowledged. "As one attains maturity," wrote Greenleaf, "one learns to live peacefully and sleep well with a submerged awareness of constant danger."[7]

Third, by seeing things whole, a Servant-Leader *loves the sheer beauty of this world.* A Servant-Leader cultivates heightened awareness, allowing him to see connections between history, people, events, possibilities, and deep intuition. Like an elegant mathematical formula, the "big picture" is all grand and beautiful, even in its stunning complexity.

Finally, Greenleaf said that *ethical conduct* is central to seeing things whole. A Servant-Leader who "zooms out" to clearly understand causes and effects, profound relationships, and outcomes of actions can no longer say, "It's not my fault," or "Let someone else fix it." A Servant-Leader takes personal responsibility and acts ethically, doing what he or she can reasonably do with the resources at hand.

## Ask Yourself

- How comfortable am I with complexity?

- What problem should I "zoom out" on to include the rest of my organization and its employees, the local and wider community, and even the environment?

- When have I reacted at an Events level rather than a Structure level with colleagues and (here's the hard one) with my family?

- Can I find real-life examples for at least two of Senge's laws of systems thinking? What price did I pay for not understanding the law?

- Do Greenleaf's four requirements for systems thinkers make me feel comfortable or generate anxiety because they seem too vague?

- Where can I put into practice at least one of Greenleaf's four principles in the next two days?

## 1. Being Comfortable with Complexity

*Behind complexity, there is always simplicity to be revealed. Inside simplicity, there is always complexity to be discovered.*

—Gang Yu

Everything is related and everything is part of a system. A Servant-Leader is a fragment of many systems—a fragment of a board, of an executive team, an organization, a family, a community, and so on. This is such a simple, profound idea that it has become a cliché. Yet we act as if it were *not* true, as if one can "fix" broken parts of an organization, or even wounded pieces of our own psyche, without considering the whole system.

Ancient Hindu mythology offers a striking image that forces us to see things systemically—Indra's net. In the heaven of Indra, there is said to be a network of pearls so arranged that if you look at one you see all the others reflected in it. In the same way, each object in the world is not merely itself but involves every other object and in fact IS everything else.[8]

Contemporary findings in quantum and particle physics tell us that Indra's net is more than metaphor: it is fact. Humans and stars are made of the same energy stuff, all connected, but all expressed in infinite varieties of matter, mind, and magnitude. The same forces that affect the organization and creativity of the hundred billion stars in our galaxy and the hundred billion other galaxies also influence the hundred billion synapses that are the working ends of our brain neurons. Fritjof Capra put it this way in his book *The Turning Point*: "The conception of the universe as an interconnected web of relations is one of two major themes that recur throughout modern physics. The other theme is the realization that the cosmic web is intrinsically dynamic."[9]

Indra's net is also a fact for our organizations. You can look at any one department and see reflected the values and policies of the whole. The ways people input data for an insurance company affect customer service. The processes and skills followed by machine operators on a manufacturing floor create the quality sold by the marketing department. Leaders sometimes believe they can keep secret any long-term power tussles or toxic policies within an organization, but there is always leakage. Customers, suppliers, and stockholders eventually find out because they, too, are part of the same system.

Think of someone in your organization who is a complainer, a person who seems to delight in pointing out what is wrong. Now think about another employee who is unfailingly positive, who sees every problem as an exciting challenge and every person as a source of solutions. Imagine each of these people as one of the pearls in Indra's net of your organization. It takes both of them to reflect a more accurate picture of the whole system. While the positive person may be more pleasant to be around, the complainer may have his finger on unpleasant truths important to face. Unless you *zoom out* and look at the system rather than personalities, you will miss the positive contributions of the complainer.

This is not so much a matter of completely understanding every person, or even every individual system. That is impossible. Neuroscientists, mental health professionals, and even religious leaders tell us that the complexity of the mental systems inside every human being far surpasses the most complicated computer.

As for understanding every system, it is a sure bet that even Bill Gates does not understand every line of code in every Microsoft process. Systems thinking is more about understanding *relationships* between people, processes, structures, belief systems, and a host of other factors.

A person can get dizzy just thinking about it all. That's why a common response to complexity is to ignore the messiness: "I'm only going to think about my little part of the world. Let others worry about the big picture." Servant-Leaders know there is an alternative response: to be comfortable with complexity and its paradoxes after seeking to understand it as deeply as possible. It is a paradox that the more you learn about the details of systems thinking, the more comfortable you will be with the overwhelming intricacies of reality.

A Servant-Leader is not comfortable with complexity because he has figured out all the answers, but because he can live with the remaining questions and trusts that it is possible to *live into* new answers as long as he is following the right direction.

## *Acting Strategically*

A high-powered consultant once admitted that he used the word *strategic* dozens of times a day but still was unsure of what it meant. He was smart and could have looked it up in the dictionary, where he would see that it generally means using all available forces to execute a plan of action in order to reach a clear outcome. However, I doubt that he was referring to a dictionary definition. I think he was speaking of the shorthand way we have come to use the word. Confession time now: when I say, "I'm going to be strategic about that opportunity!" I like it that I sound like I know what I am doing. I am a man with a plan. Strong. Clear. Smarter than most. Sometimes I actually do know what I am doing, but other times I use the word to cover up my lack of clear direction—and I am almost never smarter.

We are far better off having a strategy so we can act strategically, and a strategy depends on knowing the end goal. Middle managers frequently approached Robert Greenleaf to describe a situation and ask for his advice, and his first response was always a question: "What are you trying to do?" Without knowing that, we are doomed to failure. A good strategy also requires intermediate goals, a planned sequence of actions, a timetable, and benchmarks for evaluation.

Systems-thinking Servant-Leaders do all that, but operate a little differently in executing a strategy. When formulating the end goal, they are more likely to ask for ideas from a more diverse group of people at different levels of the organization. They use all the analytical tools of systems thinking, but because they know that everything is connected, they also rely on foresight and even intuition to play with "what if" scenarios to understand unintended consequences. They develop their bullet-point plans of action like others, but hold them more lightly so they can be revisited and modified to incorporate lessons learned along the way. They consider ethics and the greater good as they formulate and execute. They understand that *they* are not their strategy. Their ego is not offended if someone has a better idea. Finally, they model Servant Leadership while acting strategically. Like Greenleaf, they understand that "the means determine the ends" and realize they could sabotage a positive outcome by going about it negatively.

## 2. Demonstrating Adaptability

*The art of progress is to preserve order amid change and to preserve change amid order.*          —Alfred North Whitehead

A systems-thinking Servant-Leader is adaptable because he or she knows reality is fluid, and new issues call for new responses. This is a *courageous* stance! A person who "changes course in midstream" can be accused of being inconsistent or wishy-washy. Colleagues may confuse adaptability with lack of direction. Just ask any politician who has changed a position on an issue.

This is why communicating a shared vision is so important. People will accept a lot of midcourse corrections if they understand that each contributes to movement *in the right direction*, always moving toward the destination (vision) on the horizon. A sailing ship headed for a destination due north will tack back and forth from northeast to northwest, changing short-term headings to take advantage of natural forces of wind and tide so it can advance confidently in the right direction. An airplane flying directly from point A to point B makes thousands of midcourse corrections.

All of which is to say that *adaptability is a natural process, in harmony with nature's forces*. Rigid stubbornness is unnatural. The pilot of a ship or plane who simply plants his course on one compass heading will be as lost as the pilot who wanders around without knowing the right direction. Robert Greenleaf wrote about the need for leaders to be adaptable, even when setting goals with others: "The goals, both immediate and long range, emerge as the search proceeds."[10] In the systems-thinker "pearl" of Indra's net, we can see reflections of all the other Pillars of Servant Leadership. Here are just three examples:

- *Foresight.* A Servant-Leader reads the signs, anticipates the storms that come with any complex system, and corrects the course to stay headed in the right direction. She has the courage to get beneath events and examine patterns and structure.

- *Person of Character.* The Servant-Leader is humble in the face of complicated challenges, realizing that he does not have all the answers and that every other team member can contribute leadership in solving systemic problems.

- *Skilled Communicator.* The Servant-Leader finds language to share the reality and possibilities of systems thinking.

## *Beware the Seas of Change*

According to Watkins and Mohr, "Change is not a force acting on organizations, but the very water in which they swim."[11] As we facilitate organizational change efforts for client companies, we find it helpful to use a few nautical metaphors to remind them that they "can't control the winds or seas of change, but they can adjust their sails." They may not be able to control the change itself, but they can certainly control their reactions to it.

I (James) am fond of emphasizing the futility of fighting against the "seas of change" by sharing a personal experience about the first time I had a chance to swim in the ocean.

When I was around twenty-two years old, I boarded a ferry on the coast of North Carolina with my dear friend and mentor Chris Faegre, thirty years my senior. We were headed to one of the Outer Banks islands in the Atlantic, to try out a little sand camping.

It was a magnificent, sweltering day. After a brief ride, we were deposited on what looked like nothing more than a long, narrow lump of sand, along with enough supplies and fresh water to keep us comfortably sustained for the weekend.

We immediately went about setting up our homemade sand tent, constructed of rip-stop nylon and mosquito netting purchased from an Army-Navy Surplus Store. When we finished, I got into my Speedo swimsuit (back when I felt no shame wearing one) and eagerly made a beeline to the surf.

"Not so fast," said Chris. "Have you ever swum in the ocean?"

"No," I replied tersely, with a twinge of "what's the big deal" in my voice.

"Then I need to talk to you about the riptide."

I was hot, drenched in sweat and caked with sand—in no mood for a "paternal" lecture. He noticed.

"Listen to me, this could save your life!" Squatting down, he drew a picture in the sand.

"Every wave that crashes on the shore recedes back toward the ocean. This is called the 'ebb tide.' Somewhere along this island, the ebb tide flows out in a narrow channel, creating a powerful backward current under the surf."

"Oh, you mean the undertow," I exclaimed in a flash of recognition.

"Yes, it's also called an undertow, because it's under the waves—and if you get caught in it—you'll be towed out to sea."

"So how will I know where it is?"

"You'll know where it is once you're in it," he said a little too flippantly, and paused for effect. "But I'm going to tell you how to get out of it."

He pointed back down to the sand. "If you end up in this channel, and start careening out to sea, your instincts will tell you to swim against the current directly toward the shore. Unfortunately, that would be a deadly mistake. Instead, start to swim parallel to the shore until you reach the other side of the riptide. *Then*, you can start heading for shore."

"Thanks, Chris," I absentmindedly replied and made a beeline into the surf.

The water was cool and refreshing and I quickly settled into my lap swimming pace.

When I stopped to catch my breath and get my bearings, I sighted our bright green tent, a little speck in the distance. Chris's words came back to me. "You'll know it when you're in it." From the looks of things, I had been in it the whole time.

Of course I panicked and started swimming toward shore. Fortunately, I quickly came to my senses and stopped. With every ounce of faith and fortitude I could muster, I pondered my wise old friend's advice and began to swim perpendicular to the undertow, and parallel to the shore.

Sure enough, it wasn't very long until I knew I wasn't in it anymore. With a mixture of relief, pride, and humility, I proceeded at a comfortable, steady pace toward home base.

When I got back to the tent, Chris was napping peacefully. To this day I regret not thanking him for saving my life.

The story does not end there. Eight years later, my new wife Dawne and I were vacationing in Puerto Rico. We were playing in the surf, jumping waves with not a care in the world. I'll never forget the sound of my wife's screams as she called for help while I headed for the beach to wet my whistle. I looked up, and somehow she was way out there. "Damn undertow," I exclaimed. Why didn't I think to discuss it with her?

I swam posthaste to her side and, after helping her calm down, I conducted a brief in-service on riptides. Grabbing her around the waist, we swam slowly together in the way my now-deceased mentor had taught me, working with the available forces rather than against them.

Chris taught me the lesson that the intuitively obvious answer is not always the right answer. Thank you, my friend. You saved my life, and the life of my wife.

## *Change Is Inevitable; Growth Is Optional*

Change is not something that happens along once in a while, a nuisance to be addressed. The Greek philosopher Heraclitus believed that the only thing that endures is change.

In keeping with a tradition of the great Zen master teachers, we often tell our students that the fundamental truth about change can be found in the form of a riddle.

Q: How many psychologists does it take to change a light bulb?

A: Only one; but the light bulb has to really want to change!

That is, we have a *choice* in the face of change. Although we cannot always control change, we can control our eventual response to it. In other words, "Change is inevitable; growth is optional!"

This sounds good, but is too facile for most people, at least in the short term. A person in the middle of a painful divorce may not see the wonderful opportunity of the thing until months or years later and perhaps wishes this change to go away right now, thank you, in spite of all the breathless growth it supposedly offers.

How many times have you seen this Chinese symbol for crisis and been told it is composed of two ideograms that mean danger and opportunity?

The name of this compound character is wēijī (roughly pronounced "way-gee") and, according to Victor H. Mair, professor of Chinese language and literature at the University of Pennsylvania, the translation of it as CRISIS = DANGER + OPPORTUNITY is misguided hooey, even though scores of motivational speakers have made a living on it.[12] Professor Mair's more accurate translation still gives us plenty to think about, though, and is actually more interesting.

First, he asks us to call this expression a *character* or *graph* rather than an ideogram because, strictly speaking, ideograms look like the thing they represent and this one does not. Okay. It is a character.

However, it is also a word composed of two syllables, each of which could stand on its own as a word, just like the two-syllable English word *airplane*. As a whole word, wēijī does mean "crisis," and the first syllable—wēi—(on the top) really does mean "danger." But the syllable on the bottom—jī—means something like "the crucial point" when used in this context. To quote the good professor, "A wēijī indicates a perilous situation when one should be especially wary. It is *not* a juncture when one goes looking for advantages and benefits. In a crisis, one wants above all to save one's neck!" In colloquial English, we might say that wēijī means it is time to get the heck out of here, but fast!

However, that last syllable jī is the interesting one. It is an expression that generally means "the dynamic of a thing's unfolding," and is neither good nor bad until it is given context in combination with another graph. When combined with wēi to form wēijī, it lends a negative connotation. When combined with liáng ("excellent") to form liángjī, it does, in fact, mean "opportunity."

We can take away a deep learning from these Sino-linguistic analyses by focusing on what we'll call "the jī factor"—the dynamic of unfolding, or the sense of immediacy in timing. A crisis is a crisis, and it is Pollyanna-istic to paper over that nasty reality in the middle of the threat (assuming it really is a threat). If your house is on fire, put out the fire first. *Later* you can think about the "opportunity" it represents for building a bigger kitchen. Do the work. Address the crisis without sentimentality about what a wonderful opportunity it represents. But later, after making it through the worst, a Servant-Leader can reflect on what happened and reframe the jī factor in another context, with more positive associations, and use that energy to unfold dynamics never guessed at.

Here is an example—one mentioned earlier. When Johnson & Johnson faced the crisis of Tylenol contamination with cyanide in 1982, company officials addressed the immediate crisis by recalling twenty-two million bottles of Tylenol with a value of $100 million.

They went on television and asked consumers to not use the product and offered to replace any Tylenol bottles already opened and arrange a $100,000 reward for information leading to the capture of the culprit. Safety and candor came first, even though the company had quickly determined that the contamination could not have been their fault, and they were not forced into acting by any government agency. Still, the company suffered great damage. The marketing guru Jerry Della Femina claimed that J&J would never sell another Tylenol capsule.

He was wrong actually, because after the crisis came the opportunity. The jī factor, the power of associating with a positive dynamic with right timing, was now applied to the reintroduction of Tylenol with triple-seal safety measures. Consumers were offered a $2.50 coupon for any Tylenol product and thousands of J&J representatives fanned out to make presentations to physicians and other medical professionals explaining the steps that had been taken, and to share the latest research on the efficacy of Tylenol. J&J reframed the jī factor to turn wēijī—a true crisis—into liángjī—a genuine opportunity. There is evidence that some consumers switched to Tylenol after the reintroduction because their faith in the company, and the product, had soared.[13]

Is it *not* true that many critical incidents in your personal or professional life contain both disruption and then, after reflection and right action, the potential for fresh achievement? Your ultimate reaction to the stimulus depends upon your perception, how you assign meaning to what you are experiencing, and how you access the dynamic of unfolding.

## *The Dimensions of Change*

A systems-thinking Servant-Leader leads change in three dimensions:

1. Organizational (Systemic),

2. Relational (Interpersonal), and

3. Individual (Personal).

If you overlook any dimension, you will not manage change effectively or systemically.

For example, the loss of a key partner in the organization through disability, death, or retirement has ramifications on the organization in every dimension: organizational consequences that require succession planning and talent management, relational impacts through reconfiguration of the leadership team and shifting alliances of power, and individual consequences on some who may face expanding roles and responsibilities or be grieving the loss of their friend in the workplace.

Paradoxically, experts have discovered a certain amount of predictability embedded in the change process. In brief, organizational change is often perceived by individuals in the organization as something that originates "out there," upsetting the way we've always done things. Natural reactions include disbelief, denial, or active attempts to maintain the status quo.

Systems-thinking Servant-Leaders understand this and prepare to constructively channel fear and resistance. They listen, and then listen some more. They gladly and calmly explain details for the second or third or fourth time—whatever is necessary. Servant-Leaders do not preach others to change or coerce them or foolishly seek "buy-in" to a program others had no opportunity to craft. Rather, over time, they guide and empower others to explore positive possibilities for a renewed organizational culture, backed by sound strategy and achievable performance. Eventually, individuals within the organization become committed to the vision of the future. They are then willing and able to accept, even embrace, their new roles and responsibilities.

An excellent portrayal of how to implement change can be found in Kotter's book *Leading Change*. He has identified the elements that contribute to a positive change in organizations.[14]

- Establish a sense of urgency
- Create a powerful guiding coalition
- Develop a compelling vision for the change
- Communicate, communicate, communicate the vision

- Remove obstacles to change

- Create short-term wins

- Refrain from declaring victory too soon

- Anchor the change in corporate culture

Let's review a few key elements of our discussion about change:

- Anticipate and plan for change

- Constantly communicate information about change

- Listen with attentive presence, but without believing you can always "fix" another's anxiety about change

- Acknowledge the challenge of change

- Provide quality training and skill building in change management

- Foster a flexible, supportive climate

- Celebrate milestones along the way

- Attend to self-care during times of change

## *Balancing Stability, Strategy, and Change*

Vision provides an organization with the stability of moving in *the right direction*. Strategy helps it get there.

Notice that the first sentence above includes two seemingly contradictory words: *stability* and *moving*. The kind of stability provided by a Servant-Leader systems thinker is more vibrant than the stability of things that never change. It is a stability with surprises.

Part of the human makeup seeks harmony, balance, and some level of predictable security. There is odd comfort in predictable rituals like reading the morning paper over a cup of coffee or kissing your loved one before heading off to work, and there is, of course, nothing wrong with that. Our bodies also seek stability—or homeostasis—which means "the ability or tendency of an organism or cell to maintain internal equilibrium by adjusting its physiological processes." The problem arises when we quit adjusting. After all, the ultimate state of equilibrium is death.

Servant-Leaders find harmony in moving toward the shared vision rather than in embracing the security of once-and-for-all answers. They do not confuse vision with goals. Many others do, though, and that is why managing change is so difficult.

Strategic choices—those midcourse corrections—require change, especially if they address issues of structure and belief, and change is not easy. (Remember one of Senge's laws: the harder you push, the harder the system pushes back.) Realizing this, a Servant-Leader continues to communicate the relationship between changes and the shared vision. He personally lives the change even while he is honest about his own inner pull to do things the same way for the sake of tradition or harmony or just plain comfort. This is where the "lead" emerges from a Servant-Leader.

We must be careful that we do not ruin chances for responding to change by making things so stable they turn into concrete, like Hans Solo who was flash frozen at the end of *Star Wars Episode V: The Empire Strikes Back*. Poet William Blake understood this when he wrote in his poem "Opportunity,"

> He who bends himself to a joy
> Doth the winged life destroy;
> But he who kisses the joy as it flies
> Lives in eternity's sunrise.[15]

## Ask Yourself

- Can I think of a time when Indra's net was evident in my actions on the job?

- Having heard the story of James's friend and mentor Chris Faegre, can I remember a situation where the intuitively obvious answer was not the right answer?

- Is a time upon me when I can use "the jī factor" to reframe the aftermath of a crisis as a positive opportunity?

- Do I know *the right direction* for me personally, and for my organization?

- Have I succumbed to the temptation of resolving issues into neat, airtight packages for the sake of feeling good rather than addressing whole systems in context?

- Am I able to see the sheer beauty of this world even in the midst of convoluted organizational issues?

- Are ethical considerations for the greater good part of my toolkit for systems thinking?

- Do I find the language to express how I and others "see things whole?"

- Am I "strategic" in a traditional way or in a Servant-Leader way?

## 3. Considering the Greater Good

*Greater good is calling upon us here in this world to be done this day. One of my rallying calls is let's go out and do some good. This is who we are. This is what we are about.*
—John Morton, *The Blessings Already Are*

Anyone can learn the tools to analyze processes within organizations. A Servant-Leader does more. She extends her thinking to include the greater good, the impact her actions will have on individual people, families, and the larger families of community and the natural world. The purely analytical approach and the Servant-Leader approach lead to different outcomes.

Meet Brett, a smart executive who is given the goal of increasing the profit of VanTran, the transportation company he works for, by 10 percent in two years. He zeroes in on the most obvious target—expenses—and decides he can save money by replacing a number of his aging vans with diesel-powered vehicles. Diesel engines are reliable and get better mileage than gasoline engines.

The savings in fuel alone will let Brett reach the company's goal. Case closed.

Andy, a Servant-Leader who is given the same assignment, also sees diesel-powered vans as a way to meet the two-year profit goal of VanTran, but decides to investigate further by zooming out and looking at his company's needs within the context of prevailing patterns, structures, and the greater good. He asks for input from drivers, regular passengers, and mechanics. In order to gain foresight about future trends, he calls an economics professor at the local university who specializes in energy issues. He even invites an ethicist to come visit with his team for several hours to help them consider the wider impact of this decision. (This is something Greenleaf did on a regular basis at AT&T.)

Finally, Andy asks the key question: What is best for my company *and* the community *and* the environment? Notice that he never lets go of the original assignment; he simply extends his understanding to embrace issues of pattern and structure.

Andy and his team wonder if new hybrid vehicles would save enough money through increased mileage to do the trick. They run the numbers and realize that because of their increased purchase price, hybrids will take around three years to increase profits by 10 percent. Still, hybrids seem like the right thing to do; they will decrease pollution and possibly attract admiration and loyalty from a whole new generation of riders. It's just possible they could even increase ridership enough to make that two-year goal, but there is no guarantee of that.

Andy presents all the alternatives to management, including his recommendation that the company go ahead with the purchase of hybrids and decrease expenses in other areas until they deliver their return on investment (ROI). If the organization has a vision that includes the greater good, its leaders will take his proposal seriously. Even if it does not, Andy has done his best to move the company in that direction.

The point of this fictional example is not that diesel engines are necessarily bad—in fact, the newest designs dramatically decrease emissions and increase mileage—but that Andy had the courage to see things whole. He was comfortable with the complexity of the situation, showed adaptability in considering a solution that was not necessarily a sure thing, but seemed to be headed in the *right direction*, and considered the greater good in his proposal.

How would a situation play out differently in your organization if it were analyzed systemically with an eye to the greater good? And what is "the greater good?" How do we know it? Aristotle suggested that the greater good is something that embraces a value for its own sake rather than to satisfy individual wants or needs. Wholesomeness, then, is a greater good than individual pleasure.[16] American pragmatists associate the greater good with what works best for the most number of people. If you have several years to kill, you can spend it pleasantly by investigating the philosophical views on the greater good, but here is a better suggestion: check your common sense and your heart.

By "zooming out" for a systems perspective, does your common sense tell you that unregulated pollution is bad? Does your heart have sympathy for children all over the world who drink contaminated water and come down with serious illnesses? Of course! Minimizing pollution is in the greater good. If you worked for one of the Big Three American carmakers during the 1980s, could you have "zoomed out" for a systems perspective and at least dimly realized that the price of gasoline would go up and that quality would be an issue for American car buyers? Would your heart have told you that increased safety was the right thing to do for the greater good of everyone? Yes.

You need not read Aristotle to have a sense of the greater good, for yourself, your family, or your organization.

## How to Recognize a Systems-Thinking Servant-Leader

Here is a handy guide to the Top Ten Behaviors that will help you recognize one of these systems-thinking Servant-Leader critters in an organization.

- Often answers a question with a question.

- Frequently unwilling to make a snap decision on a major issue until the group looks at "wider ramifications."

- Listens carefully, restates the speaker's ideas, and asks for agreement on meaning.

- Sometimes brings up Peter Senge's pesky "Laws of Systems Thinking."

- Asks about "unintended consequences three or four years down the road" with a faraway look in her eyes.

- Has been known to change positions on several issues and somehow seemed comfortable doing so.

- Occasionally makes doodles using funny symbols she calls "reinforcing loops, flows, boundaries, and archetypes" and actually makes sense when she explains what they mean.

- Sometimes jumps up in a meeting and draws the Systems Pyramid and asks, "Is this a matter of responding to events, patterns, structure-culture, or beliefs?"

- Uses the word *paradox* in normal conversation.

- Once talked about learning from a crisis by suggesting we reframe an opportunity using "the jī factor."

We do not wish to scare good people who intend to access systems thinking as a way to serve their organizations. We only point out that, because systems thinking is still new in many institutions, it may seem a little "fringey" to old-timers. But what can you do? Sacrifice service in order to appear more "normal?" We hope not. Greenleaf said a Servant-Leader is one who "goes out ahead to show the way," and systems thinking is a well-researched method for moving ahead on the journey.

## Ask Yourself

- Do I understand that asking powerful questions is at least as important as finding powerful answers?

- How does systems thinking support the test of a Servant-Leader? "Are those being served healthier, wiser, freer, more autonomous, and more likely themselves to become servants while they are being served? And what is the effect on the least privileged in society? Will they benefit or, at least, not be further deprived?"

- Have I thought about the long-term greater good for myself, my family, and my organization?

- Am I willing to stand out as a systems thinker?

# PILLAR VII

# Moral Authority

*Moral authority requires sacrifice.* —Stephen Covey

A Servant-Leader is worthy of respect, inspires trust and confidence, and establishes quality standards for performance.

- Values moral authority over positional authority.

- Empowers others with responsibility *and* authority.

- Sets clear, firm yet flexible boundaries.

- Establishes, models, and enforces quality standards for conduct and performance.

## Core Competencies

1. Accepts and Delegates Responsibility

2. Shares Power and Control

3. Creates a Culture of Accountability

## Becoming Worthy to Lead

In college I (Don) was once part of a team charged with the task of building a float for the homecoming parade. Our elected foreman had worked construction during the previous summer but was not a strong leader. To be fair, we followers did not give him much of a chance. We were being goofy—joking, joshing, and jiving. Not much was getting done, and we had little time left. Then, we gradually noticed Larry, who was quietly picking up two-by-four boards and nailing them into place, stopping to ask others how he could help with their jobs, working with grace and efficiency to make the float take shape. He did not lecture the rest of us knuckleheads, whip us into shape, shame us, or order us around. He simply worked.

As Larry moved among us we eventually quieted down and got to work. He became the project leader by example. He proved his trustworthiness and dedication to our shared objective. He earned moral authority.

Moral authority is different from formal authority. Formal authority is the power a person holds because of his or her position. It usually includes the discretion to hire, fire, promote, demote, or correct. A CEO holds formal authority, just like a parent. Lurking in the background is the threat of coercion to make things happen, even if the person with the position would prefer to operate collaboratively. Robert Greenleaf believed the background threat of coercion could sabotage a leader's ability to persuade with open hands. He even turned down some promotions because he feared the formal authority that came with them would interfere with the most precious kind of power—moral authority. Greenleaf understood that moral authority is not something that automatically comes with a position, or even with a claim to moral authority. It is something one *earns* by following the other six Pillars of Servant Leadership.

Specifically, your followers *grant* you moral authority when they see that you consistently

- act as a person of character with humility, integrity, and a base of spirituality,

- put people first through acts of care and concern, mentoring, and serving,

- communicate skillfully with empathy and an open heart for feedback,

- collaborate compassionately, honor diversity, build effective teams, and face conflict,

- exercise foresight, nurture creativity, inspire and support an audacious vision, and

- think systemically, considering the greater good while acting strategically in complex environments.

Stephen Covey puts it this way: "Moral authority is another way to define Servant Leadership because it represents a reciprocal choice between leader and follower. If the leader is principle-centered, he or she will develop moral authority."[1]

A person with moral authority acts as servant. Robert Greenleaf summarized the principle in this famous passage:

A new moral principle is emerging which holds that the only authority deserving one's allegiance is that which is freely and knowingly granted by the led to the leader in response to, and in proportion to, the clearly evident servant stature of the leader. Those who choose to follow this principle will not casually accept the authority of existing institutions. Rather, they will freely respond only to individuals who are chosen as leaders because they are proven and trusted as servants. To the extent that this principle prevails in the future, the only truly viable institutions will be those that are predominantly servant led.[2]

If Greenleaf is right, the importance of moral authority goes beyond the esteem it brings to individuals. It could mean the survival or demise of entire organizations. This is already happening. During the era of Enron and similar scandals, billions of dollars were lost and thousands of lives disrupted because the public lost its trust in the basic moral authority of organizations. Other scandals are always occurring, even if they do not receive similar publicity. The need for moral authority prevails.

Moral authority is not to be confused with the trait of being moralistic, which is too often expressed in shallow commands like, "Do what I say, not what I do." Every parent knows this approach does not work with children, so why would it work with adults? A moralistic person frequently, and often unconsciously, operates out of the ego. A moral person operates out of love—love of self and others.

My (Don's) friend Melinda is not a moralistic person. She responds to problems by listening first rather than judging first, but she is certainly moral. Melinda taught me of the value of acting in a moral way *even when no one is looking*. Like many Servant-Leaders, Melinda expects more from herself than she does from others.

I called her one day and commented that she sounded sleepy. "I've tossed and turned all night," she said, "thinking about a situation with my health insurance." Melinda lost coverage when she left a job to start her own business and had been shopping for a new policy. She had had an interview with an agent who asked a minimal number of questions, all of which she answered honestly, but she did not volunteer much beyond what was asked. Most people would say, "Hey, smart move, Melinda!" but she did not see it that way. Melinda is generally of sound body, but like most fifty-eight-year-olds, has had a few health-related issues along the way. She did not want to be in a position she called "out of integrity" by not disclosing everything on an insurance application.

"It's interesting that not so long ago this wouldn't have bothered me," she said. "Now I'm like the princess in the Princess and the Pea fairy tale." She had to refresh my memory on that one.

"The Princess and the Pea" is a Hans Christian Andersen story. In it, a prince searched the world for a true Princess (with a capital *P*). He found plenty of princesses, but there was always something about them that did not ring true. He wanted the real deal.

One night during a terrible storm, a young woman knocked on the gate of the king's castle claiming she was a real Princess and needed a place to stay. The old queen thought, "We'll find out how real she is!" and arranged a test. She cleared off a bed and put a pea on the wooden board that held the mattress, and then piled twenty mattresses and twenty elder-down beds on top of it. The stack of bedding was so high that some illustrations show the Princess climbing a ladder to get to the top of it.

In the morning the Princess was asked how she slept. "Horribly!" she said "Heaven only knows what was in the bed, but I was lying on something hard, so that I am black and blue all over my body." That was when everyone knew that she was a real Princess, because only a true Princess could be so sensitive.

Like the Princess, Melinda has learned that the price of being moral—in essence, the price of royalty—is to suffer the bruises of sensitivity. Melinda is a Person of Character (Pillar I) who has learned to pay attention to her intuition (Pillar V) and taken radical responsibility for her own values *first*. She has learned that a prickling awareness accompanies the attempt to be a thoughtful, congruent "good person." It is too late for Melinda to sleep soundly—to literally be unconscious—about issues that define her core values.

After awakening with the bruises caused by the pea under her mattress, Melinda called her insurance agent and started over. She later told me that if she did not have credibility with herself when no one was looking, she did not see how she could have it with others while the world watched.

Credibility is a key ingredient of moral authority. James Kouzes, coauthor of *The Leadership Challenge*, summarizes the importance of credibility in a leader:

> All the techniques and all the tools that fill the pages of all the management and leadership books are not substitutes for who and what you are....My colleague Barry Posner and I have been collaborating on leadership research for nearly fifteen years, and we keep learning the same thing over and over and over. We keep rediscovering that *credibility is the foundation of leadership*. It's been reinforced so often that we've come to refer to it as the "First Law of Leadership."[3]

When you reflect on the people who have moral authority, you will recognize a common thread in their demeanor, one that Greenleaf called *awareness*. Peter Senge and his coauthors wrote a book about it titled *Presence*. Awareness—or presence—is a disturber, said Greenleaf, but it is also a grounding state of mind. Our friend, Jeffrey Dols, wrote a poem about it.[4]

## Cell Phones, PDAs and Other Assorted Gadgets

When you take your dog for a walk,
walk with your dog.

Be present to your dog.
Be present to your walking.
Stock quotes can wait until you get to work.

When you take your kids to the ballgame,
watch the game with your kids.
Be present to your kids.
Be present to the game.
Straggler e-mails can wait until morning.

When you visit the Grand Canyon,
enjoy the Grand Canyon.
Be present to the beauty.
Be present to the vastness.
Describing it to your friend in New Jersey can wait
    until later.

When you and a friend watch the sun disappear over
    the ocean,
marvel at the beauty of the sunset.
Be present to your friend.
Be present to the waves.
You can place your pizza order after the sun goes down.

When you decide to spend time alone with God,
spend time with God.
Be present to God all around you.
Be present to God within you.
Be present.
Be.

Jeffrey's accessible images remind us that if we wish to live lives of moral authority, we must first be in the room, really be there, immersed in the reality of the people and environment, open to the moment, aware of the past and the future but not focused on them. This quality of presence is frequently commented upon by people who have spent time with Mother Teresa, the Dalai Lama, and other great spirits. You can also find it in Servant-Leaders in your community; those who have somehow carved out a way of being present in our fast-paced digital world.

Servant Leadership is not only about one's *being* but also about one's *doing*. The remainder of this chapter will present three key competencies that describe how people with moral authority act in organizations.

## 1. Accepting and Delegating Responsibility

Do any of these statements sound familiar?

- "They made that decision, not me!"
- "I wouldn't touch that project with a ten-foot pole. Let someone else wreck her career with it!"
- "Word has come from on high!"
- "If you want something done right, you've got to do it yourself!"

Life is messy, and we cannot control all the messes. It is easier to blame someone else for bad decisions than to roll up our sleeves, jump into the chaos and do what we can to help, like Larry did building the float. Most frequently, some person or group of people called *they* is to blame for the problems. "They" are going to have a lot to account for on judgment day!

On the other hand, when we *must* do something and are to be held accountable, it is tough to trust anyone else to follow through. For many people, delegating responsibility to others is harder than accepting it for themselves.

That was certainly true of Jane, one of my (Don's) smart, competent former bosses. As head of our department, she was responsible for all outcomes. She willingly accepted that responsibility, but could not bear to put her fate in others' hands. Her greatest asset—her competence—became her greatest liability because she knew she could always do a project better than anyone else. Those of us who worked for her recognized that, while it was true that only she could complete a project in the precise way she wanted, it was not true that no one else could do it ably and efficiently. Funny how we see those things in others but not ourselves!

Both of these attitudes—blaming others and withholding dele-gation—reveal a victim mentality. The belief that "someone else is in charge and I can't do anything about it!" makes you "dust in the wind," in the words of the popular song. It also means you are deny-ing your God-given gifts to the universe, which is an affront to the Creator in any religion. Remember the words of the popular poster in the 1960s: "God Doesn't Make Junk!" When you cannot delegate responsibility to others, you are also making yourself a victim—of your own limitations and your often-hidden grandiosity.

Make no mistake: there *are* real victims in the world, of crime, abuse, war, illness, and, yes, victims of stupidity in the workplace. The real question is, how will you respond? Do you choose to remain a victim or change yourself—and the world—for the better?

In his classic book *The Road Less Traveled*, M. Scott Peck makes the point that most suffering in life is the result of an attempt to avoid pain. Do not take on that risky project and you will not fail. Do not delegate responsibility to others and you will not be disap-pointed in the outcome. Peck observes that avoidance of pain solves nothing in the long run. Suffering goes underground and pops back up in the most peculiar places. The same challenges will occur again and again until we address them head-on, with honesty, dis-cipline, and integrity.

People with moral authority will be asked to accept more than their share of responsibility, because they are trusted, even when others do not always agree with them. If time permits, they give it their best shot, and take every project personally. They humbly ask others to help them improve areas of weakness, keep an open mind about possibilities, and understand that some of their best contri-butions can come through playful creativity, quiet reflection, reframing of issues, and asking better *questions* rather than only focusing on answers to the old questions.

When it is time to delegate responsibility, Servant-Leaders take on partners rather than subordinates. They offer clear guide-lines and remain available to support the people they have asked for help. In fact, they see themselves as *servants* to their helping partners.

Robert Greenleaf summed up the issue of responsibility in his essay, *The Servant as Leader*:

Who is the enemy?...Granting that fewer evil, stupid, or apathetic people or a better "system" might make the job easier, their removal would not change matters, not for long....*In short, the enemy is strong natural servants who have the potential to lead but do not lead, or who choose to follow a non-servant.*[5]

The skills of delegating responsibility are easy to learn—be clear with expectations, provide the necessary resources, agree on a deadline, and be available to help. The biggest hurdle is the *decision* to delegate, in trust and without micromanaging.

For a Servant-Leader, no magic formulas can make the acceptance and delegation of responsibility risk-free; no bullet-point mantras will assure you are doing things right, or even doing the right things. There is only this: the gentle but persistent guidance of love.

## Ask Yourself

If I want others to give me moral authority:

- Do I really trust others to be responsible, or do I only trust myself?

- Am I generally "in integrity" with myself?

- Do I feel like a victim because others ask me to do so much? If so, how can I set appropriate boundaries?

- In the next week, will I accept the challenge to delegate two tasks that I prefer to do myself?

## 2. Sharing Power and Control

In his *Autobiography*, Benjamin Franklin explained how he not only shared power and control once he had the power—as a legislator, for example—but arranged things so that sharing was established from the beginning of an enterprise. When Franklin saw a need in the community, he first tested a possible solution by presenting a paper on the subject to a group of twelve close colleagues who called themselves the Junta. Cool, rational discussion followed, all out of the public eye. If the idea seemed worthy, Franklin began laying the groundwork by discussing it informally with people in the community and seeing to it that favorable articles were published in his newspaper.

When interest reached a critical mass, others began a campaign to enlist subscribers who would each contribute a small amount over several years to make the thing happen. Franklin preferred that others take over public leadership of projects, for two reasons: first, wide public support made success more likely because more people would invest their personal time to make the project happen, and second, he wanted the focus to be on the project, *not* on Benjamin Franklin. Using this strategy, Franklin established the first circulating library in America, the first firefighting company, a hospital, the University of Pennsylvania, and a score of other worthy institutions.

Robert Greenleaf preferred a similar approach during his years as an AT&T executive. In fact, Greenleaf considered himself most successful when no one realized he was the originator of an idea![6]

Both Greenleaf and Franklin learned that they would not win every issue this way, but they would win most of them, and in the process would increase moral authority, a precious commodity for the next campaign.

In this book, we use the phrase *share power and control* because people can easily understand it in the context of a typical hierarchical organization. However, let us look at that phrase more closely. In reality, it reflects a form of zero-sum thinking: some people have power and others have less. Those with more decide to give some of it away, which can be a scary thing to do, because the person who gives away power may be less able to control outcomes. Several dangers lurk in this mental model. First is the notion that there is only a limited amount of power available, and sharing it diminishes the one who shares. In truth, sharing power only increases the abundant currency of power for everyone, and the likelihood of success of the mission.

That idea seems nonsensical, but look at it using an image shared by Dr. Ann McGee-Cooper: Imagine a picnic scene on a hot, August day. Janet is the keeper of the cold lemonade and her job is to be sure everyone who wants a drink is satisfied. Two hundred people are waiting in line with empty cups. Janet has no helpers so she pours until her pitcher is empty, takes a break to refill, and then pours again. She wants to be sure the job is done right, without spilling a drop, so she refuses all offers of help. She would not want to be responsible if others wasted lemonade! Finally, after hearing grumbling from the thirsty crowd, Janet allows others to help. They find extra pitchers, fill them, and wander around, filling glasses. Every pourer becomes a lemonade leader. Leadership becomes a shared territory. If there are any problems with the lemonade's quality or delivery, the pourer can try to solve it on the spot. The lemonade leaders can still go to Janet and work out a solution with her for the really sticky issues— like running out of sugar! Most importantly, the mission of the work—to slake thirst with lemonade—is being accomplished in a more efficient way. If Janet had shared power and control from the beginning, the problem would not have grown so large. We are all Janet at times, but we can all be lemonade leaders.

The second danger of the zero-sum model lies in its implied paternalism. The person "above" graciously gives away power to those "below," thereby establishing a kind of parent-child relationship. This smacks of codependence or, even worse, flat-out dependence. It is not good for the soul. Paternalism makes leaders prone to grandiosity and tempts followers to use sneaky tactics or outright sabotage to get what they want.

Whenever possible, a Servant-Leader practices a more radical kind of power sharing, one that sees every player as an important part of the enterprise rather than as a tool to carry out the leader's wishes. This kind of leader, first, serves the common vision, which is created, supported, and frequently revised by employees themselves rather than by a small group of top executives on a weekend retreat. Second, the Servant-Leader also serves everyone in the organization by teaching, nurturing, listening, and arranging for individuals and teams to take real responsibility at the highest possible levels. Through all this he or she also "goes out ahead to show the way"—Greenleaf's definition of a leader—using traditional tools of analysis supplemented by intuition, foresight, collaboration, and a concern for the common good.

## Ask Yourself

- Do I secretly feel good about having power over others? If so, what is one thing I can do differently *today* to share power with others?

- Using the example of Benjamin Franklin, where can I allow others to assume more public visibility as leaders of an enterprise? As a beginning, where and how can I enlist broad support from the beginning of an issue rather than struggle for "buy in" after a decision has been made?

- How can I transform the ego needs that cause me to seek power *over* others—we call it the "power payoff"—into a different kind of satisfaction that comes from having power *with* others? (Greenleaf said that we all have ego needs. A Servant-Leader finds alternative ways to satisfy them.)

## 3. Creating a Culture of Accountability

How do you create a culture of accountability? Codes of conduct can be useful, but are not enough. After all, Servant Leadership is a journey for seekers, not a code for conformers. Cultures of accountability are created and sustained through moral principles, stories, congruent policies, ongoing learning, and celebrations.

### *Moral Principles*

Greenleaf believed an organization should begin with solid, enduring moral principles rather than rules. The classic example: since 1901, the Nordstrom retail chain has done just that by evolving a culture of radical accountability with one simple principle found on a sheet given to new Nordstrom salespeople on the first day of training. It reads, "Use your good judgment in all situations. There will be no additional rules. Please feel free to ask your department manager, store manager, or division general manager any question at any time."[7]

Nordstrom's strategy for advertising is to let their customers do most of it by word of mouth, and reinforcing their impeccable customer service through stories, like these:

A woman with one leg approached a Nordstrom salesperson and bet they would not sell just one shoe. She lost the bet, and Nordstrom gained a customer for life.

A man tells the story of how his "personal" Nordstrom salesman encouraged him to take home a suit and see how his family liked it before he paid.

A customer left her plane ticket at the store and her salesperson rushed to the airport in a cab to get it to her before the flight left. Top salespeople keep databases on their customers, send birthday and anniversary cards, and develop genuine friendships.

Patrick McCarthy, coauthor of *The Nordstrom Way*, says, "A relationship is everything. It's a heart experience. Most companies are head experiences—bean counters are running them. When the heart is running them, it becomes exciting."[8]

Nordstrom's total culture supports these outrageous acts of relationship and service. It is the job of the salesperson to do the right thing and the job of managers to back up their salespeople.

Great customer service alone does not make a servant-led company, but it is impossible to operate an organization on the principles of Servant Leadership and not give terrific customer service. This is one way an entire organization acquires moral authority in the eyes of the world.

## *Stories*

Insurance companies that survived the Great Depression tell stories about how they did the right thing back in the thirties and lived to tell the tale. The stories of two companies, one in Wisconsin and the other in Indiana, are similar.

Few folks had money to buy insurance in those days, which meant very little cash came in to replenish the company's coffers. Financial reserves set aside to pay claims dwindled to dangerously low levels.

The company was in trouble when a natural disaster hit, or there was an unusual string of deaths that demanded immediate payment of benefits. To meet the claims, the company's top executives mortgaged their own homes and, in one case, lower-level employees joined them. Both companies survived, and stories about holding to principles in tough times became part of their corporate cultures, because they encoded the deepest values of the organizations.

Tom's of Maine is a company that makes personal care products from natural ingredients and takes care to secure supplies only from ethical providers who treat workers fairly. In 1992, in an attempt to reduce reliance on petroleum, the company replaced a petroleum-based derivative in a deodorant with a vegetable-based glycerin. Half of their customers were satisfied with the new formulation but half complained. A recall would cost $400,000 and affect growth plans. What to do?

The company looked to its mission statement: "To serve our customers by providing safe, effective, innovative natural products of high quality." By that standard, they decided that even the old formulation didn't make the grade. So Tom Chappell authorized a recall. He wrote to thousands of customers, apologized, and sent a free sample of the new product.[9]

This story and many others about Tom's of Maine support Tom Chappell's belief in "common good capitalism." Unlike many in the Corporate Social Responsibility (CSR) movement, he does not believe in quantifying a "second bottom line" that measures human good. "Goodness is not a bottom line," he says. "It's not reducible, it's not measurable, it's only something you can feel and affirm, and share....We're talking about a business strategy that employs your head to do the calculations and the shrewdness, and your heart or spirit to be in respect and awe of the wonder and beauty of goodness in nature, in people, and so on."[10] His words would mean nothing unless there were stories to back them up.

## *Congruent Policies*

TDIndustries, a Dallas-based firm that designs and installs heating and air conditioning equipment, has followed the principles of Servant Leadership since the mid-1970s and has evolved procedures consistent with their values.

For example, evaluations at TDIndustries are multiple-layered affairs. In conversations with supervisors, Partners (all TDI employees are called *Partners*) are honestly praised for tasks well-done and given suggestions for "future areas of growth." Then it is the Partner's turn to comment on her goals, what she appreciates about the supervisor and areas that could be improved in the supervisor's actions. Supervisors understand that their role is to *serve* the needs of those who report to them. Others in the organization are free to submit comments about *anyone's* performance—from the CEO to maintenance personnel—but most frequently this is done in personal conversations. One of the criteria for all evaluations—and the one taken most seriously—is this: "How am I doing as a Servant-Leader?"

Meetings at TDI are conducted in an open fashion. Every Partner learns deep listening skills and is expected to practice them in meetings and personal encounters. When possible, decisions are made by consensus. At the end of every meeting, the designated leader asks for a "Plus-Delta" evaluation. First, everyone is invited to comment on the "pluses" of the meeting—what went well, what was learned, whom they appreciated for contributions, positive comments on the process, and so on. Then, participants are asked for the "deltas." *Delta* is the letter in the Greek alphabet that stands for change, so rather than dwell on the negative aspects of the day's meeting, team members are asked what they would like to change *in a positive way* in future meetings. When the team is dismissed, every Partner has had a chance to be heard.

TDIndustries has evolved dozens of large and small policies that support the principles of Servant Leadership, including open accounting and sharing of financial statements on a monthly basis. Some of the policies are tough, like the zero-tolerance policy about lying, stealing, and drug use.

Policies congruent with Servant Leadership begin at the hiring stage. As the CEO of a TDIndustries business partner once said, "You don't train for integrity; you hire for it!"

## *Ongoing Learning*

There has always been a strong minority of Spanish-speaking people in Texas. Historically, most companies simply expected those people to learn enough English to get by, but Partners at

TDIndustries decided they should also learn Spanish, and the company offered free Spanish classes for Partners. It was "the right thing to do" according to one executive, and also a profitable thing to do since Partners could communicate more effectively with customers. This is a learning organization. Workshops allow Partners to stretch their skill sets. Seminars pass along the latest wisdom from leadership and management disciplines. Managers do not hoard information, or complain about the cost of learning, even though the company is hypervigilant in all its expenses.

All new TDI Partners receive training in Servant Leadership. Technical training is supplemented by periodic refresher courses in the practice of Servant Leadership in the workplace. Partners even help create the training, like a series of homemade videotapes that contrasted "The Old Guard" way of doing things with "The Servant Leadership Way." The video series was premiered at a gala celebration.

## *Celebrations*

Servant Leadership is often seen as a serious, sober subject, but Robert Greenleaf himself once said, "If it ain't fun, it won't get done," and by all accounts he had a marvelous, quirky sense of humor. When he was a youngster, Greenleaf was not able to experience many celebrations because his parents had little money and did not make a "big deal" of rituals of celebration. As an adult, he could have followed their model, but decided instead to give himself and his family what he had missed as a child. He pulled out all the stops to decorate the house for Valentine's Day and other holidays. At work, he fostered an atmosphere of enjoyable companionship, even though he was a natural introvert and was not a gushy person. He carefully chose coworkers to plan formal celebrations and initiated his share of informal ones.

Servant-Leader celebration is more than staging an office Christmas party. Just ask Southwest Airlines. Southwest created a Culture Committee to ensure that *fun*, and the Southwest value called *LUV*, is integrated into all aspects of its operation. At their annual Heroes of the Heart celebration, Employees (Southwest always capitalizes the words *Employees* and *Customers*) honor their unsung heroes, like the Gate Agent who leased a private plane to fly a Customer to emergency medical care after she broke her leg on the ramp. Other Southwest celebrations abound at their centers around the country.

As a loyal Southwest Customer for years, I (Don) have witnessed many events that show how those LUV folks bring Customers in on the fun. I remember the preflight safety speech by a flight attendant who said passengers were perfectly welcome to smoke as long as they did it out on the wing! But my favorite memory happened on an Easter Sunday. The plane was pulling away from the ramp when a Flight Attendant dressed as a bunny popped out of the galley and hopped up and down the aisle wishing everyone a happy Easter!

Celebration is a natural expression of the joy and passion that undergirds moral authority.

Every organization must create its own culture of accountability, guided by its most important moral principles and supported by stories, congruent policies, ongoing learning, and celebrations. Creating such a culture requires patience. Nordstrom evolved its DNA of customer service over more than a hundred years. No one can do it alone, but you can start here, now, where you live and work.

## *Setting Quality Standards for Performance*

The examples from Nordstrom, TDIndustries, Tom's of Maine, and numerous other servant-led companies teach us five things about how to set standards for performance, to establish benchmarks that will earn individuals and companies moral authority.

1. The most powerful performance standards arise from the deepest values found in the company's mission statement. If the mission statement only contains sentences like "Our mission is to return shareholder value," work to have it changed.

2. Top performance results when employees are trusted to use their own creativity and passion to implement details of enduring principles, and are backed up by their supervisors.

3. Even though no one is perfect, the performance of top officials should be congruent with the highest standards, or

employees become dispirited. Simply put: actions speak louder than words.

4. Creating a culture of accountability requires ongoing learning, storytelling, careful scrutiny of policies, celebration, and loads of patience.

5. *All* employees should be part of the enterprise, of setting and judging standards of performance.

Listing these principles is one thing; beginning to implement them is another. But that's the joy of the Servant-Leader way: seeking fresh, exciting ways of changing your little corner of the world. Trying and failing and trying again and succeeding, but feeling solid about your own deepest values even as you constantly refine them, and feeling satisfaction at the growth of others. Marveling at the astonishing power of human passion, commitment, and creativity in an environment where it is rewarded.

As for moral authority, it is ultimately a *by-product* of acting as a Servant-Leader, not a goal in itself. It is a test of servanthood, conducted and scored by others. And that is as it should be.

## Ask Yourself

- Does the culture in my workplace nurture and reward accountability?

- What is my role in fostering accountability, not only for projects, but for persons?

- What are three things I can do this week to hold myself accountable for the growth of others?

## Jai Johnson: A Case Study in Moral Authority

I first heard about Jai Johnson when I read a profile of her in the local newspaper.[11] She was an elected representative of the La Crosse Common (city) Council and also a member of the unwieldy thirty-five-member county board. Jai, a middle-aged middle executive, told the reporter she got into politics because "I just couldn't sit on the sidelines anymore and wait around for someone else to change it." Sounded to me like a natural servant who consciously chose to lead.

The article quoted people who admired Jai's leadership because she did not preach—"She even smokes," noted the reporter—as she sought common ground and exhibited true humility while guiding legislation that committed the city to following sustainable practices. I wrote Jai a fan letter and arranged a conversation with her on the hunch that she would be a powerful example of one who has earned moral authority.[12] Mostly, I wanted to meet a natural Servant-Leader hidden in plain sight among us, someone who sounded wise, practical, and original, like Robert Greenleaf himself. I was not disappointed.

Jai grew up on a farm nestled among the breathtakingly beautiful coulees bordering the upper Mississippi River near La Crosse. Her Scandinavian background emphasized strong morals and radical humility. "To be arrogant was almost the worst sin you could commit," she remembered. "That got so burned into me that it's hard to sit here and have this conversation because it seems like I'm bragging a little. Some people say, 'Oh, wow, you're on the City Council; you're on the County Board.' I say, 'Whatever. Look at a map of the world for perspective.'"

In college, Jai took a strange assortment of courses because she simply loved learning—a seeker who relished the journey. When she graduated as an English major, jobs were scarcer than Wisconsin natives who hated cheese. She shoveled sidewalks and cut firewood before landing a job with an organization that primarily offered services for the elderly—nursing and group homes, assisted living, services for Alzheimer patients, adults with disabilities and more.

Jai was later promoted to a middle management position in charge of the people who maintained the buildings and cleaned up after residents—"the people who do the important work," as she put it. At the first staff meeting, she called together her team and said, "The residents have social workers, family members and ombudsmen looking out for them—even people at the state level—while the corporate staff needs to look after the health of the entire organization. As I see my role, I'm the only person whose job it is to look out for you."

They tested her and found she was serious. "With working class people," she says, "you have to *earn* moral authority—I mean, big time! I try to demonstrate a work ethic, to keep my promises, never break my word or betray a confidence. Always be fair. Never play favorites. Be even-handed with people. It's not that I've never slipped. I have. But that's the policy I pretty much stand on." Jai conducted surveys and initiated conversations to find out what jobs people preferred, when they would like to start their shifts, even what was *fun* for them. Then she did her best to match the people to the jobs, and was successful more often than not.

Jai was not imposing a model of change management or trying to "invert the pyramid." She was simply operating from her Scandinavian common sense and her own sense of engagement. "My crew's purpose is to serve our clients and my purpose is to serve them. Doesn't that just make sense? It may sound odd to some people, but it's *fun* for me to try and make people more happy and satisfied in their jobs. It's not that I'm purely magnanimous. In my head, that's just logical—that's how you manage people and get results."

The word *fun* appears frequently in Jai's conversation, reminiscent of Greenleaf's dictum: "If it ain't fun, it won't get done." It even appears in the Environmental Services Purpose Statement her crew lives by: "To do the best possible job in the least amount of time with the least amount of effort, the least risk to personal safety, and the least disruption to the residents' lives while having the most fun." Jai finds fun in situations where others tear out their hair. "I love that tension between upper management and the front-line staff," she says. "It's crazy-making. It's so stressful sometimes. You work on resolving the tension but you'll never get there. That's why it will continue to be challenging."

She is an advocate of the people she serves and sees herself as one of them. "I hate elitism. People like cleaners are the closest thing we have to a lower-caste system. It's open season for jokes about maids, butlers, and janitors. I don't need to tell you how inverted our value system is when football players are paid extravagantly, but someone who cleans up after a nursing home resident has an accident gets paid next to nothing. Look at your quality of life. Who's more important? The whole culture is trying to tell these people, 'You're *just* a housekeeper.' You're never *just* a housekeeper! Their leader needs to keep chipping away to convey how important they are."

Jai is an early adopter of the latest technologies for her crew and sees that as one more way of serving them—and her organization. She also demands accountability. "I don't give up on people easily. I usually spend 12–18 months trying to help those who lack good judgment or a strong work ethic, but some people you just have to cut loose because they have such a negative impact on the organization."

## *On Politics and Persuasion*

A concern for regular working folks extends to Jai's political life. She absorbed in her bones the area's history of populism and progressive politics, and finally decided to run for office. "There was way too much conservatism and nonsense going on in local government," she remembered. "The city spent about $100,000 just to keep the Ten Commandments in a city park and I thought, 'Hey! That's my money!' But in my heart I mostly just wanted to serve." She attended several seminars on Servant Leadership and, like so many others who have discovered Greenleaf's ideas, realized that she was a Servant-Leader all along, even if she had not been familiar with the language.

Ms. Johnson's preferred mode of power is *persuasion*. I asked her to summarize her "big tent" strategy for gaining agreement in politics and on the job.

- "*Always start with what you can agree on*. If you can't get everyone to see the value, you're chasing the bus right out of the gate."

- "*Put a moral spin on things* by emphasizing that this is the right thing to do. You change human behavior from the heights. I don't preach. I just try to talk to people in a way that persuades them."

- *Support the case* with accurate statistics, case studies, and financial details. "You can sell some people on the soft side, others on the hard side, so also sell it for its good business and economic sense."

- *Don't demonize others or assume moral superiority for yourself.* The newspaper profile quoted colleagues who said that Jai practices what she preaches on personal and environmental issues. "Right!" she laughs. "With my chlorinated swimming pool and my cigarettes! The courage of my convictions is an area that needs work." That kind of honest humility is precisely the reason people trust her, but they also know she is dead serious about being as congruent as possible. "I think Aristotle's argument that *ethos* [one's character as revealed by actions] is the most powerful persuasion tool."

- *"I can never listen enough."*

Her approach *works*. When Councilwoman Johnson and a colleague argued for a resolution to support the eco-friendly principles of "The Natural Step," a Swedish system for reducing dependence on nonrenewable resources and synthetics, they emphasized core values everyone could agree upon and then connected the dots with statistics, real-life examples, outside experts, and realistic financial projections, and listened respectfully to opposition voices.[13] To the surprise of many observers, the issue passed.

La Crosse citizens might be stunned to know that Jai Johnson is a dyed-in-the-wool introvert. "It taps my energy to run for political office," she says. "It's not natural for me to be on stage or television. Maybe I wouldn't be so exhausted if I learned to live outside my comfort zone a little better." Yet, her influence soars when she stands up and speaks from her heart rather than from a political playbook. That is what happened when she addressed people from a progressive political action committee who were interested in running for office. "I wasn't polished and I didn't toe the party line. I just spoke honestly about how I won my race. Later, people came up to me and said, 'I didn't think I could do this but now I think maybe I can, because you're just like me.' I didn't get much feedback from the organization that invited me, though. I didn't follow their party's manual to a 'T.'"

## *Sustained by Spirit*

How does a Servant-Leader like Jai get up every morning and face the challenges of a full, complicated life of management and politics? She just does it, but it is not always easy. "I get angry at times. Frustrated. Some days I wish there was a pill I could take so I didn't care so much, just for a couple of days, but it's just not my nature. But despite the struggles, the rewards are great and very personal to me. Like when a constituent thanks me for helping them with a problem or a client compliments my departments. When an employee says, 'I'm glad you're my boss,' that's the ultimate compliment and the greatest motivator for me."

Jai Johnson is her own person. She is a homeowner and a solid citizen, with no husband or children. She has studied religion, but rather than relying on doctrine, likes to quote the ethic in the song "Santa Claus is Coming to Town": "Be good for goodness' sake." Aristotle would agree. She is funny, thoughtful, committed, and absolutely authentic—a person of spirit. Greenleaf once wrote about this quality in a leader:

> Spirit in a leader, as I see it, is the quality that leads him to risk and venture; this is communicated to the timid and the less venturesome who are energized to follow. Spirit directs the leader when the going is rough, or uncertain, or hazardous, and gives strength and assurance to the less hardy. Spirit sustains the leader in long depressing periods when things are not going well. Spirit armors the leader for the stress of crisis and the unexpected. Spirit is an aspect of inner strength.
>
> From my limited view of things, folk in the full spectrum of belief and non-belief, from atheists and humanists to the most orthodox evangelicals, possess the qualities. I can't see that it makes much difference.[14]

Jai Johnson believes that Servant Leadership is a path well-suited for local electoral politics, but wonders how well a "true people's candidate" would fare in larger arenas, given the political maneuvering she's witnessed. She does not believe Servant Leadership is a magic bullet ideology for either politics or important issues. "You know what a magic bullet is?" she asks. "A good start! But I do see sustainability as having the potential to unite people at a time when most issues divide us, and it goes way beyond the environment for me. If you could link the Servant Leadership approach with sustainability, that would be extraordinary."

Some have urged Jai Johnson to run for office in the state legislature, or even the United States House of Representatives. She's not so sure. "There's plenty of building to be done locally," she says, "and no one in Washington would understand my Feingold and cheese jokes!"

## Ask Yourself

- Do I feel any call to exercise my role as servant in a wider arena?

- How does my way of operating compare to Jai's model for using persuasion?

- What sustains me every day to get up and act as servant in spite of the challenges and disappointments?

# Implementing the Seven Pillars of Servant Leadership

This is my thesis: caring for persons, the more able and the less able serving each other, is the rock upon which a good society is built. Whereas, until recently, caring was largely person to person, now most of it is mediated through institutions—often large, complex, powerful, impersonal, not always competent, sometimes corrupt. If a better society is to be built, one that is more just and more loving, one that provides greater creative opportunities for its people, then the most open course is to *raise both the capacity to serve and the very performance as servant* of existing, major institutions by new regenerative forces operating within them.[1]

—Robert K. Greenleaf

Robert Greenleaf wrote, "Everything begins with the individual," and throughout this book you have had an opportunity to "Ask Yourself" how the Seven Pillars of Servant Leadership may apply to your life. However, Greenleaf also claimed that "organizations are how you get things done," affirming that Servant Leadership requires both personal and communal efforts. Greenleaf believed that, given existing and available resources, we could evolve a more caring society if individuals *and entire organizations* acted as servants, with the organizations governed by trustees who not only held employees accountable for financial performance but also for mission and means.

## Where to Begin

The most common question we hear from clients is, "How do we implement Servant Leadership? Where is the road map?" The bad news is, there is no single map. The good news is, there is no single map! The geography of every organization varies too much to impose a detailed map from one to another. And there is more good news. As you survey your own organization and evolve a map that makes sense for you, you can still gain by studying the experience of others. That is a good place to begin.

Many efforts to implement Servant Leadership in organizations have fallen short due to impatience, incongruence, and a misunderstanding of the change process required to make it happen.

> *As a theoretician, I am an idealist; as a practitioner, I am a gradualist.* —Robert Greenleaf

Patience is a forgotten virtue in today's flat, wired world. It is true that decision makers must be nimble in a global marketplace where business opportunities blink on and off like distant stars. Maybe that is why CEOs act like Jack in the children's rhyme:

Jack, be nimble,
Jack, be quick,
Jack, jump over
The candlestick.

Move. Act. Be quick about it. But what is not often remembered is that the "Jack" in the rhyme was probably the pirate Black Jack. He was running *away* from accountability, not toward greatness. Look at what happens in the last verse:

Jack jumped high,
Jack jumped low,
Jack jumped over
and burned his toe.

Impatience is burning a lot of toes today, and money is frequently at the root of impatience. Companies outsource products to get them faster and cheaper, foregoing the due diligence quality control required for items manufactured in domestic plants. Then they moan at the cost of recalls. More to the point of this book, some leaders hear about Servant Leadership and decide they want to implement it *right now*, then later get "buy in" from employees, as if integrating Servant Leadership was like implementing a new accounting procedure. They bypass the deep conversations and reflections required for due diligence, and sometimes violate the core principles of Servant Leadership in the way they promote it. This leads to the second mistake: incongruence.

The authors heard about a hospital that managed to be incongruent and impatient in one fatal move. After a few conversations among its top leadership teams, the hospital issued a press release stating that Servant Leadership was now the basis for the hospital's mission and policies. Hospital employees had two problems with that. First, most of them knew nothing about this sweeping decision until they read it in the newspaper—and knew very little about Servant Leadership to boot. Second, their experiences with hospital leaders could not always be described as encounters with Servant-Leaders, nor were hospital policies always based on principles of servanthood. Employees steamed for a while and then yawned, figuring this fad would blow over like all the others—and they were right.

Contrast that with the care taken by hospitals in Michigan and Wisconsin with which we are familiar. Their top leadership teams also held months of discussion about the wisdom of adapting the principles of Servant Leadership to their organizations, but they then carried those conversations to all levels of the organization, listening, adapting, and forging practical plans to gradually transform mission, policies, and procedures. Most importantly, the leaders themselves were willing to be held accountable for their own failings as Servant-Leaders and, in fact, welcomed that feedback. They were congruent. They were also patient, and spent several years in listening, reflecting, and planning *before* beginning widespread training that nurtured systemic evolution toward a servant-led organization. They understood the dynamics of change.

One thing that *never* changes is the number of books written about change. You can alter policies and organizational charts all you want, but changing human behavior is the hardest trick. Sure, organizations can coerce changes in behavior and see grudging compliance, but they will also see passive-aggressive sabotage. That is because we humans operate from a grounding that is deeper than shifting corporate policies. We behave the way we do because of our *values*, which in turn are based on even deeper beliefs. For permanent, even joyful, changes in behavior, successful companies link changes to widely held values and beliefs.

The good news here is that the ethic of servanthood abides within the hearts of most people as both a value *and* a belief. They long to be part of an enterprise that makes a positive difference in the world, one that appeals to what Lincoln called "our higher angels" in his second inaugural address. They search for opportunities to use their peculiar passions, creativity, and competencies in the workplace. However, because so many organizations are killing grounds for the spirit, they stifle these fresh springs of hope, and everyone loses.

That can change, not by dictating answers, but by asking different questions and finding answers that make sense in the context of your organization. This chapter will help you get started.

## What You Can Do Now

*The real voyage of discovery consists not in seeking new landscapes, but in having new eyes.*　　　　—Marcel Proust

You can begin conversations around implementing Servant Leadership by reviewing each Pillar chapter and then meeting in small groups to ask others the questions related to that chapter. You can also share your responses to the quote that precedes each group of questions.

We suggest you appoint someone to keep track of the general flow of discussions, especially the items that emerge as points of consensus agreement.

This is how institutions that successfully implement Servant Leadership generally begin the process. Expect the small group conversations to take as much time as they need. Then, in the fullness of time when larger efforts are mounted to share Servant Leadership with everyone in the organization, a solid core of thoughtful, informed servants will be available not only to support the process but to act as Servant-Leader teachers.

# Pillar I: Person of Character

*Character cannot be developed in ease and quiet. Only through experience of trial and suffering can the soul be strengthened, ambition inspired, and success achieved.* —Helen Keller

## 1. Discovery

- How does our organization find, nurture, and reward persons of character?

- Do we reward "Variations" in values that deflect us from pointing our moral compass toward "True North?" If so, what are those variations?

- What Defining Moments jump out from a timeline of our organizational history? What have we learned from the positive and negative Moments of Truth?

- What is the higher purpose, the ultimate meaning, of our work together as a community of people fulfilling a mission?

## 2. Desire and Incentives to Change

- What has been the organizational impact of negative moments of truth?

- Can we afford to pay the financial and emotional price for *any* loss of institutional integrity with suppliers, customers, and each other?

## 3. Learning

- What can we do to strengthen our institutional character through hiring practices, training programs, and policies that are based on doing the right thing as Servant-Leaders?

- What books should we be reading? Which seminars should we attend? How can we document our learning so it is available to all?

## 4. Practice

- At the next meeting that requires a decision, can we try an experiment by asking these questions:

— Are we right in our analysis and in the conclusions we draw from it?

— What are our "second thoughts" based on questions we did *not* ask, like this one, drawn from Greenleaf's writings: "Are business needs being adequately served while helping the individuals affected by this decision grow as persons?"

— Are we doing the right thing?

— Are we doing the wise thing?

• Do we have conversations, and perhaps even measurements, about behaviors that build institutional character, like returning phone calls, meeting promises, and admitting mistakes? If not, where can we begin?

## 5. Feedback and Evaluation—The Best Test

• How can we have accountability if we don't have feedback?

• What could we learn by conducting a "character audit," asking internal and external stakeholders how we are doing on benchmarks of character? Using the results, ask each other, "How do we act when we are 'in character?' When are we 'out of character?' How can we stay 'in character' more consistently?"

• As an organization, do we consider feedback something to dread or an opportunity to improve? Do we reward honest feedback or make people pay a price for offering it?

The medical and mental health communities may offer a model here. Review committees in hospitals regularly discuss medical decisions made by physicians and nurses. As part of their clinical training and ongoing practice, psychologists and other mental health workers meet with someone who "supervises" their decisions. The supervisor does not tell the practitioner what to do but serves as a sounding board for his or her thinking.

— Could your organization experiment with small groups that allow employees to share, in a supportive environment, difficult decisions that call forth the dynamics of conscience and character?

— Could every important business meeting end with the question, "How are we doing as Servant-Leaders?"

Remember that character is *not* imposed from above; it bubbles up from below. Efforts to nurture character and Servant-Leader behaviors should never devolve into witch hunts or tools for coercion and manipulation. At first, people will test the sincerity of efforts to nurture character, and they should. They have been around the block and are smart enough to know when an organization is operating in good faith for the growth of persons or simply using new language to gain compliance. *Use* character as you *nurture* character.

## Pillar II: Puts People First

*I never lose an opportunity of urging a practical beginning, however small, for it is wonderful how often the mustard seed germinates and roots itself.*

—Florence Nightingale

In an ideal economic system, the decisions that are best for an organization would also be best for each individual. Unfortunately, that is not always the case, and sometimes a standard like "the greatest good for the greatest numbers" results in decisions that cause distress for individual employees and their families. On the other hand, how often do leaders consciously consider creative solutions that would "put people first" *and* protect the efficiency and survivability of an organization?

As you ask each other the following questions, know that the balance between putting people first and institutional performance can be messy. However, that does not mean we should not try.

### 1. Discovery
- Consider the last major decision made by our organization. Would we have modified that decision if the "put people first" criterion were paramount?

- Do we sometimes confuse helping each other (with its emphasis on the helper) with serving each other (with its emphasis on those being served)?

- Which specific policies and procedures in our organization do *not* put people first?

- Do we claim and cultivate "a servant's heart"?

## 2. Desire and Incentives to Change

- Financial results from the "better than great" companies profiled in the introduction of this book indicate that putting people first is more likely to result in better Profits After Taxes (PAT). Do we *believe* that could be the case in *our* organization? Do we need to *believe* that in order to put people first?

- How could putting people first result in increased retention, enhanced employee morale and performance, and help fulfill our mission? What are some likely numbers on that?

- Would *we* feel better about our careers if our institution began putting people first in concrete ways?

## 3. Learning

- Could we each read a book on the topic of putting people first and report back to the group? (A suggestion: James Autry's *The Servant Leader: How to Build a Creative Team, Develop Great Morale, and Improve Bottom-Line Performance* [New York: Three Rivers Press, 2004]).

- How can we share our learning with others in the organization?

## 4. Practice

- What are specific actions that members of our small group can take to "try out" people-first behaviors?

- Where and how can we begin to implement more people-friendly policies into our corporate culture, and have fun doing it? For example, maybe we could start a column in our internal newsletter called, "Love at Acme Corporation

Is…" and share stories of how people at all levels of the institution acted to put people first.

- Is "putting people first" something that suggests a program or a new initiative, or is it something we should simply try to live out "under the radar" for a while?

## 5. Feedback and Evaluation—The Best Test

- Would there be an advantage in conducting a system-wide survey to establish a baseline for employees' current attitudes about our people policies and ask for suggestions?

- Knowing that coworkers are usually wary of new initiatives, how could we evaluate our "put people first" efforts through the entire process instead of after the "project" is over?

- Do we have a safe way for our colleagues to provide ongoing feedback?

## Pillar III: Skilled Communicator

*Persuasion involves arriving at a feeling of rightness about a belief or action through one's own intuitive sense….The act of persuasion, thus defined, would help order the logic and favor the intuitive step. But the person being persuaded must take that intuitive step alone, untrammeled by coercive or manipulative stratagems of any kind.* —Robert K. Greenleaf

## 1. Discovery

- Do we listen to each other as keenly as we listen to our clients?

- Is empathy a value we could bring into the boardroom, or even into the general culture, like Ken Melrose did with the Toro Company (as described in the afterword)?

- In our small group (where it may be safer) are we willing to do a 360 degree evaluation of our competencies in giving and receiving feedback?

- Do we tend to act as persuaders in the workplace more than manipulators?

- How well do we tell stories in our actions as leaders and anchor our organization's mission in memorable events?

## 2. Desire and Incentives to Change

- What are two situations in our organization that would have turned out better if people had used Servant-Leader communication skills? What specific financial, organizational, or individual benefits did we lose out on?

- How could things change around here if everyone knew three great stories about this company?

## 3. Learning

- Let's face it: we are *always* busy. When is it appropriate to use "shorthand" communication—say, to simply gain information—rather than a more leisurely approach? Is time really the only factor in deciding which is which?

- Who is a great communicator in our organization? What makes that person so good? How can we learn from him or her?

## 4. Practice

- Can we practice the ABCs and XYZs right now in our small group? Are we willing to teach it to our coworkers in the next week?

- Are we each willing to identify an accountability partner to help us maintain our commitment to practicing these communication skills?

- Is someone in the group willing to bring in a new workplace story for every meeting? How can we capture and share them?

## 5. Feedback and Evaluation—The Best Test

- Using language from the short surveys in this chapter, what behavioral anchors can we use to evaluate how well we currently communicate and how we will know when we do better?

- Consider an experiment: at the end of each meeting with our other work partners, ask the question, "How well did we do in communicating with each other as Servant-Leaders?"

## Pillar IV: Compassionate Collaborator

*I have always thought that the best way to find out what is right and what is not right, what should be done and what should not be done, is not to give a sermon, but to talk and discuss, and out of discussion sometimes a little bit of truth comes out.*
—Jawaharlal Nehru, Indian statesman (1889–1964)

## 1. Discovery

- How much does the frontier ethic of "rugged individualism" affect the ways we work together? Does it impede collaboration?

- How well do we express appreciation in this organization?

- Taking this group as an example, who seems to inhabit each of Greenleaf's roles in a group?
Mediator
Consensus Finder
Critic
Meliorator (one who makes things better)
Keeper of the Conscience
Process Watcher
Titular Head

- Generally speaking, do our groups here allow for *all* roles, including critic? Do our groups tend to encourage compassionate collaboration?

- Which bird, or birds, in the "What Is Your Conflict Style?" grid does our organization as a whole most value?

- What prevalent attitudes around here discourage collaboration? Encourage it?

## 2. Desire and Incentives to Change

- What are we missing by not collaborating more?

- Do we have any problems with anger that affect performance? If so, what is that costing us?

## 3. Learning

- If we, like "The Evolution Committee" mentioned in the chapter on Pillar IV, could collaborate to design anything from scratch in this organization, what would it be? Who would be on the committee?

- Will one person in this group be willing to read a book on collaboration and report on it at our next meeting?

## 4. Practice

- What would happen if we shared with everyone—not just managers—the five tips for giving praise and asked them to praise someone at least once per week?

- Can we each find a situation to try out the Peace R.U.L.E.S!™ Negotiation Guidelines in the next week?

- How can we teach the model of compassionate collaboration to all of our colleagues in the organization *in a fun way*, like an original skit that shows confrontation versus evaluation or contest that awards the "collaborator of the month?" Is it worth doing that?

## 5. Feedback and Evaluation—The Best Test

- Is it possible for us to measure the benefits we would gain from compassionate collaboration rather than confrontation, both with internal and external stakeholders? What could those factors be besides efficiency?

- Does the return on investment benefits of collaboration make it worth the effort or should we simply think about collaborating more because it's the right thing to do?

# Pillar V: Foresight

*Practice foresight as an* ethical *responsibility.*

Robert K. Greenleaf

## 1. Discovery

- Can any member of the group remember a situation where planning based on raw numbers and straight-line projections turned out to be inadequate?

- Foresight, as it is defined here, only happens when intuitions are brought to the attention of the conscious mind. Is each member of the group willing to reflect on events and decisions where intuition played a part?

- Does our organization have a process to welcome foresight from every level? For example, a sales representative who speaks with clients every day may have a stronger sense of emerging needs than her bosses who plan production. The same is true in nonprofit organizations, even though their "products" are different. How can we capture and use the wisdom of foresight that is scattered throughout our organization?

- Do we encourage creative people or consider them a pain in the neck?

- Does our review process penalize colleagues who come up with different and better solutions rather than follow the rules whether they work or not?

## 2. Desire and Incentives to Change

- What positive outcomes could we expect if we had the foresight to predict fairly accurate conditions eighteen months from now?

- How can we reward colleagues who contribute creative ideas to our workplace community? For example, in the next four months, can we find one creative idea worth at least $100,000 to the organization? What would be an appropriate reward for such an idea?

## 3. Learning

- Take a current, relatively simple problem and work the rules for foresight to see what new learnings may emerge.

- What do our work partners think about our current vision statement? Are we willing to invite them to help revise it?

- Ask three people in the group to each find a vision statement so good it gives them chills and come back and share it at the next meeting. What makes it so good? What can we learn from it?

- Choose a common object in the room and ask, "What is this *like*?" No rules allowed that would prevent nutty answers! Now, choose a business or organizational challenge and ask again, "What is *this like*?" Scan the answers for possible solutions.

- What would happen if we saw our organization as a garden rather than a machine?

## 4. Practice

- How can we combine foresight, visioning, creativity, and bold action? For example, perhaps we could stage a "Foresight Fair" that includes fun and learning, or ask our colleagues to paint, draw, or sculpt a desired vision.

- When any members of our small learning group are present when a major decision about the future is taken, are they willing to ask the question that Native American leaders ask about big choices? "What will be the impact of this decision seven generations from now?" Or even, one generation from now?

- How can we go beyond the mythology of the heroic, top-down leader and develop a new mythology of the heroic team that can use foresight, vision, and creativity to take bold actions?

## 5. Feedback and Evaluation—The Best Test
- What are some reasonable metrics we could develop to measure the impact of foresight on our organization? Creativity? A vibrant mission?

## Pillar VI: Systems Thinker

*We live in webs of interdependence.*      —Peter Senge

In 1971, Apollo 14 astronaut Edgar Mitchell was on the way back home from the moon when he saw the earth floating in the vastness of space. Suddenly he *knew* that everything was connected and that all humans were involved in an ongoing process of creation. Two years later, he founded the Institute of Noetic Sciences, an organization that seeks to understand the inner and outer worlds of interconnections.[2]

It does not take a mystical revelation in space to intuitively *know* that every individual and system in an organization is interconnected. The following questions can help your thoughtful small group participate in the ongoing process of creating an institution that integrates systems thinking.

## 1. Discovery
- Do we know what *the right direction* is for our organization, even if we are sometimes unsure of the details? Do others in the organizations know it?

- Do we use our vision as a practical criterion for everyday decision making?

- Have I enlisted a sympathetic team of cohorts who will help with conversations and assist in shepherding changes in systems and attitudes?

- Do we operate in silos or have petty turf wars that impede systems thinking?

- How could we have responded differently to our most recent challenge if we had analyzed it using the Systems Pyramid levels of Events, Strategies, Culture, and Beliefs?

- How can we be "strategic in a Servant-Leader way?"

- Are we a learning organization?

## 2. Desire and Incentives to Change

- When has it cost us money because we failed to "zoom out" and look at the systems picture?

- When have we failed to reflect on a crisis and missed learning of "the jī factor"—the dynamic of unfolding?

- Do ethics play a role in our overall *modus operandi?*

## 3. Learning

- Assign a group member to visit the Pegasus Communications website (www.pegasuscom.com) to read online articles about the basic tools of systems thinking and recommend the best way for others to learn the analytical tools of systems thinking and share them.

- If you have not already done so, is everyone in the group willing to read Peter Senge's 1990 classic *The Fifth Discipline: The Art and Practice of the Learning Organization?*

## 4. Practice

- Consider an organizational change that is likely to occur soon. How can we incorporate each of the suggested principles for managing change?

  —Anticipate and plan for change

  —Constantly communicate information about change

  —Listen with attentive presence, but without believing you can always "fix" another's anxiety about change

  —Acknowledge the challenge of change

—Provide quality training and skill building in change management

—Foster a flexible, supportive climate

—Celebrate milestones along the way

—Attend to self-care during times of change

- Can we consider creating a company-wide exercise that will help all our colleagues understand that "what I do counts!"? Encourage creativity—a mind map, a mobile, sculpture, or painting that expresses each person's job in the context of other jobs within the company and also demonstrates the impact on external stakeholders, and even the world at large. The goal is to provide a vivid example of the interconnectedness of *everyone* in the enterprise.

- Ask managers to explain the Systems Pyramid to their teams and encourage them to use it during discussions until it becomes second nature.

## 5. Feedback and Evaluation—The Best Test

- Conduct a survey. Ask employees if they can describe negative "unintended consequences" they observed as a result of programs or policies that were started with the best of intentions, and unintended *positive* consequences from any initiative. Report results in an executive summary. This will illustrate one of the key benefits of systems thinking. Invite employees to share their thoughts on possible unintended consequences *before* changes are made.

- Ask employees which "greater good" they think the organization serves, or should be serving.

## Pillar VII: Moral Authority

*Actions do speak louder than words. Manuals don't count. Leadership is good work, not simply good talk.*
—Max DePree

## 1. Discovery

- How well do we trust each other in this organization?

- How well do our external stakeholders trust this organization?

- Does this organization reward delegation of tasks?

- As a corporate community, how do we use power?

- Where could we exercise our servant role better in the wider community?

## 2. Desire and Incentives to Change

- If some people in this organization have a "victim mentality," what does that cost us?

- How much less "pushback" could we expect if we created a culture of respectful persuasion?

## 3. Learning

- Assign one group member to read Janet Hagberg's book *Real Power: Stages of Personal Power in Organizations* and share a summary with the rest of the group.

- The next time we introduce a new policy or program, what can we learn from Jai Johnson's model of persuasion?

## 4. Practice

- What specific jobs can we delegate in the next week?

- Can we implement some form of a 360 degree evaluation?

- Could we consider a series of positive articles in our newsletter titled "What Sustains Me," contributed by employees at all levels?

## 5. Feedback and Evaluation—The Best Test

- Could we ask our employees to fill out a "character audit" survey *on the organization* to set a baseline for our level of moral authority?

- Go through Greenleaf's "Best Test" a line at a time and benchmark our outcomes by his ideals.

## No Magic Bullet

I (Don) am indebted to my friend Dr. Earl Madary for an image that describes how organizations successfully integrate Servant Leadership. Earl, the chair of the Religious Studies Department at Viterbo University, walked into the office one day and I asked how he was doing with his chemotherapy treatment for an especially scary form of cancer. As he explained the details, I interjected, "Cancer is such a complex condition. There is no magic bullet, is there?"

"That's my biggest learning through this whole experience," he said. "Before I got cancer, I assumed there was a magic bullet for every area of life. It's not true. There is no magic bullet. There is only a hammer and chisel. Every day, you patiently chip away what is not necessary—what doesn't work—and reveal the perfect form underneath."

It was the last conversation I had with Earl before his death several months later.

As you "Ask Others" the questions in this chapter, think of them as hammers and chisels that can help you and your colleagues slowly chip away at the unnecessary barriers to a servant-led culture and reveal the ideal form that lies beneath.

# The Seven Pillars in Action

On August 1, 2007, Tom Sorel was eating at a restaurant in Washington, DC, when the call came that would change his life. Sorel, the division administrator for the Federal Highway Administration (FHWA) office in Minnesota, was in town for meetings and consultations with federal transportation authorities.

The first few times his phone rang, Tom ignored it, but when the calls persisted, he answered and learned that the I-35W bridge over the Mississippi river in Minneapolis had collapsed. Even as he was being informed of the tragedy, a school bus with sixty-three children from a poor neighborhood tilted precariously against a mangled guard rail on a surviving piece of the bridge. Jeremy Hernandez, a twenty-year-old staff member for the Waite House Neighborhood Center, was kicking out windows and leading frightened kids to safety. Nearby, a semi-truck trailer was burning with searing heat. Down in the river, an off-duty firefighter named Shannon Hanson was swimming up and down the river looking for survivors. Before it was all over, thirteen people had died and 145 more were injured.

By the time Tom was rushing to the airport for the next flight home that night, three high-level officials from the Minnesota Department of Transportation (MnDOT), including state traffic engineer Bernie Arseneau, were standing next to the school bus alongside Hennepin County Sheriff, Rick Stanek, Governor Pawlenty, and other state officials as they inspected the damage. It was a time for unsung heroes, a time for horror, a time for leadership.

The state was flat-out lucky that a person with Tom Sorel's qualifications was available at precisely the right time. He had spent a lifetime gaining competence as a transportation engineer and growing as a Servant-Leader.

# The Making of a Servant-Leader

Tom Sorel fits Greenleaf's definition of a natural Servant-Leader. As a kid he loved baseball. He was not only a darn good player but was also recognized as the de facto leader on nearly every team he joined. "I found myself watching out for the kids who were not the most talented," he said, "making sure they felt part of the team. Frankly, I didn't think a lot about it at the time, but now I realize what I was doing."

He was intuitively applying the principles of Servant Leadership. Even as a young man in his twenties, Tom was reading leadership books and thinking about what leadership philosophy he wanted to follow in his life and career. When he discovered Greenleaf's writings on Servant Leadership, everything clicked. "I liked what I read," he said, "and tried to figure out how to apply this stuff. It wasn't easy. Today, I tell everyone that they need to figure out their leadership philosophy and be able to articulate it." Tom had found the language for the natural impulses of his head, heart, and spirit.

In 1989 he was part of a team barnstorming Nicaragua for a program called Baseball for Peace when he met an American who invited him to put a team together, come to Minneapolis, and compete in a Senior World Series. Tom convinced a few baseball pals from Albany, New York, to hop on a plane with him and fly to the Twin Cities. Their first game in the tournament was also the first time they had all played together, yet they finished in fourth place. Tom called it a "high-performing team" because every player knew his own strengths and weaknesses and those of every other player. They gelled as a team precisely because they were all *different* and transcended individual egos to work together and supplement each other's play. It was a lesson he would apply again and again in his work as a public servant.

By the time of that first trip to Minnesota (a state he grew to love), Tom had earned a bachelor's degree in civil engineering and an MBA, with advanced study certificates from places like Cornell, George Washington University, and the Wharton School. In 1978, he began working for the Department of Transportation's Federal Highway Administration and spent the next thirty years as a peripatetic leader and collaborator. Wherever he landed, he worked with the team he was given and built them into the best they could be. People noticed—important people.

In 1999, he joined another high-performing team in Salt Lake City that was building the transportation infrastructure for the 2002 Olympic Games. Tom was the USDOT's liaison to multiple local, state, and federal entities, including the White House. He helped plan and get funding for projects like an interstate expansion and two light rail lines that would allow athletes and visitors to get around the Olympic Games quickly, comfortably, and safely. "If you run across anyone today who worked on the Olympics," he said, "they always use the word *we*. *We* did this, *we* did that. It didn't matter if you were with the feds or the state or a contractor. *We* did it together. You won't experience that very many times like that in your life."

## Collaboration (Pillar IV) Pays Off

Prior to the bridge collapse, Tom served as the FHWA administrator for Minnesota, where he oversaw the distribution of $600 million in federal highway funds and was responsible for seeing that regulations were followed. According to him, many people who hold that position around the country "kind of sit there, administer programs, and sign off on things. If they don't like something they speak up and create some hoopla." It is a cushy, well-paying job. But that was not Tom Sorel's style.

"Here was my philosophy," he said. "If I was going to deliver a project or a program, I wanted to be ingrained with all the players—the Federal Department of Transportation, MnDOT, the contractors, and other stakeholders—so they knew me and trusted me. That way, if something problematic happened, we could have a discussion and it would go away quickly rather than being projected out for years and years."

In his federal role, he hosted several years of meetings and collaborative projects. Some of the parties at the table had a history of conflict based on protecting turfs and competing for projects. Over time, people who would later be responsible for rebuilding the bridge became comfortable with his leadership, and with each other. They also knew that he believed in something called Servant Leadership because he talked about it frequently and seemed to live by its principles. In fact, the authors of this book first met Tom when he asked us to conduct a Servant Leadership workshop for his federal staff of twenty to twenty-five people.

All that collaboration paid off after the bridge tragedy. Behind the scenes, Tom was involved in getting federal funding for the tremendous costs of building the new bridge. He worked with engineers to help investigators understand why the bridge had failed, and took an active role in planning for a new bridge. He joined discussions with law enforcement and community leaders as they sought to heal wounds and move ahead.

Once again, important people noticed. President George W. Bush eventually gave Tom the President's Award for his work on the I-35W bridge.

## Commissioner Sorel

In February 2008, the Minnesota Senate refused to confirm Lt. Governor Carol Molnau to continue in her "second job" as MnDOT commissioner. Without Tom's urging, a parade of people who had worked with him the last three years recommended that Governor Pawlenty appoint him as the next MnDOT commissioner because he was not only competent but a Person of Character (Pillar I). His collaborations had earned him Moral Authority (Pillar VII). Moreover, Tom would be the first engineer to head the agency in twenty-two years. The governor made the appointment and the *Bemidji Pioneer* reported that "The 'Wedding March' would have been appropriate background music as a Minnesota Senate committee gave its blessing to the state's new transportation commissioner." Committee chair Senator Steve Murphy said, "Communication is better in some marriages, and this is as good as marriages get."[1] Sorel was praised by legislators on all three sides of the aisle. (Minnesota has more independent legislators than most states.)

Sorel was surprised by the turn of events. "I was just a guy who worked for the local federal highway office," he said. "I had planned to retire early and go work at—oh, maybe Home Depot—but then this thing happened. After the governor called, I asked for a few days to talk with my family because that's what we do in my home. By accepting the job, I would take a big pay cut and lose the security gained from thirty years of working with the federal government, but I saw the opportunity as a *calling*, as corny as that sounds. I felt I could help the healing process with these good people of MnDOT, and the whole state.

"Eventually, I found myself over at the Governor's office for a crazy press conference. Before I went in front of the microphones, the communications people said, 'Say this! Don't say that!' But I thought, 'My gosh, I'm just going to go out there and be natural about this.'"

That he was. After his introduction, Tom thanked the appropriate people and said, among other things, "I'm just a Servant-Leader with a passion for transportation and innovation! Servant Leadership is a philosophy that has served me well and a philosophy that I hope to bring to this department." A few big shots on stage exchanged confused looks and later a speaker hastened to remind the media that Tom Sorel was indeed a certified *engineer*! Tom's optimism and down-home authenticity carried the day. Bill Salisbury of the *Pioneer Press* said about him, "Flashy, he is not."[2] That calmness and competence was just what the state needed.

When Commissioner Sorel took over MnDOT, public trust in the agency had been shaken. Various minority communities were demonstrating to increase the percentage of minority hiring on highway projects. The legislature, while generally friendly toward their new commissioner, was suspicious of his agency.

Five years later when he left, the agency had increased minority participation in hiring and contracts from 2.8 percent to over 10 percent. Public trust in MnDOT had increased so quickly that it was almost a nonissue after the commissioner's first year, when the sleek new bridge opened only fourteen months after the collapse. Satisfaction among MnDOT's employees ranked around 90 percent—higher than any other Cabinet-level agency. The legislature trusted and admired their commissioner and his agency. Moreover, he left an enduring legacy of Servant Leadership.

Mr. Sorel would be embarrassed at the suggestion that MnDOT's story is about an individual, heroic Servant-Leader who charged in to make things right. That is not how Servant-Leaders operate. Besides, as MnDOT veteran Bernie Arseneau observed, the agency was a good one even before the bridge collapse, resilient and highly functional. The positive changes that happened required all five thousand MnDOT employees and hundreds of others from various communities. Still, Tom Sorel was the visionary who went out ahead to show the way with Servant Leadership. Here is how he did it.

## Say It; Live It; Act on It; Measure It

Commissioner Sorel's five years at MnDOT were a whirlwind of innovations, program initiatives, and collaborations. The first thing he did was rearrange the organizational chart, putting the citizens at the top, then the governor, then the commissioner and his MnDOT people at the bottom. The message was clear: we ultimately work for the people.

Then he began speaking and acting strategically, using Servant Leadership-based principles that can guide us all.

### Declare Your Leadership Philosophy

Bernie Arseneau first heard about Servant Leadership from his friend, Tom, before he was Commissioner Sorel. Bernie knew that explaining this philosophy to MnDOT employees would be one of the new commissioner's priorities, but *how* he explained it would make all the difference. Based on his twenty-four years at the agency, Bernie offered a little guidance on the subject.

"I explained that every four years or so the agency had been introduced to a new leadership style or a new quality management approach which was more or less mandated. That meant it finally faded away. If we just started laying Servant Leadership out there for people to grab if they wanted—and if we lived it—the impact would be more powerful than to say, 'Here it is. We're all going to be Servant-Leaders now!' Wouldn't that have been an oxymoronic approach?!"

One of the authors witnessed an early presentation to employees where the commissioner explained Servant Leadership and can testify that he offered the ideas in accessible language and ended with an invitation rather than a mandate: "This is a philosophy that has worked well for me and I try to live by it. You will have plenty of information about it if it's something you want to consider."

Before long, Tom created a small "Servant Leadership card" that he passed out everywhere he went. On one side, Servant Leadership is defined using terms important to MnDOT. Listed on the other side are Larry Spears's Ten Characteristics of Servant-Leaders and the Seven Pillars of Servant Leadership. (An aside: shortly after the first edition of this book was published, the commissioner contacted me [Don] to ask if he could use it within the agency. I said, "Sure, that's what it's for. My only suggestion is that you change it to meet MnDOT's needs." He said, "Don't worry. I've already done that!") After a few months, every MnDOT employee was familiar with the basics of the Servant Leadership philosophy and either carried the card or posted it in the workplace.

To reinforce the message, Tom frequently brought Servant Leadership-related books to meetings "with a million colored Post-it Notes on the pages," according to MnDOT employee Abe Hassan. He frequently gave books to staff, often paying for them from his own pocket. He established a Commissioner's Reading Corner in the main office and started a monthly book club. "At the book club meetings," explained marketing and communications specialist Jeff Ostrom, "people took turns reading books or articles related to leadership and presenting the findings to colleagues. My presentation group compared leadership lessons in one of John C. Maxwell's books to leadership principles in the TV program *Seinfeld*."

"A book club?" says Bernie Arseneau. "Come on! You wouldn't see other commissioners doing that. But it forced people to begin thinking out of their comfort zone."

According to Abe, one reason for Tom's flurry of education about Servant Leadership was to explain the word *servant*. "I can't begin to tell you the reaction on people's faces when he used the word *servant*," Abe remembers. "Like, what was he talking about?

But he always explained it. Besides, people saw that *he* was a Servant-Leader. Even when he was in the cafeteria you could see that the cashier or the people making the hamburgers loved this guy. He talked to them like they were just normal human beings."

## Share the Vision, Mission, Core Values, and Priorities

When Tom took over the agency, it lacked relevant vision and mission statements. "This was a new world after the bridge collapse," he recalled, "a new environment. We were going through a healing process. We couldn't just pull out something old and move on. We needed new energy. I didn't have time to monkey around with this for a couple of years like a lot of companies do. So I assigned some interns to write it."

Interns?

"Sure. We had a summer internship program for college and high school kids. I called the coordinator one day and said, 'I want to pull together some of your brightest people in these programs and I want them to work on a strong vision and mission statement. We will give them some mentors but will not tell them what to write. I do want them to take a look at our Core Values, though.'

"I got pushback from the veterans who said, 'Well, why aren't we involved in this?' I said, 'You will be involved in it, but these guys are our future. They will be driving this place when you and I are no longer here.'

"The kids loved it and did a remarkable job. We changed very little in their small document that outlined MnDOT's Vision, Mission, Core Values, Critical Issues and Responses, and the five Strategic Directions: Safety, Mobility, Innovation, Leadership, and Transparency.

"Mike Barnes, our Division Operations Director, is a super guy. After I asked him to explain our Strategic Directions to audiences a few times and he hesitated, he came up with the acronym SMILT to remember the key categories. Everything is there in the words these kids provided in only a few months. It was phenomenal. Using them as an example, I always challenged my leadership team to harness the power of diversity."

## *Innovate*

Tom promised innovation at his first press conference and delivered in spades, especially on the new I-35W bridge, which was completed under budget and earlier than the stated deadline. A new bridge of that size normally requires two to three years to build. This one was completed in eleven months from the time of groundbreaking, three months earlier than the deadline.

The new bridge was elegantly simple and fit seamlessly into the landscape. Beneath the surface, however, it was crammed with new features like sensors that measured the bridge's response to vibrations and loads and evaluated the effects of Minnesota's notoriously frigid winters on the roadway. Other sensors and cameras fed traffic flow data to a central management system that made data available for download and analysis. The bridge had its own anti-icing system and security monitors.[3]

In 2012, the aging Maryland Avenue bridge over I-35E was replaced in just three months, with only sixty days of road closure. This was astounding to bridge engineers. Sorel contracted with a company that built both sections of the bridge off-site and then dropped them into place with a giant "self-propelled modular transporter."

Sorel, who was already well-known in national transportation circles for his writings and presentations on innovation, extended that passion from bridges to every phase of the agency's operations. In his first year at MnDOT, the agency issued the booklet *Innovative Contracting Guidelines* to suggest ways contractors could save time and money and minimize problems with traffic flow.

Tom borrowed an idea from IBM and set up something called an *E-Jam*—short for E-Magination Jam, a sophisticated online outlet for MnDOT employees to submit innovative ideas. Many were acted upon, like the idea of grading the edge of new four-inch asphalt so drivers whose wheels wander off the road can get back on without flipping the car. (This happened to Abe Hassan's son.) When the governor heard of E-Jam's success, he told other Cabinet agencies to stage their own versions of it.[4]

Commissioner Sorel introduced the idea of *predicting conflict* in a project beginning with the planning process through public participation, environmental challenges, and the final build. The idea was to anticipate conflict and mitigate it before it became serious. Typically for Tom, he explained the model he had in mind and assigned the details to staff members who brought in experts to help.[5] The process amounts to a powerful tool for practicing foresight (Pillar V).

When he was on the federal side, Sorel developed an innovative *risk-management system* in collaboration with around fifty stakeholders and taught it to others in workshops. It was a tool for prudent decision making, with financial considerations only one marker. "Feds don't do that," said Tom. "They normally just handle regulations." When Tom became MnDOT commissioner he brought the risk management model over to MnDOT and refined it to align the process with MnDOT's vision, mission, and strategic directions.[6] The process was taught to MnDOT employees around the state in over seventy workshops. "In my mind it was all related to how you spend public dollars and how you influence quality of life," said Tom. "But what is 'quality of life' for Minnesotans, we wondered. So we set out to define it."

## *Research—Act—Evaluate—Translate*

Research is a way of asking important questions and listening deeply to the answers, which is the first step in becoming a Skilled Communicator (Pillar III). Perhaps that is why Robert Greenleaf once wrote a paper on the need for a "research mindset" in an organization. The entire MnDOT culture is based on serving citizens with transportation opportunities that enhance their safety and quality of life, but until Commissioner Sorel arrived, no one had bothered to ask Minnesotans what "quality of life" meant to them. Karla Rains, the MnDOT's Director of Customer Relations, knew how to find out.

Karla is a research and marketing wizard who worked for MnDOT for ten years, left for five years to work as a market researcher in the private sector, and was hired back by Commissioner Sorel. When she tackled the quality of life measurement, Karla knew it was "big, a *very* big exercise in Systems Thinking (Pillar VI). I mean, how far can you zoom out? But we truly needed to understand these issues so we could align MnDOT's services to them."

The research included focus groups and a snail mail survey. Karla explained that 40 percent of households now only have cell phones, so an old-fashioned phone survey would not have worked. Since the survey questions filled a small booklet, her team, which included people from the University of Minnesota, figured a 10 percent response rate would be dandy. However, this is Minnesota, and the people who received surveys either thought they should return them because that's what Minnesotans do or, as Karla hypothesizes, were intrigued by a questionnaire that asked about things that really mattered to them. The response rate was 43 percent, an outcome that hard-core researchers can only dream about.

The study found eleven factors that contributed to quality of life, ranging from safety and health to spirituality/serenity/faith, and, yes, transportation.[7] Researchers dug deep into that transportation bucket and found eleven predictors of transportation satisfaction, and also discovered that transportation affected other areas in significant ways.

Now MnDOT—and other state agencies—had solid data to begin tweaking their services and strategizing how to communicate them. Karla's team was able to start making connections between quality of life, risk assessment, risk management, and the agency's vision and mission. MnDOT used the findings to develop a twenty-year plan and even a *fifty*-year plan. Partly because of the survey results, Tom Sorel realized the profound link between health care and transportation. After all, how will you get to the doctor or hospital when you get sick? He attended and presented at so many health care conferences that the health commissioner told him folks were starting to think Tom had his job. Tom said, "I'm just trying to help you. Transportation is one of the ways you can help public health."

Another of Karla's projects is the Online Customer Community website, which is far more than a simple place to post comments. Four hundred and fifty (450!) Minnesotans engage with the website every week. Ever the research professional, Karla chose the participants by aligning them with census criteria so they truly represented the state. Members of the Community are paid a nominal amount to give feedback on services, communications, and a variety of other topics. "For example," Karla reports, "we asked what transparency means to them; we explored the topic of financial accountability and integrity. Some weeks, we simply ask them, 'What should we know?'"

Every year about 30 percent of the participants are replenished to keep the community fresh. The nominal amount spent is probably the best research bargain of any state agency because every quiver of new concerns or changing attitudes is detected immediately and addressed by MnDOT.

Karla was surprised that citizens were surprised—much less grateful—when government asked their opinions. Yet the public *was* both surprised and grateful, as you can see from a sampling of comments from the *Online Customer Community*:

> "Too few government agencies as well as corporations solicit opinions and ideas from their 'clients' except on election day or by looking at the 'bottom line.'"
> "I feel like my concerns are going directly to people who can make changes according to my concerns and surprised by the quick responses to my message to MnDOT."
> Here is my favorite: "A department of government is proactive? It must be a mighty cold day in hell!"

That is servanthood in action, right down to the policy and program level.

"Karla is a true Servant-Leader" says Tom Sorel. "I went to her one day and said, 'Hey, we have data on the performance of our systems, but none of that matters if we have bad relationships. She got a group together and generated a database to reflect *performance-based relationships*. Now, if the numbers start to go down with contractors or the feds, MnDOT can do something about it and figure out mitigation strategies. This was groundbreaking work and it was fun to watch."

Research may not sound like a compelling enterprise. But it is, because research guides actions and *actions are how we serve*.

## Be Accessible and Transparent

When Commissioner Sorel said his door was always open, he meant it. He was accessible to the media, the public, and MnDOT employees. "I was probably a media person's nightmare," he said. "If I didn't know the answer to a question, I'd simply say 'I don't know.' I was just being honest. And I would talk to anybody—*anybody!*"

"When I got to MnDOT, I think people were shocked to have access to me. Most of the previous commissioners parked in a nice corner office and asked their secretaries to set up appointments. I especially liked to be available to interns. They would see my open door and stop to say hi. Then I would invite them to have an ice cream together. I'm comfortable with that. If I could have an impact on some of those kids, that's what I'm here to do. Sure, I'm here to build a transportation system, but at the end of the day, you need to have an impact on people's lives."

Accessibility and transparency together work to build stakeholder trust. Karla remembers that "when we asked the public what transparency meant to them, they told us that it is open, honest, and timely information regarding operations, planning, funding, and expenditures. They said they welcome, encourage, and expect transparency in state government."[8]

Hearing Karla and other MnDOT employees makes me reflect on the various organizations with which I have worked. I wonder what we could have learned if we had simply asked customers and stakeholders what *they* would have liked to see in accessibility and transparency, instead of assuming that we already knew what they wanted and needed.

## *Trust First*

One of the top priorities of the new commissioner was to rebuild trust with the legislature, public, contractors, and staff. He developed a deliberate strategy for a trust turnaround. First, he acknowledged the pain caused by the bridge collapse. "I said that we were all feeling sad. We would come out better from this but first we needed some time to heal. It was OK to acknowledge the sadness, not gloss it over."

Second, he spoke frequently about the principles from Stephen Covey's book *The Speed of Trust*. "I explained that in order to have trust, you must function with integrity. You have to follow through on what you say you're going to do. You declare your intent, and you need to have a positive intent. I just kept building with those principles through very consistent messaging." The trust message was given in scores of meetings with staff and community groups, and it paid off not long after Tom took over MnDOT when two new bridge crises hit.

First, the mile-long bridge connecting Duluth to Superior, Wisconsin, was closed for repairs following an inspection of the bridge's gusset plates, the components implicated in the collapse of the I-35W bridge. A month later, the Main Channel Bridge over the Mississippi at Winona was closed, also because of gusset plates. "I had to get in front of the media and explain what the closings meant," said Tom. "They didn't like it, but I kept talking about public safety, and this is the right thing to do. You know, I think the more people saw of me, they felt comfortable asking more questions, because I was honest."

Tom Sorel's notion of trust extends to his own staff. One talented employee on MnDOT's leadership team seemed to need validation from Tom before she acted. "She'd come in and say, 'I don't know what to do about this,' or 'Well, I heard from this group and they don't like this or that.' And I would say, 'What would you do as a Servant-Leader?'"

"Sometimes her response was, 'I didn't come in here for you to put a philosophy on me,' or, 'I told them I'd come talk to you.'"

"I would respond, 'I'm not telling you what to do!'"

"She and I would talk like a brother and sister and I would tell her, 'You are a leader in this agency. I'm depending on you to explain why these things are important. Don't just come to me.'

"After some time, she learned. I kept pushing back, saying, '*You* are a Servant-Leader; you are a leader in this agency. *You* should be leading these people and helping them move in the right direction in a positive way instead of listening to their complaints all the time.'"

Some might say this employee was simply trying to survive by following the familiar top-down pattern of authority. Or, that she was testing the idea that she had permission to fail. One is reminded of the famous experiment with fleas in a jar covered by a lid. The flea learns not to jump too high or it will bang its little flea head on the lid, but once the lid is removed, the flea will *still* not jump high enough to escape, even though it is perfectly able to hop to freedom. Using this (rather awful) analogy, you could say that Tom coaxed this employee—and many others—to keep jumping higher until they felt safe enough to operate with autonomous freedom.

Tom says that 99 percent of the time he starts with trust because a trusting relationship allows people to work through almost any problem and support each other. But he is not naïve. He and Jeff Ostrom—a former communications specialist in the governor's office—had numerous conversations about the idea of "smart trust" in Covey's book *The Speed of Trust*, and Jeff learned a leadership lesson from those talks, and from Tom's model.

"Most leaders say, 'You have to earn my trust,' says Jeff. "No. Transformational leadership is about extending that trust, but not blind trust. As a friend, employee, or colleague, you want to reward trust that is offered. You don't want to disappoint. That's one reason Tom was able to find and keep terrific talent at MnDOT."

"I do have a hard time with people who violate trust with sabotage," says Tom. "I'm fine with people disagreeing with me, but be respectful. Don't sabotage what I'm trying to do here. There was a bit of that happening when I first came to MnDOT, but after a while, when a few people started doing that, others around them would shut it down."

## *Wear Out the Soles of Your Shoes*

Tom spent much of his tenure on the road speaking to everyone from community groups to other government agencies. He sometimes made public appearances under tense circumstances, like the meeting about Highway 14.

For years, Highway 14 between New Ulm and Rochester had been known as the most dangerous road in the state. Not long after Sorel became commissioner, a young man died in a motorcycle crash on the heavily traveled two-lane highway. The victim's vocal family and outraged citizens scheduled a public rally to protest road conditions, and most of their ire was directed toward MnDOT.

The MnDOT leadership team met to discuss how to handle the situation. Some thought the agency should handle it with PR and isolate the commissioner from the fracas. Bernie Arseneau disagreed and suggested that he and Tom go down for the meeting. Tom agreed. "You don't run from criticism," he said, "that's gutless. We needed to be there not to 'face them,' but to engage with them."

Hundreds of angry people attended and several patrolmen were on hand in case trouble bubbled up. Tom sat in front with the local district engineer and a few community leaders. One by one, people stood and talked about the young man who died, and this went on for an hour. "I just listened, and listened, and listened," Tom remembers. "I tried very hard not to have any negative or judgmental body language." Tom did not bring up the fact that the governor had vetoed a bill that would have provided money for road upgrades, even during the current deep recession. Nor did he make any other excuses.

"I didn't speak much, but I did finally say, 'Look, I have heard everybody. Trust me; we are going to come up with some solutions. I can't tell you what they are today but we are going to be responsive to your concerns.'" Things calmed down and he was faithful in reporting new developments to the local Highway 14 Partnership.

Several months later he received a letter from the family of the deceased motorcycle rider expressing appreciation for his attendance at the meeting. It is one of his most treasured mementoes.

## *Initiate Compassionate Collaboration (Pillar IV)*

Before he took office, Tom Sorel's collaboration with a colleague began at a personal level. His friend, Bernie Arsenau, later promoted to deputy commissioner, deeply understood Tom's working strengths, based on his experience with the man when he was working for the feds. "Tom was such a visionary, with forward-thinking ideas about impacts on stakeholders and so many other things. He was also a dedicated collaborator. If Tom had a weakness, it might have been in implementation, and I feel like I may have filled in that area with my own strengths." Bernie would have fit right in as a player on Tom's old baseball team where each player meshed his strengths with others' weaknesses. And, just like the baseball team, no one objected when a teammate ran onto the field to help. After all, as Bernie said, "We all have our strengths and weaknesses."

Tom had a deep belief that if he could just get all stakeholders in an issue around the table, they could arrive at solutions through collaboration. That assumption was tested early in his stewardship at MnDOT.

Tom decided to bring together the communities who had been protesting MnDOT's lack of minority participation and see what they could do. Minnesota, especially the Twin Cities area, is surprisingly diverse, as explained on a Minneapolis website promoting the city:

> Minneapolis is home to a robust African American community, a strong Native American heritage, the largest Somali population in the U.S., the largest Hmong population outside Laos, the second-largest Vietnamese and Ethiopian populations and one of the fastest-growing Latino/Hispanic populations.[9]

Representatives from most of these communities, plus religious and civic organizations, responded to Tom's call for a get-together. "I asked Phil Barnes to facilitate this," said Tom. "He was in our Office of Policy, Analysis, Research & Innovation, and was darn good at running meetings. It was a challenge because very different kinds of interests were represented.

"It did not gel. People were nipping at each other's heels and sending nasty e-mails around. Some destructive conflicts were afoot. At one point, we almost had an altercation and called the cops. Phil was doing his best to moderate it, but at one point a guy from a religious organization stood up to question my leadership and just ripped MnDOT. I had to stop him. I said, 'Do not come here and behave that way. That's not the norm that would be acceptable in our building.'

"I recognized that we were in over our heads with the deep-rooted feelings between some of these groups, and some of it had nothing to do with MnDOT but more to do with history. Still, I didn't anticipate these dynamics particularly well, and that's on me.

"I finally announced that we were ending the meeting. Some of them said, 'We can't stop!' but I said, 'There are some unacceptable behaviors here. Look, none of us are being forced to do this. I could just sit here as commissioner, implement regulations, provide the minimum minority participation for projects, give statistics, and we could all go on our merry way for years and years. But what I'm trying to do is make your communities strong partners in our transportation systems and work with contractors. We're trying to build a workforce in this state to help all of our communities. MnDOT wants to be a player.'

"'We need to stop. We'll get it going again in a month or two when we can regroup with a professional facilitator who can help us set norms for the group and get this off on the right foot again.' In the interim, I went to four or five pizza parties with these groups because I wanted to have personal contact with them.

"When we got back together the whole thing took off and it became a pretty successful group. After they had done some work in project committees, I met with them again and reminded them of how we had started. I reflected on our commitments and asked how they felt about the current situation. One Asian woman owned a painting company. She was a minority business owner trying to get contracts, but it had been tough. She said, 'You guys absolutely saved me.' We said, 'That's all we wanted to do.'

The contractors were not always open because they'd had some bad experiences with these folks, so we also had to work with the contractors. They needed to trust us a little bit, you know, when we said, 'We're going to do this.' You need to bring these people along in their jobs. That was no small feat. Some did well and some didn't, but we stayed the course."

Several years later, Mark Dayton was elected as the new Minnesota governor. His first appointment, before he was even sworn in, was to keep Tom Sorel as MnDOT commissioner. He was only following the advice of the growing parade of people who lobbied to keep their innovative commissioner in place. When Tom Sorel later accompanied the governor and other new commissioners to a public meeting near the Urban League, Tom was probably one of the few people known by the audience because he had visited there many times. An African-American man named Robert Woods stood up and said, "Governor, you have Tom Sorel standing over there. I'll tell you, Mr. Governor, we are so proud of MnDOT and how MnDOT is really helping our community."

"That made me feel so good, remembers Tom. "It was unsolicited; he just happened to see me there, and he knew me."

## *Honor Your Heroes*

Soon after Tom arrived, MnDOT began highlighting stories of their heroes, ordinary people who acted courageously or provided meritorious service in response to extraordinary or dangerous circumstances. Some of the first honored heroes were snowplow drivers, who routinely save lives in the frigid Minnesota winters. The heroes were first recognized in online stories and videos. Then, starting in 2011, the governor invited recipients to the state capitol to receive the Heroes of MnDOT award. The last year Bernie Aresneau was at MnDOT, he handed out the awards with the governor. Tom recalled that Bernie was near tears because he was so proud of the MnDOT employees.

## *Sustaining the Servanthood*

Tom Sorel may not be flashy in the way of media stars, but he is absolutely electric in his authenticity and compelling as a Servant-Leader. He gets things done while building people up. Those who work with him, feel trusted, inspired to hope and to perform. He also has a knack for finding other servants to be part of the team, like Abe Hassan, a Sudan native who was running an innovative program to train minorities when Tom met him and quickly hired him, seeing Abe as a brilliant and creative collaborator.

The Seven Pillars of Servant Leadership are evident in Tom's thinking, and especially in his actions. "I used the material in that book all over the darn place," he said. "It is most effective when you ask the questions, 'What could that idea mean for us? How, specifically, could we implement it?'

"This is a hard philosophy. No matter where I am, when I talk about Servant Leadership, people can generally understand some of the principles, but when you live it and act on it, too many people see you as weak. If they are accustomed to a leader who is loud, aggressive, and dictatorial, you appear tentative when you plant seeds and encourage collaboration.

"However, look at the outcomes. Look how MnDOT reestablished our relationship with the legislature who blamed us after the collapse. Why? This stuff doesn't just happen; it's all about embracing the philosophy of Servant Leadership, moving forward consistently using these values.

"I continue to expect people to take responsibility for their actions, knowing that sometimes they will fail, but also knowing they will never grow if they are micromanaged to be dependent. Some folks around have said, 'I know they're going to learn from mistakes, but it's hard for me to watch. I want to jump in and tell them what to do.' Truth is, it's hard for any of us, but people need to be reminded that they are Servant-Leaders wherever they may be, and whatever their jobs.

"One day a man who I respect said, 'Why do you make this look so easy?' I said, 'Trust me, it is not easy, even if it appears that way.' It's easy for somebody to slam a fist on the table and say, 'I want you to do this! Do that!' But that is not transformational in nature. That is not going to last or be sustainable for a lifetime of the person's life or agency or whatever you're trying to affect. Sure, we can all be leaders like that, but is that effective? I don't think so.

"I believe that the purpose of government service is to help people, to make their lives better. That opinion is shared by thousands of MnDOT employees. The Servant Leadership philosophy gives language and strategic direction for living out that mission."

# Afterword

When I began my career at The Toro Company in Minneapolis, Minnesota, in the 1970s, I had never heard the term *Servant Leadership* used as a business idea. No one had written about it, it wasn't taught at business schools, and even Peter Drucker, who believed in its principles, never mentioned it.

I came upon the concept of leading by serving quite fortuitously when I was thrust into my first general management assignment in 1973. At the time, I was director of marketing in Toro's Consumer Products Division. The CEO of the company approached me with an opportunity to become the president of GameTime, Inc., a new Toro subsidiary in Litchfield, Michigan. GameTime was a leading commercial playground and park equipment manufacturer. When Toro bought the company a year earlier, management kept its founder at the helm. Unfortunately, as is often the case, the shared journey of the acquired entrepreneur and the acquiring corporation was short-lived. I accepted the opportunity with much apprehension, partly due to the new position in an industry I knew nothing about, but also because I was moving my young family from Minneapolis to Litchfield, a rural community of just under one thousand people.

On the job, I found myself in a familiar predicament. Managers came to me asking for decisions regarding their functions. For example, the accounts payable manager wanted to know what bills should be paid; the traffic manager needed a decision about which orders to ship. I, of course, did not know the answers and tried to push the decision back to the department head. Their replies were often the same, "Well, Bob—the former president and founder—always made the decision." Fear of failure permeated the organization and I sensed that mistakes were frequently followed by redress or punishment.

I reasoned that if anyone left the company in a town of 973 individuals, I would have a hard time filling the vacancy. So, as a process-oriented person, I wanted to find a way to help these managers make their own decisions and be accountable for the outcomes, all within a safe environment.

The next time the purchasing manager asked me how much steel we should procure for swings, I responded with a series of probing questions: "How much inventory of steel do we have? How many swings shall we build? How many units do we plan to sell?"

His reply was usually, "I don't know."

I then suggested we invite the inventory manager, the production manager, and the sales manager to meet with us.

During the meeting, each shared what they knew. A certain number of swings were forecast, the production run size was so many, and we had so much steel in the barn. We then did the math.

Gazing at the numbers, the purchasing guy had a flash of insight, "Aha...looks like we need six tons of steel." It was a reasonable conclusion. Unfortunately, he was wrong. Very wrong!

I asked, "Why do you think we were so far off?" This led to a discussion of the sales forecast and we discovered that it too was considerably off. I asked the sales manager how he arrived at his decision. His explanation afforded an opportunity to collectively identify some better ways to forecast.

The sales manager was happy to strengthen his skills, the purchasing manager was happy he did not get fired, and the whole group was happy to be part of a collaborative team.

This kind of activity went on for months. People started to look to a team approach to solving problems. And when they began to comprehend that mistakes became opportunities to learn, rather than to "catch hell," they all became more accountable. As their processes made them better decision makers, they began to take pride in their work and their confidence grew. The purchasing manager told me a year or so later, "I've learned that I am a pretty good purchasing manager and I finally feel valued around here."

We owned GameTime for about four years before Toro's executives and board concluded it was not a good fit. But during this time GameTime was very successful. It enjoyed solid growth, an improving PAT (Profits After Taxes) percent to sales, and achieved the highest return on invested capital of all of Toro's businesses.

What happened to its people was more impressive. They blossomed in self-esteem, confidence, and initiative. They were productive and accountable, trusting, and trustworthy, which encouraged working in well-functioning teams. I realized that I could not manage them as a "top-down" boss—they all knew more about their jobs than I did. Instead, I became a facilitator, coach, mentor, and servant, engendering in them a spirit of "I/we can do this."

Was this Servant Leadership in some form? I didn't know—to me it was common sense, coupled with an upbringing of a philosophy of serving others. It was not until some years later, after reading Robert Greenleaf's *Servant Leadership*, that I saw the correlation.

I tried to develop and practice Servant Leadership principles upon my return to Minneapolis. But I was one of several division managers in the late 1970s who resided within a different culture and management style, so nothing took root. Still, I continued to reflect on how to translate the GameTime learnings into leadership principles and styles, organizational culture, values, and structures. How did all these factors work together to bring value to the company and its shareholders?

In 1981, when I was made head of Toro, I thought this was my chance to "GameTime" the company. But I simply didn't know how. The team and I brought in Stephen Covey, Ken Blanchard, and Tom Peters to help us form our cultural values and leadership principles, but it was still tough sledding. These business gurus had great Servant Leadership concepts, but we didn't know how to make them part of the Toro fabric. It took a great deal of trial and error, and many years before we were successful.

Even though Servant Leadership was starting to percolate in pockets of corporate America, the "larger-than-life" CEO genre reigned supreme.

I do not fault this "CEO as hero" mentality. It is a product of the world we live in. The Wall Street environment is overly focused on short-term results, quarter after quarter, so that today, Servant Leadership the GameTime way would not get out of the starting blocks. What is needed today is an architecture that can build a Servant Leadership environment much more quickly than what I had at my disposal in 1973. This is exactly what James Sipe and Don

Frick construct for us in their book *Seven Pillars of Servant Leadership*. They clearly describe the leadership behaviors necessary to create and sustain a servant-led company, plus they show us how to build the skills, capacities, and systems to support them. In essence, *Seven Pillars of Servant Leadership* provides the reader with a practical, step-wise "blueprint" that I wish I had back in the 1970s.

The gratifying thing about Servant Leadership is how it affects the organization. It gives employees the freedom to be as much as they can be. It builds an environment for continuous improvement and self-direction. Its culture of collaboration and accountability fosters good ethics naturally. It builds intrinsic value in the company. And in the end, everyone wins, including the shareholder.

The principles of Servant Leadership are timeless and universal. As James and Don say, "We didn't make this stuff up." They have spent years studying and practicing Servant Leadership. I believe their book will have enduring value, just like the concept of Servant Leadership.

And the ego issue? As Robert Greenleaf says, "Everything begins with the individual." An effective Servant-Leader in today's world needs two things: an ego that values humility and the Seven Pillars of Servant Leadership!

*Ken Melrose*
*Former CEO & Chairman, The Toro Company*
*Founder & Principal, Leading by Serving, LLC*

# Notes

## Preface

1. Robert K. Greenleaf, *The Servant as Leader* (Indianapolis: The Robert Greenleaf Center for Servant Leadership, 1970). This essay was Greenleaf's first published formulation of the principles of Servant Leadership as they apply to individuals. His 1972 essay, *The Institution as Servant*, explores how Servant Leadership could be implemented in organizations, and his 1974 essay, "Trustee as Servants," expands upon the role of trustees who act as Servant-Leaders. The seminal 1977 book, *Servant Leadership* (Paulist Press, 1977) includes these early essays plus additional writings about Servant Leadership in education, religion, and other arenas.

2. Ibid., 9.

3. Stephen Covey, *Insights on Leadership: Service, Stewardship, Spirit, and Servant Leadership* (New York: John Wiley & Sons, 1998), xi.

## Introduction

1. Robert K. Greenleaf, *The Servant as Leader* (Indianapolis: The Robert Greenleaf Center for Servant Leadership, 1970), 7.

2. Ibid., 1.

3. James Collins, *Good to Great: Why Some Companies Make the Leap and Others Don't* (New York: HarperCollins, 2001), 30.

4. The Magellan Executive Resources research project chose eleven publicly traded companies most frequently mentioned in the literature as implementing the principles of Servant Leadership: The Toro Company, Southwest Airlines, Starbucks, AFLAC, Men's Wearhouse, Synovus Financial, Herman Miller, ServiceMasters, Marriott International, FedEx, and Medtronic. Because some of these servant-led companies had not yet implemented servant

leadership during the time period studied by Collins, both the Collins companies and the servant-led companies were compared for financial performance from 1994–2004. Here are the results over that ten-year period:

*Percentage of pre-tax profit returns*
S&P companies—10.8 percent,
Collins' Good to Great companies—17.5 percent,
Servant-led companies—24.2 percent.

Our special thanks to Jeff Pauley, cofounder of Magellan Resources, for being the champion of this research effort.

5. Rajendra S. Sisodia, David B. Wolfe, and Jagdish N. Sheth, *Firms of Endearment: How World Class Companies Profit from Passion and Purpose* (Upper Saddle River, NJ: Wharton School Publishing, 2007), 6.

6. *Firms of Endearment*, http://www.firmsofendearment.com.

7. Larry Spears has published his "Ten Characteristics" in various venues, including "On Character and Servant Leadership: Ten Characteristics of Effective, Caring Leaders," *Concepts & Connections*, 8, no. 3 (2000). University of Maryland, National Clearinghouse for Leadership Programs. You can also access a version of it online at http://www.regent.edu/acad/global/publications/jvl/vol1_iss1/Spears_Final.pdf.

The Ten Characteristics include:

1. *Listening*—A deep commitment to listening intently to others as well as to one's own inner voice.

2. *Empathy*—Understanding others deeply, accepting them and valuing them for their special and unique spirits.

3. *Healing*—Manifesting the potential for healing oneself and one's relationship to others, and to help make others whole.

4. *Awareness*—Fostering general awareness, and especially self-awareness, to aid in understanding issues involving ethics, power, and values.

5. *Persuasion*—Relying on persuasion rather than positional authority. Convincing rather than coercing—the clearest distinction between the traditional authoritarian leadership model and that of Servant Leadership.

6. *Conceptualization*—Going beyond concern for short-term operational goals and day-to-day realities to nurture one's ability to dream great dreams.

7. *Foresight*—The "lead" in leadership; to understand the lessons from the past, the realities of the present, and the likely consequence of a decision for the future.

8. *Stewardship*—First and foremost a commitment to serving others and to holding the institution in trust for the greater good and benefit of society.

9. *Commitment to the growth of people*—The belief that people have an intrinsic value beyond their tangible contributions as producers; a determination to nurture the personal, professional, and spiritual growth of each individual.

10. *Building community*—To regain the lost sense of community spirit by building community back into the workplace environment among all those who work there.

8. James O. Prochaska, John Norcross, and Carlo DiClemente, *Changing for Good: A Revolutionary Six-Stage Program for Overcoming Bad Habits and Moving Your Life Positively Forward* (New York: Collins, 2007).

9. *The Development Pipeline* integrates research from adult learning and human development into five conditions for change: Insight, Motivation, Capabilities, Real-World Practice, and Accountability.

## Pillar I: Person of Character

1. Stephen R. Covey, foreword to *Servant Leadership: A Journey into the Nature of Legitimate Power & Greatness 25th Anniversary Edition*, by Robert K. Greenleaf (Mahwah, NJ: Paulist Press, 2002), 1–14. Dr. Covey's foreword not only speaks to the differences between Servant Leadership and other approaches to leadership, but also identifies Servant Leadership as an underlying principle for all ethical approaches to leadership.

2. Bill George "True North," *Georgia Tech Alumni Magazine*, Fall, 2007, 47, http://issuu.com/gtalumni/docs/2007_84_2. This

article excerpts passages from Bill George, David Gergen, and Peter Sims, *True North: Discover Your Authentic Leadership* (San Francisco: Jossey-Bass, 2007). See also other features on George's website: http://www.billgeorge.org/page/true-north.

3. William James, quoted from an 1875 letter to his wife Alice Gibbons James in Jill M. Kress, *The Figure of Consciousness: William James, Henry James and Edith Wharton* (New York: Routledge, 2002), 161.

4. For an excellent discussion of Aristotle's virtues, see Jody Palmour, *On Moral Character: A Practical Guide to Aristotle's Virtues and Vices* (Washington, DC: The Archon Institute for Leadership Development, 1986).

5. Michael Novak, quoted by Christina Casanova in "Character Education in Our Schools: What Is Good Character?" *Guidance Channel Ezine*, June 2007.

6. See Thomas A. Teal, "The Human Side of Management," in *Harvard Business Review on Leadership* (Boston: Harvard Business School Publishing, 1998), 147–70.

7. Frederick F. Reichheld, *Loyalty Rules: How Today's Leaders Build Lasting Relationships* (Boston: Harvard Business School Press, 2003). Reichheld describes leaders' behaviors that foster loyalty, and marshals impressive research to show the relationship between loyalty and bottom-line results.

8. Warren Bennis, "The Leadership Advantage," *Leader to Leader* 12 (Spring 1999). Bennis cites a study that shows a dramatic advantage in bottom-line performance for companies that are perceived as being well-led: "The stock price of companies perceived as being well led grew 900 percent over a 10-year period, compared to just 74 percent growth in companies perceived to lack good leadership."

9. John P. Kotter and James L. Heskett, *Corporate Culture and Performance* (New York: Simon & Schuster, 1992). Even though the rigorous, ten-year empirical study that supported this book's conclusions ended in 1990, Kotter and Heskett's research about the link between corporate culture—including the culture's leadership—and economic performance have been validated since the book's 1992 publication.

10. Thomas Lickona, *Educating for Character: How Our Schools*

*Can Teach Respect and Responsibility* (New York: Bantam Books, 1991), 51.

11. Joseph Badaracco, Jr., "The Discipline of Building Character," *Harvard Business Review on Leadership* 76, no. 2 (1998): 114.

12. Jan Carlzon, *Moments of Truth* (New York: Collins, 1989), 3.

13. James M. Kouzes and Barry Z. Posner, *The Leadership Challenge* (San Francisco: Jossey-Bass, 2002), 29.

14. Rob Goffee and Gareth Jones, "Managing Authenticity," *Harvard Business Review*, 83, no. 12 (2005): 90.

15. Jim Collins, *Good to Great: Why Some Companies Make the Leap and Others Don't* (New York: HarperCollins, 2001). Throughout this classic book Collins elaborates on the paradox of humility and strong will, at one point using Abraham Lincoln as an example of one of the few United States presidents who was a "Level 5 Leader."

16. Stacy T. Rinehart, *Upside Down: The Paradox of Servant Leadership* (Colorado Springs, CO: NavPress, 1998). Rinehart bases his take on leadership on the model of leadership supplied by Jesus in the New Testament.

17. Luther's short book *The Magnificat* is included in *Luther's Works*, ed. Jaroslav Pelikan, vol. 21 (St. Louis: Concordia Publishing House, 1956), 313.

18. Johan Hinderlie and James W. Sipe, "Well Done, Good and Faithful Servant" (unpublished manuscript, 2006).

19. Paul T. P. Wong and Don Page, "Servant leadership: An Opponent-Process Model and the Revised Servant Leadership Profile," *Regent University Servant Leadership Research Roundtable*, 2003, http://www.regent.edu/acad/global/publications/sl_proceedings/2003/wong_servant_leadership.pdf.

20. Ibid., 7.

21. Joseph Jaworski, "Destiny and the Leader," in *Insights on Leadership: Service, Stewardship, and Servant Leadership*, ed. Larry Spears (New York: John Wiley and Sons, 1998), 259.

22. The popular Charles Handy quote found at: http://www.brainyquote.com/quotes/authors/c/charles_handy.html. It was originally published in Charles Handy, "The Search for Meaning," *Leader to Leader*, no. 5 (1997): 14–20.

# Pillar II: Puts People First

1. Jeffrey Pfeffer, *The Human Equation: Building Profits by Putting People First* (Boston, MA: Harvard Business School Press, 1998), 292–306. In the course of explaining a detailed strategy for creating a "people first" company, Pfeffer refers to the extraordinary profits of companies like Service Masters, Southwest Airlines, and others.

2. A. Gregory Stone, Robert F. Russell, and Kathleen Patterson, "Transformational versus Servant Leadership: A Difference in Leader Focus," *Leadership & Organization Development Journal* 25, no. 4 (2004): 349.

3. John Barbuto Jr. and Daniel W. Wheeler, "Becoming a Servant Leader: Do You Have What It Takes?" *NebGuide*, University of Nebraska–Lincoln Extension, http://www.ianrpubs .unl.edu/epublic/live/g1481/build/g1481.pdf.

4. Shankar Vedantam, "If It Feels Good to Be Good, It Might Be Only Natural," *Washington Post*, May 28, 2007, A01.

5. Lynn O'Connor, "Altruism as a Fundamental Unconscious Motivation," *SFPRG Process Notes*, Spring, 1996, 11, http://www. eparg.org/publications/altruism.pdf.

6. Ibid., 12.

7. Robert K. Greenleaf, *Management Ability*. (Indianapolis: Robert K. Greenleaf Center Archives, Joseph Distefano Collection, undated). Originally published by Pacific Telephone.

8. Tom Gegax, *Winning in the Game of Life* (New York: Harmony Books, 1999), 57.

9. Abraham Maslow, *Maslow on Management* (New York: John Wiley & Sons, 1998). Yet Stephen Covey, speaking at an international conference on Servant Leadership hosted by the Greenleaf Center, said that at the end of his life, Maslow commented that he had learned that "self-actualization" was not the ultimate human need, but *self-transcendence*.

10. James Autry, *Love and Profit: The Art of Caring Leadership* (New York: Avon Books, Inc., 1991). In this book you will also find some of James Autry's award-winning poetry for the workplace.

11. Kouzes and Posner, *The Leadership Challenge*, 305.

# Pillar III: Skilled Communicator

1. In two classic books, both Stephen Covey in *Seven Habits of Highly Effective People* (New York: Fireside, 1989) and Peter Drucker in *The Effective Executive* (New York: HarperCollins, 1967) emphasize the value of clear, respectful communications.

2. Gerard Egan, *The Skilled Helper: A Problem-Management Approach to Helping*, 6th ed. (Pacific Grove, CA: Brooks/Cole Publishing Co., 1998).

3. Carl Rogers, *A Way of Being* (Boston: Houghton Mifflin, 1980), 142.

4. Vittoria Gallese, "The Roots of Empathy: The Shared Manifold Hypothesis and the Neural Basis of Intersubjectivity." *Psychopathology* 36 (2003): 176.

5. Daniel Goleman, *Social Intelligence: The New Science of Human Relationships* (New York: Bantam, 2006).

6. Inbal Ben-Ami Bartal, Jean Decety, and Peggy Mason, "Empathy and Pro-Social Behavior in Rats." *Science* 334, no. 6061 (9 December 2011): 1427–30.

7. Although the quote is from the Peace Prayer, popularly attributed to St. Francis and certainly reflecting the spirit of Francis of Assisi, recent scholarship has shown that it did not originate with him. See Pat McCloskey, O.F.M., "Where Did St. Francis Say That?" *St. Anthony Messenger: Ask a Franciscan*, http://www.americancatholic.org/messenger/Oct2001/Wiseman.asp.

8. Robert K. Greenleaf, *The Servant as Leader* (Indianapolis: The Robert Greenleaf Center for Servant Leadership, 1970), 10.

9. Ibid., 301.

10. Arthur Schnabel quoted in *Chicago Daily News*, June 11, 1958.

11. Greenleaf, *Servant Leadership*, 18.

12. St. Thomas Aquinas is quoted by Episcopal priest Father Ronald Ketteler in the *Catholic Conference of Kentucky Newsletter*, March 20, 1998, revised December 19, 2001. Ketteler notes that "a more idiomatic translation [of the final sentence] reads: 'For both study to find the truth and in this way are collaborators.'"

13. You can find strands of the "as if" notion in both philosophy and psychology. In 1911, the philosopher Hans Vaihinger pub-

lished *Philosophie des Als Ob* (Philosophy of As If), a manuscript he had written thirty years earlier. In it, he argued that we behave *as if* the world matched our models of it. And it works the other way, too. A therapist, for example, may ask a shy person to act as if she were outgoing for two weeks. That behavior may then become integrated so that it becomes an authentic part of her repertoire of behaviors.

14. Greenleaf made these comments in his essay "Growth through Groups" in the unpublished *Receptive Listening Course Leadership Manual* that he and his wife Esther wrote for the Wainwright House in Rye, New York, in the early 1950s.

15. Robert Burns, from verse 8 of the poem "To A Louse, On Seeing One on a Lady's Bonnet at Church, 1786"—offered here with a modern expression of Scottish dialect, http://www.robert burns.org/works/97.shtml.

16. For more information on these and other principles, see Fred Nickols, "Feedback about Feedback," *Human Resources Development Quarterly* 6, no. 3 (1995): 289–96.

17. Robert Bolton, *People Skills: How to Assert Yourself, Listen to Others, and Resolve Conflicts* (New York: Simon & Schuster, 1976).

18. Greenleaf, *The Servant as Leader*, 7.

19. If you are interested in a scholarly approach to understanding research on feedback, especially as it has been translated for use in the behavioral sciences, consult George P. Richardson's excellent book *Feedback Thought in Social Science and Systems Theory* (Philadelphia: University of Pennsylvania Press, 1991).

20. Robert K. Greenleaf, *On Becoming a Servant-Leader*, eds. Don M. Frick and Larry C. Spears (San Francisco: Jossey-Bass, 1996), 129.

21. For a comprehensive, more traditional treatment of influence and persuasion, see Robert B. Cialdini, *Influence: The Psychology of Persuasion* (New York: William Morrow & Company, Inc., 1984).

22. Robert McKee and Bronwyn Fryer, "Storytelling That Moves People: A Conversation with Screenwriting Coach Robert McKee," *Harvard Business Review*, June 1, 2003, 5–8. See also Robert McKee, *Story: Substance, Structure, Style, and the Principles of Screenwriting* (New York: HarperCollins, 1997).

## Pillar IV: Compassionate Collaborator

1. The authors are indebted to Dr. Ann McGee-Cooper and Duane Trammel of the Dallas-based firm Ann McGee-Cooper and Associates for graciously granting permission to feature their Synergy Box exercise.

2. Facts about camels accessed online from the following URLs: http://camelfarm.com/camels/camels_about.html http://www.acsamman.edu.jo/~el/2/camels/index.html http://www.llamaweb.com/Camel/Info.html.

3. David D. Crislip and Carl E. Larson, *Collaborative Leadership: How Citizens Can Make a Difference* (San Francisco: Jossey-Bass, 1994), 5.

4. Comments by Anja White from personal interview with James Sipe, September 26, 2007.

5. Gary Vikesland, "Part II: An Unseen Force in Your Company," *Employer-Employee.com*, 2001.

6. John P. Kotter and James L. Heskett, *Corporate Culture and Performance* (New York: Simon & Schuster, 1992).

7. Robert K. Greenleaf, *Seeker and Servant: Reflections on Religious Leadership*, ed. Anne Fraker and Larry C. Spears (San Francisco: Jossey-Bass, 1996), 96–98.

8. Ibid., 97.

9. Ibid., 98.

10. Wendall Walls, "Anatomy of Collaboration: An Act of Servant Leadership," in *Practicing Servant Leadership: Succeeding Through Trust, Bravery, and Forgiveness*, ed. Larry C. Spears and Michelle Lawrence (San Francisco: Jossey-Bass, 2004), 131.

11. Standards are adapted from D. Johnson and F. Johnson, *Joining Together: Group Theory and Group Skills* (Englewood Cliffs, NJ: Prentice Hall, 1975).

12. James Allen, "Brawn Puts Faith in Brain Power; Ross Brawn Is Shumacher's Closest," *The Sunday Herald*, August 27, 2000, http://www.highbeam.com/doc/1P2-19055983.html.

13. James Allen, "Ciao for Now, Ross," *F1 Racing*, January 2007, as quoted in "Corporate Mental Health," *The Agile Manager*, February 19, 2007, http://www.rosspettit.com/2007_02_01_archive.html.

14. "What Is Your Conflict Style?" is adapted from Kenneth W. Thomas and Ralph H. Kilmann, *Thomas-Kilmann Conflict Mode Instrument* (Mountain View, CA: CPP, 2002) and the work of Robert Blake and Jane Mouton in *The Managerial Grid* (Houston: Gulf Publishing, 1964).

15. THE CHILL DRILL® guidelines from James W. Sipe, *Your Anger Management Tool* (Detroit: Performance Resource Press, 1994).

16. Roger Fisher, William Ury, and Bruce Patton, *Getting to YES: Negotiating Agreement Without Giving In* (New York: Penguin, 1991).

17. Roger Fisher and Daniel Shapiro, *Beyond Reason: Using Emotions as You Negotiate* (New York: Viking Adult, 2005).

18. Peace R.U.L.E.S!™ guidelines from James W. Sipe, *Your Conflict Resolution Tool* (Detroit: Performance Resource Press, 1994).

# Pillar V: Foresight

1. Robert K. Greenleaf, *The Servant as Leader* (Indianapolis: The Robert Greenleaf Center for Servant Leadership, 1970), 14.

2. Larry C. Spears, "The Understanding and Practice of Servant Leadership," in *Practicing Servant Leadership: Succeeding Through Trust, Bravery, and Forgiveness*, ed. Larry C. Spears and Michelle Lawrence (San Francisco: Jossey-Bass, 2004), 15.

3. Greenleaf, *The Servant as Leader*, 16.

4. Ibid., 18.

5. Daniel H. Kim, "Foresight as the Central Ethic of Leadership," in Spears and Lawrence, *Practicing Servant Leadership*, 204.

6. World Future Society, "The Art of Foresight: Preparing for a Changing World," *The Futurist* 38, no. 3 (May/June 2004): 31–37.

7. Paul Pearsall, *The Heart's Code: Tapping the Wisdom and Power of Our Heart Energy* (New York: Random House, 1998).

8. Robert K. Cooper, "A New Neuroscience of Leadership: Bringing Out More of the Best in People," *Strategy & Leadership Journal* 28, no. 6, (2001): 11–15.

9. Robert K. Greenleaf, *On Becoming a Servant-Leader* (San Francisco: Jossey-Bass, 1996), 317.

10. Daniel Gilbert and Randy Buckner, "Time Travel in the Brain," *Time*, Jan. 19, 2007, http://www.time.com/time/magazine/article/0,9171,1580364,00.html.

11. James McSwinney, personal interview with Don M. Frick, January 18, 2003.

12. Josh Bartok, ed., *More Daily Wisdom: 365 Buddhist Inspirations* (Somerville, MA: Wisdom Publications, 2006), 292.

13. Claus Otto Scharmer, "Every Institution Is a Living System: Conversation with Arie de Geus," *Dialog on Leadership*, September 22, 1999.

14. Baran's comments may be found in Judy O'Neill, "An Interview with Paul Baran," March 5, 1990, Menlo Park, CA, transcript OH 182, *Oral Histories Collection*, Charles Babbage Institute, Centre for the History of Information Processing, University of Minnesota, Minneapolis, Minnesota.

15. Coauthor Don Frick first heard this comment from Jack Lowe Jr. during a conversation at TDIndustries in 1996.

16. Lao-Tse, *Te-Tao Ching*, number 42, http://home.pages.at/onkellotus/TTK/English_Heider_TTK.html.

17. Ibid., number 36.

18. Teresa Amabile, *The Social Psychology of Creativity* (New York: Springer-Verlag, 1983).

19. Scores of useful books about practical creativity have been published in the last twenty years, including Roger von Oech's 1986 classic, *A Kick in the Seat of the Pants* (New York: Perennial). Don Frick is especially indebted to Dr. Ann McGee-Cooper's original work on creativity. Her 1982 book *Building Brain Power* (Dallas: Ann McGee-Cooper & Associates) is the earliest of her publications, and specifically addresses creativity. Many of the same insights are incorporated into her better-known books, including *Time Management for Unmanageable People* (Austin: Bard Productions, 1993) and *You Don't Have To Go Home from Work Exhausted!* (New York: Bantam Books, 1990).

20. Stewart Brand, "Founding Father: Interview with Paul Baran," *Wired* 9, no. 3 (March 2001), accessed online at http://archive.wired.com/wired/archive/9.03/baran.html.

21. Pierce J. Howard, "Creativity and Problem Solving," in *The Owner's Manual for the Brain: Everyday Applications from Mind-Brain Research*, 2nd ed. (Atlanta: Bard Press, 2000), 616–17.

22. Don DeGraaf, Colin Tilley, and Larry Neal, "Servant Leadership Characteristics in Organizations," in Spears and Lawrence, *Practicing Servant Leadership*, 150.

23. For Greenleaf's succinct overview of conceptual vs. operational skills, see Greenleaf, *On Becoming a Servant-Leader*, 217–20.

24. Alfred North Whitehead, *Dialogues of Alfred North Whitehead as Recorded by Lucien Price* (New York: Atlantic Monthly Press, 1954), 98.

## Pillar VI: Systems Thinker

1. The 9/11 Commission Report details these and other tragic examples of failures of systems thinking leading up to the World Trade Center attacks. See the report at http://www.gpoaccess.gov/911/pdf/fullreport.pdf.

2. For a brief summary of systems theory including applications in a few leadership theories, see *The Systems Approach to Management* (circa 1945–75). For one of the clearest introductions to systems thinking, see Daniel H. Kim, *Introduction to Systems Thinking* (Waltham, MA: Pegasus Communications, Inc., 1999). See also Kim's *Toward Learning Organizations: Integrating Total Quality Control and Systems Thinking* (Waltham, MA: Pegasus Communications, Inc., 1996, 1997).

3. Andy Grove quoted in Andrew Tellijohn, "Culture Hounds," *UpsizeMag.com* (2007), http://www.upsizemag.com/cover-story/best-practices-people-workp.

4. See https://answers.cbfl.net/answers/threadview?id=526155.

5. Peter M. Senge, *The Fifth Discipline: The Art and Practice of the Learning Organization* (New York: Doubleday Currency, 1990), 57–67.

6. Robert K. Greenleaf, *The Power of Servant Leadership* (San Francisco: Berrett-Koehler, 1998), 260. The essay, *My Debt to E. B. White*, from which this quote was taken, was originally published by the Greenleaf Center for Servant Leadership in 1987.

7. Ibid., 277.

8. Francis Cook, *Hua-Yen Buddhism: The Jewel Net of Indra*, Iaswr Series (Philadelphia: Pennsylvania State University Press, 1977). For reflections on the nature of Indra's Net, see http://www.heartspace.org/misc/IndraNet.html.

9. Fritjof Capra, *The Turning Point: Science, Society, and the Rising Culture* (New York: Bantam, 1984), 87.

10. Robert K. Greenleaf, "Some Rough Notes on Growth Through Groups," from the *Receptive Listening Course Leadership Manual*, unpublished document (Indianapolis: Greenleaf Center Archives, no date). Greenleaf originally wrote this material for the Wainwright House in Rye, New York.

11. Jane Magruder Watkins and Bernard J. Mohr, *Appreciative Inquiry: Change at the Speed of Imagination* (San Francisco: Jossey-Bass, 2001), xxxi.

12. Victor H. Mair, "How a Misunderstanding about Chinese Characters Has Led Many Astray," http://www.pinyin.info/chinese/crisis.html.

13. "The Tylenol Crisis," *Training World* 1, no. 2, August 28, 2000, http://finance.groups.yahoo.com/group/trainingworld/message/2.

14. John Kotter, *Leading Change* (Boston: Harvard Business School Press, 1996).

15. Alexander Gilchrist, *The Life of William Blake, with Selections from his Poems and Other Writings* (New York: Macmillan & Co., 1880), 126.

16. Aristotle, *Rhetoric*, book 1, chapter 7.

# Pillar VII: Moral Authority

1. Stephen R. Covey, foreword to *Servant Leadership: A Journey into the Nature of Legitimate Power & Greatness 25th Anniversary Edition*, by Robert K. Greenleaf (Mahwah, NJ: Paulist Press, 2002), 12.

2. Greenleaf, *Servant Leadership*, 23–24.

3. James Kouzes, "Finding Your Voice," in *Insights on Leadership: Service, Stewardship, Spirit, and Servant Leadership*, ed. Larry C. Spears (New York: John Wiley & Sons, 1996), 323.

4. Jeffrey Dols, unpublished. Other original poems by Jeffrey Dols may be found in his book, *One in Spirit: Reflections from a Seeker's Journey to God* (Minneapolis: Lulu.com, 2006), available for purchase or download at http://stores.lulu.com/jdols.

5. Robert K. Greenleaf, *The Servant as Leader* (Indianapolis: The Robert Greenleaf Center for Servant Leadership, 1970), 34–35.

6. Newcomb Greenleaf, "Reflections on Robert K. Greenleaf," *Reflections on Leadership: How Robert K. Greenleaf's Theory of Servant Leadership Influenced Today's Top Management Thinkers*, ed. Larry C. Spears (New York: John Wiley & Sons, 1995), 318–19.

7. Robert Spector and Patrick D. McCarthy, *The Nordstrom Way: The Insider Story of America's #1 Customer Service Company* (New York: John Wiley & Sons, 1999), 16.

8. Patrick McCarthy, quoted in Alexandra DeFelice, "A Century of Customer Love," *CRM Magazine*, June, 2005, http://www.destinationcrm.com/Articles/Editorial/Magazine-Features/A-Century-of-Customer-Love-42958.aspx.

9. Tom Chappell, "Someone Was Listening," in *Chicken Soup for the Soul at Work*, ed. Jack Canfield et al. (Deerfield Beach, FL: HCI, 2001), 133–35.

10. Douglas S. Barasch, "God and Toothpaste," *N.Y. Times Magazine*, Dec. 22, 1996, 27.

11. Reid Magney, "Jai Johnson: Put Up the Big Green Tent," *La Crosse Tribune*, August 6, 2007, http://lacrossetribune. com/news /monday-profile-jai-johnson-put-up-the-big-green-tent/article _287db3eb-730f-50cc-8044-3948f90ccbfb.html.

12. Interview with Jai Johnson conducted by Don Frick in La Crosse, Wisconsin, September 2, 2007.

13. See Sherrie Gruder et al., *Toward a Sustainable Community: A Toolkit for Local Government* (Madison, WI: UW Madison, 2007), http://www4.uwm.edu/shwec/publications/cabinet/reduction reuse/SustainabilityToolkit.pdf.

14. Robert K. Greenleaf, confidential note to Robert Lynn, Robert K. Greenleaf Archives at Andover-Newton Seminary.

# Implementing the Seven Pillars
## of Servant Leadership

1. Robert K. Greenleaf, *The Institution as Servant* (Indianapolis: Robert K. Greenleaf Center for Servant Leadership, 1972), 1.

2. Dr. Mitchell's story is told in Edgar D. Mitchell and Dwight Williams, *The Way of the Explorer: An Apollo Astronaut's Journey through the Material and Mystical Worlds* (New York: Putnam Adult, 1996). The history of the Institute for Noetic Sciences may be found at http://www.noetic.org/about/history.cfm (accessed January 8, 2008).

# The Seven Pillars in Action

1. *The Bemidji Pioneer*, http://beta.bemidjipioneer.com/event/article/id/20661/.

2. Bill Salisbury, *Pioneer Press*, http://www.twincities.com/ci9008519. Posted 4/22/2008.

3. "Minnesota Bridge Reopens a Year After Collapse." *Lede*, The New York Times News Blog, September 18, 2008, 11:59 am. Accessed on March 19, 2014, http://thelede.blogs.nytimes.com/2008/09/18/minnesota-bridge-reopens-a-year-after-collapse/?_php=true&_type=blogs&_r=0.

4. As of September 2014, a presentation explaining the process of the first E-Jam and its resulting ideas about sustainability was available at http://prezi.com/sd2rh5v5urkl/mndots-e-jam-and-sustainability-initiatives/.

5. A PDF document that explains MnDOT's process for predicting conflict can be found at http://www.dot.state.mn.us/pm/pdf/csp.pdf.

6. MnDOT's Enterprise Risk Management process is explained at http://www.dot.state.mn.us/riskmanagement/.

7. A paper describing the survey, its methodology and results can be downloaded from http://www.dot.state.mn.us/research/TS/2013/201305.pdf.

8. The full report on MnDOT's transparency research can be found in MnDOT, "Accountability and Transparency Policy Review Team Summary Report."

9. From the website *Minneapolis: City by Nature*, "Diverse Minneapolis," accessed on April 4, 2014, http://www.minneapolis.org/visitor/diverse-minneapolis.

# Bibliography

Allen, James. "Brawn Puts Faith in Brain Power; Ross Brawn Is Shumacher's Closest." *The Sunday Herald*. August 27, 2000, http://www.highbeam.com/doc/1P2-19055983.html.

————. "Ciao for Now, Ross." *F1 Racing*. January 2007, as quoted in "Corporate Mental Health." *The Agile Manager*. Sunday, February 19, 2007, http://agilemanager.blogspot.com/2007_02_01_archive.html.

Amabile, Teresa M. *The Social Psychology of Creativity*. New York: Springer-Verlag, 1983.

Aristotle. *Rhetoric*. Translated by W. Rhys Roberts. Mineola, NY: Dover Publications, 2004.

Autry, James. *Love and Profit: The Art of Caring Leadership*. New York: Avon Books, Inc., 1991.

Badaracco, Joseph Jr. "The Discipline of Building Character." *Harvard Business Review on Leadership* 76, no. 2 (1998): 114.

Barasch, Douglas S. "God and Toothpaste." *N.Y. Times Magazine*, Dec. 22, 1996, 27.

Barbuto, John Jr., and Daniel W. Wheeler. "Becoming a Servant Leader: Do You Have What It Takes?" *NebGuide*, University of Nebraska—Lincoln Extension, http://www.ianrpubs.unl.edu/epublic/live/g1481/build/g1481.pdf.

Bartok, Josh, ed., *More Daily Wisdom: 365 Buddhist Inspirations*. Somerville, MA: Wisdom Publications, 2006.

Bennis, Warren. "The Leadership Advantage." *Leader to Leader*, 12 (1999), http://www.leadertoleader.org/knowledgecenter/journal.aspx?ArticleID=53.

Bolton, Robert. *People Skills: How to Assert Yourself, Listen to Others, and Resolve Conflicts*. New York: Simon & Schuster, 1976.

Brand, Stewart. "Founding Father: Interview with Paul Baran." *Wired* 9.03, Mar 2001. http://archive.wired.com/wired/archive/9.03/baran.html.

Burns, Robert. "To a Louse, On Seeing One on a Lady's Bonnet at Church, 1786." *Burns Country*. http://www.robertburns.org/works/97.shtml.

Camel Facts: http://camelfarm.com/camels/camels_about.html; http://www.acsamman.edu.jo/~el/2/camels/index.html; http://www.llamaweb.com/Camel/Info.html.

Canfield, Jack, et al. *Chicken Soup for the Soul at Work*. Deerfield Beach, FL: HCI, 2001.

Capra, Fritjof, *The Turning Point: Science, Society, and the Rising Culture*. New York: Bantam, 1984.

Carlzon, Jan. *Moments of Truth*. New York: Collins, 1989.

Casanova, Christina. "Character Education in our Schools: What Is Good Character?" *Guidance Channel Ezine*, June 2007.

Cialdini, Robert B. *Influence: The Psychology of Persuasion*. New York: William Morrow & Company, Inc., 1984.

Collins, James. *Good to Great: Why Some Companies Make the Leap and Others Don't*. New York: HarperCollins, 2001.

Cook, Francis H. *Hua-Yen Buddhism: The Jewel Net of Indra*. Philadelphia: Pennsylvania State University Press, 1977.

Cooper, Robert K. "A New Neuroscience of Leadership: Bringing Out More of the Best in People," *Strategy & Leadership Journal* 28, no. 6 (2001): 11–15.

Covey, Stephen. *Seven Habits of Highly Effective People*. New York: Fireside, 1989.

Crislip, David D., and Carl E. Larson. *Collaborative Leadership: How Citizens Can Make a Difference*. San Francisco: Jossey-Bass, 1994.

DeFelice, Alexandra. "A Century of Customer Love." *CRM Magazine*, June, 2005, http://www.destinationcrm.com/Articles/Editorial/Magazine-Features/A-Century-of-Customer-Love-42958.aspx.

Dols, Jeffrey. *One in Spirit: Reflections from a Seeker's Journey to God*. Minneapolis: Lulu.com, 2006.

Drucker, Peter. *The Effective Executive*. New York: HarperCollins, 1967.

Egan, Gerard. *The Skilled Helper: A Problem-Management Approach to Helping*. Pacific Grove, CA: Brooks/Cole Publishing Co., 1998.

Fisher, Roger, and Daniel Shapiro. *Beyond Reason: Using Emotions as You Negotiate*. New York: Viking Adult, 2005.

Fisher, Roger, William Ury, and Bruce Patton. *Getting to YES: Negotiating Agreement Without Giving In*. New York: Penguin, 1991.

Gallese, Vittoria. "The Roots of Empathy: The Shared Manifold Hypothesis and the Neural Basis of Intersubjectivity." *Psychopathology* 36 (2003): 176.

Gegax, Tom. *Winning in the Game of Life*. New York: Harmony Books, 1999.

George, Bill, David Gergen, and Peter Sims. *True North: Discover Your Authentic Leadership*. San Francisco: Jossey-Bass, 2007.

Gilbert, Daniel, and Randy Buckner. "Time Travel in the Brain." *Time*, Jan. 19, 2007, http://www.time.com/time/magazine/arti cle/0,9171,1580364,00.html.

Gilchrist, Alexander. *The Life of William Blake, with Selections from his Poems and Other Writings*. New York: Macmillan & Co., 1880.

Goffee, Rob, and Gareth Jones. "Managing Authenticity." *Harvard Business Review* 83, no. 12 (2005): 90.

Goleman, Daniel. *Social Intelligence: The New Science of Human Relationships*. New York: Bantam, 2006.

Greenleaf, Robert K. Correspondence to Bob Lynn. Robert K. Greenleaf Archives at Andover-Newton Seminary, March 9, 1982. Box 4.

———. *The Institution as Servant*. Indianapolis: Robert K. Greenleaf Center for Servant Leadership, 1972.

———. *Management Ability*. Originally published by Pacific Telephone. Indianapolis: Robert K. Greenleaf Center Archives, Joseph Distefano Collection, undated.

———. *On Becoming a Servant-Leader*. Edited by Don M. Frick and Larry C. Spears. San Francisco: Jossey-Bass, 1996.

———. *The Power of Servant Leadership*. Edited by Larry C. Spears. San Francisco: Berrett-Koehler, 1998.

———. *Receptive Listening Course Leadership Manual*. Indianapolis: Robert K. Greenleaf Archives at the Greenleaf Center for Servant Leadership, c. 1952.

———. *Seeker and Servant: Reflections on Religious Leadership*. Edited by Anne Fraker and Larry C. Spears. San Francisco: Jossey-Bass, 1996.

————. *The Servant as Leader*. Indianapolis: The Robert Greenleaf Center for Servant Leadership, 1970.

————. *Servant Leadership: A Journey into the Nature of Legitimate Power & Greatness*. 25th anniversary edition. New York/ Mahwah, NJ: Paulist Press, 2002.

Gruder, Sherrie, et al. *Toward a Sustainable Community: A Toolkit for Local Government*. Madison, WI: UW Madison, 2007.

Handy, Charles. "The Search for Meaning," *Leader to Leader* (1997), http://www3.interscience.wiley.com/cgi-bin/jissue/113 455611.

Hinderlie, Johan, and James W. Sipe. "Well Done, Good and Faithful Servant." Unpublished manuscript, 2006.

Howard, Pierce J. *The Owner's Manual for the Brain: Everyday Applications from Mind-Brain Research*. 2nd ed. Atlanta: Bard Press, 2006.

Jackson, Michael C. *The Systems Approach to Management*. Kindle edition. New York: Springer, 2000.

Johnson, David W., and Frank P. Johnson. *Joining Together: Group Theory and Group Skills*. Englewood Cliffs, NJ: Prentice Hall, 1975.

Ketteler, Ronald. *Catholic Conference of Kentucky Newsletter*, March 20, 1998, revised December 19, 2001.

Kim, Daniel H. *Introduction to Systems Thinking*. Waltham, MA: Pegasus Communications, Inc., 1999.

————. *Toward Learning Organizations: Integrating Total Quality Control and Systems Thinking*. Waltham, MA: Pegasus Communications, Inc., 1997.

Kotter, James P., and James L. Heskett. *Corporate Culture and Performance*. New York: Simon & Schuster, 1992.

Kotter, John. *Leading Change*. Boston: Harvard Business School Press, 1996.

Kouzes, James M., and Barry Z. Posner. *The Leadership Challenge*. San Francisco: Jossey-Bass, 2002.

Lao-Tsu, *Tao te Ching*. Translated by Jonathan Star. New York: Tarcher, 2003.

Lickona, Thomas. *Educating for Character: How Our Schools Can Teach Respect and Responsibility*. New York: Bantam Books, 1991.

Magney, Reid. "Jai Johnson: Put Up the Big Green Tent." *La Crosse Tribune*, August 6, 2007.

Mair, Victor. H. "How a Misunderstanding about Chinese Characters Has Led Many Astray," http://www.pinyin.info/links.html.

Maslow, Abraham. *Maslow on Management*. New York: John Wiley & Sons, 1998.

McCloskey, Pat, OFM. "Where Did St. Francis Say That?" *St. Anthony Messenger: Ask a Franciscan*, http://www.american catholic.org/messenger/Oct2001/Wiseman.asp.

McGee-Cooper, Ann. *Building Brain Power*. Dallas: Ann McGee-Cooper & Associates, 1982.

———. *Time Management for Unmanageable People*. Austin: Bard Productions, 1993.

———. *You Don't Have To Go Home From Work Exhausted!* New York: Bantam Books, 1990.

McKee, Robert. *Story: Substance, Structure, Style, and the Principles of Screenwriting*. New York: HarperCollins, 1997.

McKee, Robert, and Bronwyn Fryer. "Storytelling That Moves People: A Conversation with Screenwriting Coach Robert McKee." *Harvard Business Review* 8, no. 6 (2003): 51–55.

Mintzberg, Henry et al. *Harvard Business Review on Leadership*. Boston: Harvard Business School Publishing, 1998.

Mitchell, Edgar D., and Williams, Dwight. *The Way of the Explorer: An Apollo Astronaut's Journey through the Material and Mystical Worlds*. New York: Putnam Adult, 1996.

National Commission of Terrorist Attacks Upon the United States. *The 9/11 Commission Report*. Washington, DC: U.S. Government Printing Office, 2005.

Nickols, Fred. "Feedback about Feedback." *Human Resources Development Quarterly* 6, no. 3 (1995): 289–96.

O'Conner, Lynn. "Altruism as a Fundamental Unconscious Motivation." *SFPRG Process Notes* Spring 1996: 11, http://www.eparg.org/publications/altruism.pdf.

O'Neill, Judy. "An Interview with Paul Baran." *Oral Histories Collection*. Transcript OH 182. Minneapolis: Charles Babbage Institute, Centre for the History of Information Processing, 1990.

Palmour, Jody. *On Moral Character: A Practical Guide to Aristotle's Virtues and Vices*. Washington, DC: The Archon Institute for Leadership Development, 1986.

Pearsall, Paul. *The Heart's Code: Tapping the Wisdom and Power of Our Heart Energy*. New York: Random House, 1998.

Pelikan, Jaroslav, ed. *Luther's Works*. Vol. 21. St. Louis: Concordia Publishing House, 1956.

Pfeffer, Jeffrey J. *The Human Equation: Building Profits by Putting People First*. Boston: Harvard Business School Press, 1998.

Prochaska, James O., John Norcross, and Carlo DiClemente. *Changing for Good: A Revolutionary Six-Stage Program for Overcoming Bad Habits and Moving Your Life Positively Forward*. New York: Collins, 2007.

Reichheld, Frederick F. *Loyalty Rules: How Today's Leaders Build Lasting Relationships*. Boston: Harvard Business School Press, 2003.

Richardson, George P. *Feedback Thought in Social Science and Systems Theory*. Philadelphia: University of Pennsylvania Press, 1991.

Rinehart, Stacy T. *Upside Down: The Paradox of Servant Leadership*. Colorado Springs, CO: NavPress, 1998.

Rogers, Carl. *A Way of Being*. Boston: Houghton Mifflin, 1980.

Scharmer, Claus Otto. "Every Institution Is a Living System: Conversation with Arie de Geus." *Dialog on Leadership*. September 22, 1999.

Schnabel, Arthur. *Chicago Daily News*, June 11, 1958.

Senge, Peter M. *The Fifth Discipline: The Art and Practice of The Learning Organization*. New York: Doubleday Currency, 1990.

Sipe, James W. *Your Anger Management Tool*. Detroit: Performance Resource Press, 1994.

———. *Your Conflict Resolution Tool*. Detroit: Performance Resource Press, 1994.

Sisodia, Rajendra, David B. Wolfe, and Jagdish N. Sheth. *Firms of Endearment: How World Class Companies Profit from Passion and Purpose*. Upper Saddle River, NJ: Wharton School Publishing, 2007.

Spears, Larry C. "On Character and Servant Leadership: Ten Characteristics of Effective, Caring Leaders," *Concepts &*

*Connections*, 8, no. 3. College Park, MD: University of Maryland National Clearinghouse for Leadership Programs, 2000.

Spears, Larry C., ed. *Insights on Leadership: Service, Stewardship, Spirit, and Servant Leadership*. New York: John Wiley & Sons, 1996.

————. *Reflections on Leadership: How Robert K. Greenleaf's Theory of Servant Leadership Influenced Today's Top Management Thinkers*. New York: John Wiley & Sons, 1995.

Spears, Larry C., and Michelle Lawrence, eds. *Practicing Servant Leadership: Succeeding Through Trust, Bravery, and Forgiveness*. San Francisco: Jossey-Bass, 2004.

Spector, Robert, and Patrick D. McCarthy. *The Nordstrom Way: The Insider Story of America's #1 Customer Service Company*. New York: John Wiley & Sons, 1999.

Stone, A. Gregory, Robert F. Russell, and Kathleen Patterson. "Transformational Versus Servant Leadership: A Difference in Leader Focus." *Leadership & Organization Development Journal* 25, no. 4 (2004): 349.

"The Tylenol Crisis." *Training World* 1, no. 2 (August 28, 2000), http://finance.groups.yahoo.com/group/trainingworld/message/2.

Vedantam, Shankar. "If It Feels Good to Be Good, It Might Be Only Natural." *Washington Post*, May 28, 2007.

Vikesland, Gary. "Part II: An Unseen Force in Your Company." *Employer-Employee.com*, 2001.

Von Oech, Roger. *A Kick in the Seat of the Pants*. New York: Perennial, 1986.

Whitehead, Alfred North. *Dialogues of Alfred North Whitehead as Recorded by Lucien Price*. New York: Atlantic Monthly Press, 1954.

Wong, Paul, and Don Page. "Servant Leadership: An Opponent-Process Model and the Revised Servant Leadership Profile." *Regent University Servant Leadership Research Roundtable*. Virginia Beach, VA: 2003, http://www.regent.edu/acad/global/publications/sl_proceedings/2003/wong_servant_leadership.pdf.

World Future Society. "The Art of Foresight: Preparing for a Changing World." *The Futurist* 38, no. 3 (2004): 31–37.

# Index

# More Praise for *Seven Pillars of Servant Leadership*

"*Seven Pillars of Servant Leadership* is the most valuable book on Servant Leadership out there. It makes the philosophy of Servant Leadership understandable, applicable, and recognizable, which is critical if we are to take a deep, personal leadership journey and make a contribution to the common good of society. It is required reading for my graduate students from all walks of life, who say that *Seven Pillars* is 'a keeper.'"

—*Dr. Carolyn Crippen*
graduate advisor and associate professor,
Leadership Studies
Faculty of Education, University of Victoria, Canada

"*Seven Pillars of Servant Leadership* is a comprehensive and practical description of the traits and competencies of Servant-Leaders, all well-supported by research. The authors invite each of us, and our colleagues at work, to answer key questions, undertake important conversations, and act on exercises that will help implement the wisdom of leading by serving."

—*Dr. Kent M. Keith*
CEO of the Greenleaf Centre for
Servant Leadership (Asia)

"*Seven Pillars of Servant Leadership* is required reading for all officers who want to take a promotion exam in our police department because the values explained in this book are the same ones required by exceptional public servants."

—*Mac Tristan*
chief of police, Coppell, Texas

"This book is both engaging and practical and is a key resource for teaching, learning, and consulting about Servant Leadership. The questions in each chapter bring home the material by encouraging the reader to reflect on how to apply the pillars at work, home, and in the community."

—*Jeff Miller, PhD*
president and senior educator,
Innovative Leadership Solutions, Inc.

"Sipe and Frick vividly illustrate Servant Leadership with practical concepts and stories that encourage the reader's personal growth. Above all, *Seven Pillars* triggers self-reflection and a realization that one's success and true happiness come from the heart and show outwardly through loving and serving others."

—*Dr. Eric J. Russell*
author, *The Desire to Serve:*
*Servant Leadership for Fire and Emergency Services*

"*Seven Pillars of Servant Leadership* offers a thorough menu of skills, and insights into how to put them to work. My business partners and I use this as a primary resource to strengthen our own practice and teach trust-building skills to others, and recommend *Seven Pillars* to our clients with consistently positive results."

—*Dr. Ann McGee-Cooper*
author, lecturer, and business consultant

"This book challenges you to ask, what is it really like to be the receptionist, copywriter, or salesperson in your firm? It makes one realize that effective leadership requires introspection and empathy…a deeper dive into every person and process affecting your company, community, and family. You may soon learn that the rewards of this leap of faith greatly outweigh the risks."

—*Mike Sullivan*
founder, Halo Creative Group (advertising agency)

"*Seven Pillars of Servant Leadership* provides a guide for learning about Servant Leadership and covers the broadest scope of ideas for application I have seen anywhere. Each pillar presents stories, insights, and thought-provoking questions that can lead you to discover the next right step for bringing Servant Leadership into your team or organization."

—*Deborah Welch, PhD*
core faculty member, Capella University
author and leadership coach

"The framework of *Seven Pillars* invites readers to examine the tenets of Servant Leadership personally, in relationship to others, and in the context of larger systems. It is my key resource when planning our leadership learning circles and monthly Servant-Leader conversations."

—*Christa Williams*
executive director, Sophia Foundation